D0953776

The
Dream
Team

The Dream Team

Stafford Hildred
& Tim Ewbank

BLAKE

Published by Blake Publishing Ltd,
3 Bramber Court, 2 Bramber Road, London W14 9PB, England

ISBN 185782 3893

All rights reserved. No part of this publication may be
reproduced, stored in a retrieval system, or in any form or
by any means, without the prior permission in writing of the
publisher, nor be otherwise circulated in any form of binding
or cover other than that in which it is published and without
a similar condition including this condition being imposed
on the subsequent purchaser.

British Library Cataloguing-in-Publication Data:
A catalogue record for this book is available from
the British Library.

Typeset by John Davies

Printed in Great Britain by CPD, Wales

1 3 5 7 9 10 8 6 4 2

© Text copyright Stafford Hildred and Tim Ewbank

Pictures reproduced by kind permission of All Action, Alpha,
Capital, Channel 4, PA Photos, Rex Features and UPP.

Every effort has been made to contact the original
copyright holders. In the case of any problems
we would be grateful if those concerned would contact us.

Papers used by Blake Publishing Ltd are natural, recyclable products
made from wood grown in sustainable forests. The manufacturing processes
conform to the environmental regulations of the country of origin.

Contents

Prologue

When it comes to comedy, David Jason and Nicholas Lyndhurst are The Dream Team. It's almost 20 years since they were first cast together as the unlikely brothers Del and Rodney Trotter in John Sullivan's wonderfully well written situation comedy *Only Fools and Horses*.

The brilliant double act is at the heart of the best comedy British television has ever seen. Certainly, Sullivan's sensational scripts give the pair a perfect comedy platform but it's the relationship between the inspirational actors who play the benevolently battling brothers that has become our favourite source of screen laughter.

Every fan of *Only Fools and Horses* has his or her favourite clips but two scenes from the series which have stood TV comedy's most demanding test, the test of time, are the scenes which have come to be known as 'the chandelier' and 'the barflap'.

The first was from the 1982 episode *Where Fools Rush In*, in which Del and Rodney are standing on ladders ready to support a chandelier which is supposedly being unscrewed by Grandad on the floor above. They wait for it to drop ... but, by mistake, it's the chandelier at the other end of the room which comes crashing down.

The following year saw what most people would agree was David's funniest moment as Del Boy in *Yuppy Love* when he and Trigger are trying to impress some yuppies in a bar. Del has been leaning on the bar, but when he turns away he doesn't notice the barman has lifted up the barflap. He turns to lean on it once more, playing it cool, and topples through the gap like a felled tree.

In a series noted for its consistent level of comedy, both 'the chandelier' and 'the barflap' remain unique scenes which have stayed firmly, and so warmly, etched in the public's memory. And now those two golden moments can truly claim to be the two funniest ever seen on TV following a special survey to find the most hilarious clips in TV sitcom history.

In the summer of 2000, a panel of experts, which included some of Britain's top comedy actors and writers, named the chandelier shenanigans and David's barflap prat-fall as the top two golden comic moments on TV over the past 40 years.

The survey was conducted for *Radio Times* and the panellists included comedy stars Ronnie Barker, Caroline Quentin, June Whitfield, Victoria Wood and Morwenna Banks. Among the writers involved were *Birds of a Feather* creators Laurence Marks and Maurice Gran, *Men Behaving Badly* writer Simon Nye, and Barry Took.

They all spent a day debating the order of merit, but it was eventually agreed that top of the Top 40 was 'the chandelier' followed closely by 'the barflap'. It was no mean accolade for David and Nicholas, for writer John Sullivan and for the rest of the *Only Fools and Horses* team since the Top 40 also included five entries from the '70s classic *Fawlty Towers* which starred John Cleese. The Top 10 included two from *Dad's Army* as well as two manic moments involving Basil Fawlty.

David and Nicholas's most magical moment in 'the chandelier', saw them crowned as all-time comedy kings ahead of such talented comedians and actors as Tony Hancock, Warren Mitchell as Alf Garnett, Eric Sykes, James Bolam and Rodney Bewes in *The Likely Lads*, Rik Mayall in *The Young Ones*, Lesley Joseph in *Birds of a Feather*, and Jennifer Saunders as Edina in *Absolutely Fabulous*, collapsing in a flowerbed outside her home after a liquid lunch.

Both David and Nicholas agree that the chandelier sequence ranks high among their own favourites, but the barflap remains one of David's own personal choices because he and the director had worked so hard at constructing what was, in fact, an extremely difficult stunt. Nicholas says, 'I also liked the sequence where Del is strapped up as a hang-glider and believes Rodney is going to save him. But he's not.'

The two actors got the chance to name their favourite clips and to reminisce about their remarkable years together one last time when they helped to launch the final three-part mini-series of *Only Fools and Horses* on 19 November 1996, before a specially invited small group of journalists and critics, including one of the authors.

At this time, of course, no one had seen the brilliant episodes which had Del and Rodney ending up walking off into the sunset as millionaires, and the first question David and Nicholas were asked was, 'Are you confident it will be a fitting farewell to the Trotters?'

'We're confident, but not over-confident,' was David's honest reply. 'You should never be over-confident as far as comedy is concerned. Yes, we are quietly confident that this is going to be a fitting tribute to the Trotter family and a nice way to end a very wonderful, happy and successful series.'

It had been three years since *Only Fools and Horses* fans had seen new episodes and there were many who had felt in some strange way that, without Del and Rodney around on their TV sets at Christmas for three years, an essential, cheerful ingredient, unique to the festive season, had been missing.

David was certainly in tune with what Del and Rodney meant to people at Christmas. 'The weight of responsibility is not missed on us,' he said. 'We're all aware of that, but we are reasonably confident — it's very, very funny.'

'We have a fan following and they've had three years of expectation,' added Nicholas. 'Hopefully, we can live up to that. I thought, Brilliant! It's coming back! But then you suddenly say to yourself, "Gosh! I hope it's funny." Also I wasn't sure I could do Rodney's voice like I had done it before, so I raided my mum's video library and watched one of the tapes. But when we are working, I really do feel David and I are brothers.'

'It's a bit like riding a bike,' David commented. 'We'd done so many series and had worked so closely together it instantly came back as soon as we started to speak, although a lot of the subtleties didn't at first.'

Turning to Nick, David said, 'There's nothing like coming back to the *Only Fools and Horses* scripts. It's such a joy working with funny material and you realise how much you missed it and how much you missed making each other laugh.'

Nicholas agreed, and warming to the subject, chipped in, 'That reminds me — we were on a night shoot and had been working for 18 hours, it was a very cold night and the crew were huddling around us listening to the rehearsals not once but several times. And the guy with the clapperboard couldn't say the numbers because he was laughing so hard. And that was before we filmed it.'

As they chatted about the series that had taken them to the heights of stardom, it was evident just how much the two actors appreciated each other and their respective talents, and the opportunities that had come their way because of their success in *Only Fools and Horses*.

'How will you feel at the end?' Nicholas was asked.

'I'll probably cry,' was his straightforward reply. And he meant it. '*Only Fools and Horses* has made my career. I've grown up with *Only Fools and Horses* and it's been a delightful process.'

David was at pains to point out how the series had launched both him and Nicholas into the professional and public eye. 'It made people in the TV industry consider us for much more valuable parts than perhaps they might have done otherwise,' said David. 'It was like a showcase. Over the years, instead of it being a sitcom, John Sullivan managed to move it into a much more emotional area where there was more demanded from the actors' point of view. We were asked to produce more emotional material as well as comic material. That began to shine through, so people began to think, There's more to those guys than comics and making us laugh. They've got some heart and soul in there. So, as actors, we were taken a bit more seriously.'

For David, it meant the chance to be accepted by viewers as a detective in *A Touch of Frost*. For Nicholas, it was the chance to play one of Charles Dickens' most insidious characters, Uriah Heep, in a BBC dramatisation of *David Copperfield* alongside such acting luminaries as Sir Ian McKellen, Bob Hoskins and Trevor Eve.

Worthy and thoroughly deserved that these roles were for David and Nicholas, it was apparent that the public could not get enough of them as the Trotter brothers. 'The series has been given such warmth and such a welcome by the public since 1981,' David observed. 'It's maintained such a high standard and the audiences have been behind it all the time so that it's going to be extremely difficult to leave them, especially when you know people want more. If there was a danger of people saying, "I don't like 'em now," we wouldn't want to do it. But if there is still a tremendous love and acceptance of the family, it's another story.

'Where John Sullivan was so clever was that he made the family move on. We started out with things out of a suitcase, then moved on to the yuppie stage, then Rodney started going out with Cassandra, then he got married, then Del had a baby. Each time there was a development, they continued their lives and they took the audience with them.

'Also, there's no hurt, no malice. Even when Del or Rodney gets angry, it's only a superficial anger. It's amusing, it's funny they get angry, good fun to watch them bicker. You don't believe it, you just enjoy them having a go at each other like a couple of old queens!'

As TV's record books now show, the audiences for the final farewell episodes of *Only Fools and Horses* were phenomenal. The public's affection for David Jason and Nicholas Lyndhurst remained undiminished, even if David himself knew he personally would find the final Trotter trilogy somewhat uncomfortable viewing. 'You don't ever really settle down,' he explained. 'You're watching for the mistakes and things you didn't do right. It's not really that pleasurable.

'But I shall have a two-minute weep on Christmas Day. It's a sad time for Del and a sad time for us and the nation. I'll certainly miss it if that is to be the end. It ends with Del as the eternal optimist. "This time next year we'll be millionaires," has always been his phrase and always will be.'

As for David and Nicholas as Del and Rodney, 'Well,' said David. 'It's never say never again. You never know, we might be forced to bring the buggers back!'

1

Realising the Dream

As brothers Derek and Rodney Trotter in one of Britain's greatest-ever comedy shows *Only Fools and Horses*, David Jason and Nicholas Lyndhurst have become the viewers' perfect partnership. Their down-to-earth professionalism has become a legend in a business where many stars possess egos which far outweigh their talent.

So smooth has their working relationship become in the nation's favourite comedy series, that it came as a severe shock to producer, cast and crew when, out on location in April 1982 in the back streets of Ealing, an argument apparently developed between the two actors while they were lunching together in their camper van.

Their van was parked close to the 'butty wagon' which meant that the rest of the team had to file past it as they queued for their lunch. They could hear every word as first David and Nicholas raised their voices at each other then suddenly launched into a vicious argument. It became a full-blown slanging match and nervous glances were exchanged among the crew as they heard shouts coming from inside the van and sounds of a struggle. Judging by the din, the two stars were swapping blows and throwing each other against the camper's walls. This was shocking and unprecedented. For years, the two actors had built up a friendship and mutual respect which was understood to be one of the bedrocks of British comedy. Now it seemed that was all about to come crashing down.

Ominously, all went quiet and then the door of the van burst open and out stormed David hurling some well-chosen insults over his shoulder at Nicholas, which were duly returned with equal venom. The crew watched open-mouthed as David slammed the camper van door behind him and strode off down the street muttering to himself in a fury.

The director and crew were aghast. A whole series and four months of filming stretched ahead of them and the two stars had fallen out on the very first day.

Gradually, David was coaxed back and filming continued but with David and Nicholas sniping away at each other and communicating only through a production assistant. The air of tension lasted through the afternoon until the tea-break when David and Nicholas could keep up the pretence no longer. In a rollicking outburst of relief and glee, they happily announced that their violent row had been merely a wind-up, and they could keep up being snappy and unpleasant no longer. Everyone heaved a vast, collective sigh of relief.

David and Nicholas enjoyed their joke hugely. The camper van in which they had engineered their fake row was fitted with a smoked-glass window and they had been able to watch the worried faces of the director and crew as they listened to the argument seemingly reaching a violent crescendo. In fact, David and Nicholas were splitting their sides inside the van as they threw cutlery, boots and shoes at the walls to make it sound as though they were engaged in a massive fight.

It was one of the many unscripted and unscreenable *Only Fools* moments which has helped to bond David Jason and Nicholas Lyndhurst together as closely as brothers could ever be.

Yet one of the greatest partnerships in British television history was born out of desperation. A brilliant writer called John Sullivan came up with his finest work because his back was financially up against the wall. And then, just when a comic masterpiece was in danger of foundering because of a lack of vision and enterprise, a crusading producer fought to link together two tremendous talents — David Jason and Nicholas Lyndhurst.

The story of *Only Fools and Horses* is the story of the transformation of two brilliant actors into stars, and of a pair of comedy craftsmen into a national institution. But it could have all been so very different.

Back in the late 1970s when *Only Fools and Horses* was just another idea in writer John Sullivan's fertile mind, David Jason was then merely a highly regarded comedy actor. Granted, he was best known for his superb slapstick abilities in ITV shows like *A Sharp Intake of Breath* and as perky shopworker Granville, the comic feed to Ronnie Barker, in the BBC's *Open All Hours*.

Nicholas Lyndhurst was a child actor who had become known as Wendy Craig's laconic screen son Adam in the popular BBC comedy series *Butterflies* and had also played Ronnie Barker's cockney son Raymond in *Going Straight*, the sequel to the BBC hit *Porridge*.

Jason was 40, twice Lyndhurst's age and, not surprisingly, they had never even considered working together, yet were about to become British television's favourite comedy team.

At the time, writer Sullivan was the man with his finger firmly on the pulse of verbal London. His sensational skill as a wordsmith has always provided the essential strength of the series. Brought up in Balham, Sullivan credits his inspirational English teacher Jim Trowers as the man who opened his eyes to books and first sparked his love of writing.

'We had two books at home,' said John Sullivan. 'The Bible and a Pools guide. Most blokes have to hide porno magazines under their jacket but, after Mr Trowers got me interested in reading, I hid Charles Dickens novels under mine, so my dad wouldn't laugh at me.'

And Mr Trowers' council flat in Farnham with its wildly clashing walls and carpets certainly provided John Sullivan with food for thought when he was first describing Del's colourful home in Nelson Mandela House.

Sullivan openly admits that he sat down to write *Only Fools and Horses* for one reason. Quite simply, it was out of desperation. 'I wrote the pilot out of a desperate need to get some money,' he declared.

Sullivan got the idea of writing for a living back in 1966 when he was working in a brewery in Balham, near his place of birth. 'A friend I knew from school also worked there,' recalls Sullivan. 'It was a very boring job, it was almost like being one of those white mice waiting for a bell to ring. When it rang, these crates would come and we had to stack them. My friend Paul Saunders and I used to laugh at the same sort of things and one day he read about the kind of money Johnny Speight was making and he suggested we had a go at writing a script.'

The two friends came up with a situation comedy set in a public toilet called *Gentlemen*, but that was swiftly flushed away. 'It was a bad idea,' admits Sullivan now. But over the next ten years he refined his talent and eventually took a job as a scene shifter at the BBC, in a bid to get nearer the action. It worked. Sullivan said, 'I met the legendary producer Dennis Main Wilson at the BBC. I had this one thing called *Citizen Smith* which was my ace card. I always thought if this was rejected I'd give it up. Dennis was the most perfect person to go to because he would give you a chance. He said to me, "I don't need you telling me about it, just go and do it."

I took two weeks off to write it and he got it on the screen within eight weeks in a *Comedy Playhouse*.' A new writer had arrived.

Daring for its day — 1977 — Citizen Smith was a comedy about a six-man political movement, the Tooting Popular Front, with Robert Lindsay starring as Wolfie Smith, South London's black-bereted answer to Che Guevara.

The series ran for four years and Sullivan had high hopes of following up with another sitcom he had written for the BBC called *Over the Moon* about a failed football manager.

He had produced a very funny script and a pilot was duly made, with Brian Wilde of *Last of the Summer Wine* fame starring as a somewhat sad soccer figure who had taken over a middle-ranking Third Division club. Within two seasons in charge, he had managed to take them right out of the Football League.

The comedy centred around the appointment of a new chairman, played by George Baker, who realised his manager was an incompetent idiot but discovered on looking at his contract that he was not in a position to be able to fire him.

Sullivan was hopeful for the show's chances but the BBC comedy bosses relegated it to the bin. They decided to kill it after Sullivan had already written three episodes. Sullivan was sick as a parrot about the decision. Suddenly, he did not even have a ball to play with. *Citizen Smith* had finished and now *Over the Moon* had been eclipsed before it had even been given a chance to shine.

It was then that Sullivan turned to *Only Fools and Horses*. He had originally broached the idea verbally with his BBC bosses but had received only a lukewarm response. Sullivan had envisaged *Readies*, as he had initially called the series, being set in a modern, multi-racial London which could be a bit violent and where the language was certainly colourful. In retrospect, he feels it was the lively language of the streets which at first frightened off his BBC superiors.

'The attitude was "We're not keen on this", he recalls. 'But with

Citizen Smith finished and my new show killed, I had nothing. I didn't know what to do.'

Sullivan had one ace left to play. At that time, the BBC's policy was to enter into an eight-part contract with its writers in which a seven-part series was commissioned plus a pilot for something new.

'I had a contract with the Beeb to write a pilot show and so away I went,' he says. 'I thought, To hell with what they think of it. I don't really care. I've got to write something to earn some money anyway. So I wrote *Only Fools and Horses* out of a desperate need to get some money. It was the only other idea in my head.

'I suppose, maybe, they were over a bit of a barrel because of this contract. But they saw it and they must have seen something in it because they didn't even pilot it. They said they would go with it as a series. So then I had to go away and do another six episodes and that kind of solved the bank manager's problem!'

Only Fools and Horses had been born from a conversation Sullivan had one night with TV producer Ray Butt in the BBC club. The two men had worked together on *Citizen Smith* and now they were relaxing over a drink and talking about their origins and their childhood. Butt's parents, it transpired, had a stall on Roman Road market and Butt had himself worked on street markets as a kid. Sullivan had also worked in the market when he was at school. Several of the people in his street were market folk, too, he remembered.

'We started talking about the various characters,' Sullivan remembers, 'and we both finally agreed that the most interesting people were the fly-pitchers with their suitcases and total disregard for licences. They would turn up sometimes for an hour, sometimes for ten minutes, and then they would be away on their toes. They were always funny characters, always selling absolute rubbish like mock perfume.'

Just talking about the fly-pitchers set Sullivan's fertile mind wondering. Where did they come from? What was their background? And what were their names? Invariably, they were somewhat secretive and they did not allow anyone to get to know them well.

Over the next few weeks, Sullivan and Butt would meet up at Butt's local, The Three Kings, on the corner of London's North End Road and Talgarth Road, and sit talking until gradually Sullivan began forming the idea of a family with two brothers separated by a large age gap. Sullivan had a sister 15 years older than himself and Colin, the Best Man at his wedding, also had a brother who was much older. So Sullivan envisaged a fraternal relationship where one brother was a man and the other was a little kid so that the relationship was one that was protective. The idea of an arm-round-the-shoulder fraternal love fascinated Sullivan.

From there, Sullivan began weaving in various characteristics. Crucially, he decided that Rodney, the younger brother, should be earnest and artistic and would not enjoy the life that elder brother Del lived. And yet he simply had to be tolerant of brother Del's ways. He had no choice in the matter because that was where the money was coming from.

'There was a guy I knew called Chicky Stocker and I used him for an awful lot of Del. He's dead now, poor chap, but he was very much the template for Del. I was using real people and real situations from my own life. And to represent the older generation there would be this wonderful grandad, grumpy but loveable.'

Finally, Sullivan sent Butt a script.

'It was marvellous,' Butt remembers. 'Simple as that.'

Bursting with enthusiasm Butt took the script to revered BBC comedy boss John Howard Davies, the man behind comedy classics like *The Good Life* and *Fawlty Towers*. This time, to Butt's joy, the response was more than encouraging. There would be no pilot, but there would be a series.

Sullivan believes that this change of heart from the BBC hierarchy had much to do with ITV's success with *Minder*, starring

George Cole as a London wide-boy with Dennis Waterman as his bone-headed bodyguard. *Minder* had shown that the new multi-racial London with shots of breaker's yards and railway arches in areas like Fulham and Camden could work on screen. But it was also because Howard Davies knew an exceptional script when he saw one.

Butt and Sullivan were elated but casting proved to be a problem. Nicholas Lyndhurst was the first to be signed up to play Rodney. He had enjoyed great success as teenager Adam going through growing pains in another BBC sitcom *Butterflies* and John Howard Davies knew from the start he was ideal for the part and Butt agreed he was an excellent choice. Sullivan wondered if the young actor wasn't a little too middle-class, having watched him mainly in *Butterflies*, but as soon as he saw Nick in action he enthusiastically agreed he was perfect.

Nicholas Lyndhurst was confident from the start that *Only Fools and Horses* would be a success. He said, 'A lot of people upstairs at the BBC did not believe that David and I could be brothers, and rightly so. But that was part of the appeal. I was pretty tall even then and it was only when we started reading that you could tell there was a chemistry between us. Although it has been worked on and polished a lot ever since, at that very first reading Lennard Pearce, who played Grandad so beautifully, and David and I just hit if off straight away. There was something there that leaped straight off the page. So off we went. There were still people saying, "I don't think they work as brothers," but we did the series anyway and I don't think anyone ever questioned it after that.'

Nicholas cleverly used his own naturally gangly frame to accentuate Rodney's awkwardness and the endless cleverly constructed friction between the brothers became the core of the success of the show. Yet both actors instilled such a warmth and humanity to their characters the viewers knew that, however angry and frustrated they became with each other, if the chips were down they would each do anything to support the other.

Nicholas said, 'Rodney would grumble about having all the dirty and difficult jobs to do but he would still do them. He knew how much he owed to Del for looking after him and bringing him up. Of course, they argue with each other all the time but they care very deeply about each other. I think that is one of the things that appeals to the viewers, the family togetherness. They might be a strange family but they are very caring.'

In spite of the age difference, there was an immediate bond between the two actors. Both had built up a deserved reputation in the business for professionalism. This can sometimes be short-hand for 'difficult', but not in their case. *Only Fools* quickly built up a tightly-knit team as the quality of the whole operation became a legend inside the BBC. Even the most experienced cameramen and technicians have been known to quietly cry with laughter when the Trotter brothers get going.

Nick recalls, 'I had actually met David before when I was in a London Weekend TV children's morning show called *Our Show*. It was pretty dire stuff really, all done in a panic, and I was one of five kids who had to interview David about his new show, which was *Lucky Feller*. I was about 16 and very nervous and David didn't remember it at all, but I've got the tape somewhere.'

The two men became firm friends very quickly. Nick said, 'It was pretty much instant between us, getting on together. We are never at a loss for words to each other. We can talk across the board about most things.'

At first, the vastly more experienced David treated young Nicholas as a genuine younger brother as they worked through the early scripts together. David Jason benefited greatly from his long screen partnership with comedy great Ronnie Barker and David was delighted to have the chance to pass on some of his mentor's advice to his new screen partner. But friendship was quickly bolstered by respect. David soon realised that while Nicholas was young in years, he was still a very fine actor.

Producer Ray Butt told the authors, 'Neither David nor Nicholas suffer fools gladly. They both have the very highest standards and they were delighted to find that they really enjoyed working with each other. I think that one of the secrets of the success of the show is that David and Nicholas gelled so well together. They are two of the best actors I know and the characters were just so good for both of them. The early years of *Only Fools* became a magical time for me. I used to look forward to going to work to see this wonderful script, which I had already chortled over several times, come to hilarious life. David and Nick are both very generous actors as well. So once they had gained each other's confidence, they each did everything they possibly could to help the other out. That makes an enormous difference to a show. *Only Fools and Horses* is one of the few comedy shows that was as much fun to make as it was to watch.'

Next to be cast was Lennard Pearce as Grandad. Butt got on the phone to an agent he knew and said he was looking for an old man in the Steptoe mould. He considered Wilfrid Brambell, who had played old Albert Steptoe, and was still around and popular at that time, but Butt decided not to use him because of his strong *Steptoe* identification. The agent said she could not help but passed him on to another agent which resulted in Lennard Pearce duly being auditioned.

Sullivan, who has generally had a big say in the casting of his shows — he cast Paul Nicholas in *Just Good Friends*, Robert Lindsay in *Citizen Smith*, and Ralph Bates in *Dear John* — knew Lennard Pearce was perfect for Grandad the minute he opened his mouth. 'It was that lovely voice of his,' says Sullivan. 'It was a deep, croaky voice, a great voice. As soon as Lennard went, I said, "That's him!"'

The biggest problem now remained. Who could they get to play the key role of Derek Trotter? Butt and Sullivan racked their brains but no obvious names presented themselves.

After much deliberation, their first choice for the role of Del-Boy was Enn Reitel, who with his long face bore more than a passing resemblance to Nicholas Lyndhurst. They could certainly have passed as brothers.

An accomplished actor, Reitel concedes he would love to have played Del-Boy. 'I was doing a series for Yorkshire TV at the time and I simply wasn't available,' he explains. 'Sure, it was disappointing, particularly when you consider what *Only Fools and Horses* has grown into. But you can't live your life with hindsight. It might have run for only one series then bombed.'

Had he taken the role, Reitel's face might now be as famous as David Jason's. But on that score he has absolutely no regrets. 'I prefer the anonymity,' he says firmly. Since then, Reitel has starred in his own ITV series, the highly forgettable *Mog*, and has provided the voices for a whole range of *Spitting Image* characters from Lester Piggott to Dustin Hoffman.

With Reitel out of the reckoning, the then little-known Jim Broadbent was the next actor to be offered the part of Del-Boy. But Broadbent had just opened in a play at Hampstead and it was transferring to the West End. A fine, conscientious actor, Broadbent felt he would be unable to give all his energy to the play if he was doing a TV series as well. Ray Butt could only admire him for his honesty and later used him in another role in *Only Fools and Horses* as the loathsome policeman Roy Slater, Del's former schoolmate and Raquel's ex-husband.

Continuing his search, Butt went to look at an actor appearing in a play called *Moving* with Penelope Keith. He didn't find his Del but he did find another important member of the *Only Fools and Horses* cast — Roger Lloyd-Pack who plays Trigger.

The moment Lloyd-Pack walked on stage Butt was immediately struck by his likeness to Sullivan's description of Trigger. In the very first episode, the explanation is given for Trigger's name. Is it because he packs a gun? No, it's because he looks like a horse.

At that time, Lloyd-Pack had a strange, almost Mohican haircut and it looked to Butt like a horse's mane. The moment Butt first saw him, he said to himself, 'That's the man for Trigger.'

Roger Lloyd-Pack is delighted by the role. He says, 'Trigger is great fun to do. It sort of developed as it went along. We do enjoy it and always have a lot of fun rehearsing. The characters John Sullivan writes are real characters. They are people he knows. They're not prototype sitcom characters written to a format like so many are on television. They all have a kind of real life and I think that's really what makes the series successful. Everyone identifies with those characters. You feel you know these people. They are real. I think that is why actors enjoy Sullivan's scripts so much.

'I guess there's a real Trigger somewhere. I am not sure I have ever met him, though. He is a bit of a one-off really. There is a Trigger in every group. There is always someone who gets everything wrong. There is always someone who is the butt-end of the joke. He is just slightly slower than everyone else and always misses the point.

'A lot of people think I am Trigger. They talk down to me, and they think I'm a bit stupid. They are patronising and that is annoying. Some people do sort of jeer. But my dustman is quite sweet. He keeps coming round saying, "Can I have your autograph for my son?" And, of course, he's a dustman and Trigger is a dustman so I feel a sort of affinity with him.'

But they still had no Del-Boy.

By now, filming dates were being firmed up for *Only Fools and Horses*, deadlines were approaching, and Butt concedes, 'I was stuck.'

The course of David Jason's career was changed when Butt, still racking his brains for the right Del-Boy, sat down one night to watch a repeat of the Ronnie Barker comedy *Open All Hours*.

Up came a scene where David had something of a solo performance as Granville the ageing errand boy clowning around in the back store of the old shop and Butt looked at him and suddenly the solution to his problem was obvious. He thought to himself, David's absolutely perfect for Del-Boy!

The next day, Butt went into the office and rang Sullivan and put forward his idea of David Jason for Del-Boy. But Sullivan was not happy at all. He could not see David in the role and when Butt then went to his bosses, they were not keen on the idea either, precisely because of David's strong connection with *Open All Hours*.

As creator of the character of Del-Boy, Sullivan felt genuine misgivings about David Jason taking on the role. 'I'd only seen him in *A Sharp Intake of Breath*,' he reasoned, 'and that was all very slapstick, falling over on the floor, opening the washing machine and all the water coming out. I thought that was his style and I was saying that Del had to be sharp, very sharp, tough, an aggressive little guy who has lived in the streets and survived.'

David later recalled, 'John couldn't believe it because I'd played this dopey, wonderful, loveable, Northern character Granville, and thought there was no way I could play this brash, up-front, smart, fast-talking, fast-thinking South Londoner. John was not impressed at all. I will always be indebted to Ray. He stuck to his guns.'

Butt staunchly refused to take 'no' for an answer. He was convinced that David would fill Del's shoes admirably and he wasn't going to give up that easily. He dug his heels in, then fought, quarrelled and argued his case.

David believes, too, that his cause was aided by Sydney Lotterby who had directed *Open All Hours*. Lotterby happened to mention David's name to Ray and reminded him of the time both he and Jason had worked together on a BBC pilot written by Roy Clarke which had eventually come to nothing.

Butt's very strong London accent had intrigued David and when the two men played pool after a day's filming, David always used to talk to Butt as if he was a Cockney. 'David used to take the right Mick out of you,' was Lotterby's timely reminder to Butt.

Finally, Butt sent David a script after winning an agreement from everyone on the production that David should at least be allowed to come in and read with Nick Lyndhurst.

David could hardly believe his eyes when the script arrived. He found himself laughing out loud and having to pause for breath. 'I couldn't wait to turn to the next page,' he remembers. 'It was one of the best scripts I'd ever read to that point — and certainly one of the best characters.'

Although the script leaped off the page at David, astonishingly he was unclear which role was being earmarked for him. 'Apart from playing Granville, I'd played old men,' he explains. 'I didn't obviously think they wanted me to play Grandad, but the thought struck me because I had always been playing silly old characters. I'd worked with Ronnie Barker as his 100-year-old gardener Dithers and played an old man in *Porridge*. I thought Ray might want me to play Grandad. There was no reason I should naturally be the right casting for someone nearer my own age because that had never happened to me. But when he said, "What part do you think you'd be right for?" I immediately said, "Del-Boy. He's a great character."'

Sullivan remembers the read-through vividly. 'They had a little read and although they'd never met before, it was immediate — just like you see it now. They both went into their characters. It was incredible. They had this wonderful chemistry. David was perfect all along and I didn't realise just how perfect he was for the part.'

In fact, David and Nicholas did not know each other although they had previously met briefly some three years before when Nicholas was working on a children's programme for London Weekend Television called *Our Show*. Nicholas had actually interviewed David about his series *Lucky Feller*.

After just five minutes of David and Nicholas reading together, Butt and John Sullivan grinned at each other, nodded, and agreed, 'We've got our Del and Rodney.' And Lennard revelled from the start in Grandad's idleness. When Del described him in Episode One as 'The out-of-work lamplighter waiting for gas to make a comeback', he had real difficulty in containing his own laughter.

Now Sullivan had come round to his way of thinking, Butt set about winning the approval of his BBC bosses. They were worried David had been over-exposed by the long success of *Open All Hours* and was too well established in the role of Granville. Butt could understand their reservations but said he could not agree. He stressed that David would be so very different as Del-Boy.

'I knew David could do it,' he says. 'He was just absolutely right — and still is right.'

'They tried to dissuade Ray,' David recalls. 'The hierarchy said, "No, that's not a good idea." They said they don't even look like brothers. Ray said, "That's the fun of it!"'

Sullivan, his blind spot about David suddenly swept away, was especially pleased that David Jason and Nicholas Lyndhurst looked so very different. Nicholas was just 19 years old when the first episode was filmed and he was tall, very slim and gangling, whereas David was small by comparison and squat.

Sullivan had indicated in the scripts that he wanted the younger brother to be tall and the elder not so. Thinking ahead, Sullivan wanted them to look different to plant the doubt about whether they shared the same parentage. He also wanted to make it look as though they were the only two people in the world who believed they were brothers. Having sown the seeds of doubt from the very start, Sullivan was able to make great capital out of and exploit the suspicion in years to come.

What was beyond question was David's own belief that he could be Del-Boy once he had read the script. 'I knew I could do it. I was convinced. And at the final reading they said to Nick, Lennard and me, "We are going with you three!"'

Nicholas Lyndhurst knew straight away that the new threesome would work, and that he would thoroughly enjoy working with the

Only Fools team — and David Jason in particular. 'As soon as we started reading the scripts together, it was obvious there was a chemistry between the two of us and with Lennard as well,' he said.

'We struck up an instant friendship that has lasted ever since. We are never at a loss for what to say to each other. We can talk about anything. We have completely different ways of switching off, of becoming totally detached from work when we want to be. He hand-builds vintage motorcycles and is brilliant with anything mechanical. I love the outdoor stuff — like watersports and flying. But most important we just have tremendous respect for each other.

'When I read a script I know how he is going to play a scene and say a line and I'm sure he knows in advance how I'm going to play my lines. So there are no big surprises when we get together. We just get on terribly well.'

Remarkably, even at that earliest stage, David was acutely aware that *Only Fools and Horses* was something very special, not just another comedy series. 'I remember going to the bar with Nick and Lennard and I remember I said, "This is not an ordinary sitcom. This is not sitcom, it's more drama. There's an unknown title for this. Everyone calls it sitcom but what John Sullivan has done has superseded that." I sensed it.'

2

Two Boys,
One Dream

The tidy, terraced houses in Lodge Lane, Finchley are more than 200 years old. They were first built as farm cottages for workers on the agricultural estates that swept right down into the edges of North London which have long since been swallowed up by suburbia. On 2 February 1940, as World War II raged bitterly across Europe, one of the coldest winters in years had encouraged most residents to stoke up the fires and stay indoors. But Billingsgate fish porter Arthur White and his sprightly Welsh wife Olwen, who lived at 26 Lodge Lane, were otherwise occupied at the nearby North Middlesex Hospital bringing twin baby boys into the world.

They already had a seven-year-old son, also called Arthur, and they were delighted to doubly increase the size of their young family. Four days later, a neighbour generously used some of his precious petrol ration to ferry Olwen and the baby boys home and for a few days their joy at their domestic bliss was undimmed, even by the horrors of war. But one of the boys was weak and ailing.

His breathing was failing as a massive infection took hold of his fragile frame. Olwen did everything she could to try to breathe life into her sickening son but tragically he died, after just two short weeks of life.

'I was in such despair,' said Olwen bleakly, years later. 'We had decided to call the twins David and Jason. David was healthy but Jason was so sickly he never had a chance and I felt so helpless. I just had to watch him go. I don't even know what was really wrong with him. I buried the tiny body myself, out the back. I didn't know what else to do. We didn't tell anybody. We had no money for a proper burial. It was war and I had it to do.'

The healthy twin thrived and his birth was registered a month afterwards when Arthur and Olwen later trudged to Edmonton Register Office on 19 March to record, sadly, only a single addition to the family. David John White was a lively baby with a powerful set of lungs which he was always eager to exercise for his grieving parents. Olwen and Arthur were devastated by their loss. But they were also determined that their tiny son should not be forgotten, and would often quietly wonder together what might have become of Jason had he been strong enough to survive. Olwen was naturally especially delighted when her surviving twin eventually went on to make the two names so well-loved and famous throughout the land.

Yet, in fact, it was not until David was 14 that he discovered the stunning truth that he was a twin and that his baby brother had died soon after birth. It came as an enormous shock to the teenager. To outsiders, David has always tried hard to look deeply unimpressed by the revelation but in reality it had a shattering effect on the young man. When asked by the authors about his lost brother, he quickly became very businesslike and matter of fact and insisted coolly, 'It just came out during the course of some conversation with my mother that apparently I had had a twin.'

David is typically anxious to play down any hint of the family trauma and would say only, 'The bottom line of the story is that one survived and one did not. It happens all the time. Many years ago, my brother Arthur's wife was pregnant with twins and she lost both of them. They now have a son called Russell which is wonderful.' David insists publicly that he does not feel his determination to do well is any sort of compensation for the death of his brother. 'It has never, ever occurred to me,' he said. 'Two little dots came out. One dot lived and one did not. I just found out casually in the course of a conversation. "You did have a twin, you know," said my mother. I just said, "Oh did I? Oh really." At that time, my mother was great and there was no problem. It was never given any weight and it was not a problem for me. I was not made to feel any responsibility. The irony is that we are all made from a moment in time.'

But one schoolfriend remembers it very differently. 'When he came to school the day after his mum told him about his twin dying, he looked terrible. He was shaking with emotion and he looked absolutely shattered. He swore us to secrecy about it and I don't think he hardly ever mentioned it again. But that day he looked awful, as though all his humour and energy had drained out of him. That day he said he felt guilty but to be honest I think afterwards he somehow drew strength from it, as if he had an added responsibility to achieve things on behalf of his brother as well as himself.'

David's parents were determined to do the very best for all their children. Olwen insisted that the long family tradition of looking after your own was very strongly in her mind. In any case there was a war on and tragedy was an everyday occurrence.

England in 1940 experienced a bitterly cold winter and it was a shivering London that welcomed baby David. The River Thames froze over as temperatures tumbled to the lowest of the century. But inside the humble terraced house, with its outside toilet and its tin bath hanging on a nail in the back door, David White spent his first months and years of life in a home which was always warm and happy, air-raids permitting.

Baby David did his bit for the family war effort by noisily resisting attempts to put on his tiny gas mask. Whenever the air-raid sirens sounded and the family started to move to the relative safety of the shelter erected in the house, David's screams of protest began. 'It used to worry me a lot, that gas mask,' recalls Olwen. 'He just screamed like mad when I put it on him.'

Often David's cries had to compete with the noise of German air-raids which used to inspire his mother to retaliate by hurling curses in the direction of Berlin as she crashed dishes around angrily in her tiny kitchen. Once, the Luftwaffe almost silenced these fearsome attacks with a near miss of a bomb which left the house structurally undamaged but somehow managed to blow out Olwen's cooker. Happily, the only casualty was the cake she was baking at the time.

The war ensured its grim effects were felt as food rationing was brought in and, just four days after the birth of the twins, that most famous of Government campaigns was launched to combat the threat of German spies in our midst: 'Careless Talk Costs Lives'. Olwen was determined to protect her brood from the worst of the war. She brought her brisk efficiency and warm sense of humour from her native Wales. A baby girl, June, completed the family four years after David was born. And while there was never much money to go around, the fiercely independent Olwen supplemented her husband's meagre wages by going out and working as a cleaner.

The wartime blackouts frequently disrupted Arthur's trips to work. He had to get up at about 4.00am to cycle to Billingsgate and early on in the war he overslept. Arthur looked like being very late and was urgently pedalling through a dark and gloomy North London when the road simply disappeared and he went careering into a bomb crater about 50ft wide and 40ft deep.

Arthur was knocked out cold. When he came round about 20 minutes later, he found he was trapped at the bottom of a huge hole and, try as he might, he was unable to scramble up the sides and out. He started shouting for help and after a further 15 minutes two men arrived and shone their torches down on the anguished Arthur.

'Go on,' said Arthur, 'get me out of here, will you, lads?' The faces looking down were shocked and wide-eyed with amazement. Then one of the rescuers said, 'Bloody hell! He's had a 50-ton bomb dropped on him and the bugger's still alive!'

There always was a black side to war-time humour. David's older brother, Arthur Jr, was growing up fast and was quick to capitalise when a German air-raid on North London blasted a part of a human arm up on to the gutter on the roof at the back of number 26 Lodge Lane. Enterprising Arthur was charging the other children 2d a look at the gruesome debris until his sideshow was interrupted by angry adults. The local doctor was called to remove the arm and take it away in a bag, much to the irritation and disappointment of Arthur and his ghoulish young customers.

Arthur was always a boisterous lad and came close to ending one of Britain's most promising acting careers some 20 years before it began, with a badly aimed house brick. Arthur recalled the incident with a wince.

'When we were schoolboys, David wanted to come to a camp I had made with my mates. I wouldn't let him, and he was hanging about trying to get in. Unfortunately, he got in the way of a brick I was throwing at our "enemies". It hit him on the head and nearly killed him. I was shattered and to this day he still carries the scar.'

Olwen was the driving force of the family and, on most matters, whatever she said went. Neighbours were always treated with just enough friendliness and respect but kept firmly at a safe distance. The family was well-liked but Olwen saw to it that they always kept themselves very much to themselves.

David's early explorations of his locality were conducted by means of a somewhat unusual form of transport — a rickety wooden wheelbarrow. Next-door neighbour Ernie Pressland recalls David as, 'a little, ragged-arsed sod in a barrow. His brother Arthur used to get lumbered with pushing him around. All the kids from Lodge Lane used to stick together in one great big sprawling gang. Arthur was our leader, we used to call him "King Arthur", and we used to go scrumping apples over near the posh houses in Totteridge.'

The Whites were one important social step up on the Presslands in that their air-raid shelter was an indoor Morrison device while their neighbours relied upon an outdoor Anderson version to save them from the Germans. But after young Eileen Pressland caught what tragically became a fatal dose of pneumonia after a night of shivering in the cold, the family shunned either form of shelter. Ernie recalls, 'After Eileen died, we all slept together in the same bedroom, all six kids and my mum and dad. My mother said, "We'll all go together if we go." But we all became close in the Blitz. The Whites were good friends and neighbours.'

Young David was known as 'Whitey' and, it seems, had a real dramatic talent right from his early days. Ernie Pressland remembers, 'I had been firing potato pellets from a toy gun and David reckoned I'd copped him one in the ear. I didn't really know if I hit him but he went through such a dying spasm act that my mother went bananas and broke the gun to pieces over my back.'

It was certainly obvious to all the family that David's flair for acting was there from a very early age. Olwen found her children's favourite game was dressing up. Her frilly blouses and floppy hats, dresses and coats and her husband's trousers and shirts were all in constant demand from the three youngsters who loved to act out their own little plays. Arthur, the oldest, generally took the early lead in the junior White dramatic society but David and June always seemed to be playing the biggest parts by the end.

When they got older, they pestered their mother to take them to scour junk shops for even more outlandish outfits. Olwen encouraged the artistic side in her offspring. She was steeped in the Welsh family tradition of creating your own entertainment with large gatherings with every relation called upon to deliver a song or a monologue.

In fact, when the children moved on to nearby Northside School, it was June who impressed dramatically with a spirited portrayal of Queen Victoria in an early school play. At Northside, David's cheeky sense of humour certainly began to develop. His best friend was a lad called Mike Weedon who lived just two streets away in Grange Avenue. The two youngsters made sure that life was never dull for their English teacher, an endlessly harassed lady called Miss Holmes. Mike recalls that one of David's early pranks was to spray on a little extra decoration to her dress.

'I remember once, as Miss Holmes walked up the aisle between our desks with a smart blue dress on, David got a pen full of ink and flicked it on to the back of her dress. She never knew it was him as the ink blended in with the colour of the dress.'

David was always the form clown and his high-spirited partnership with Mike Weedon made sure both boys were regularly in trouble with some teachers. 'We were always getting separated because of our antics,' recalls Mike Weedon. 'Every lesson seemed to begin with "White, get down to the front of the class. Weedon, get to the back of the class." We always tried to sit next to each other, but we played up too much.'

Certainly, Miss Holmes did not always fully appreciate David's irrepressible sense of fun. She once caned him in front of the class, and caned him very hard and on his wrist as well as his hand.

Mike Weedon says, 'She was so mad at something he had done

she struck him haphazardly across the wrist and we couldn't believe it when David turned round and said, "I'm going to report you to the Headmaster." And he went right along to the Headmaster, Mr Maurice Hackett. Huge weals had come up on his wrist and he just stormed out of the classroom and into the Head's office. She got into trouble and was told to ease off by the Head. She missed his hand and hit his wrist and it could have been quite damaging.' David was never shy at sticking up for himself. He was well below average height but somehow his energy and his ready wit meant that he was rarely picked on by bigger boys.

But Mr Hackett was not always so sympathetic. David and Mike packed countless scrapes into their school careers. A favourite way to start the day was to devise a new way of avoiding assembly in the morning. One day, the pair dodged down into a darkened tunnel area that ran underneath school to get out of the tedious ceremony. Unfortunately, the tunnel contained a drain which swiftly soaked them up to the ankles in water. And much worse was to come when they squelched out after assembly.

Mike remembers, 'We kept quiet until everybody had gone and crept up the stairs and round to the front door. Who should be standing there, but Mr Hackett. He caught us fair and square and we had to wait outside his room before we finally got the cane. One stroke on the hand.'

David certainly did not shine in his first years at school. He was painfully shy and in his early teens lacked any sort of confidence in himself. But a perceptive and thoughtful teacher helped him to develop. David said, 'When I first started at school I was not very bright and I did not do very well. I always seemed to be very backward. Then I found that there was something I could do well and that helped me a lot. I was always very physical and we had a very good young teacher, called Mr Joy, who taught us gymnastics. Because I was agile and could do things he said, "That is very good," and he told the rest of the class to watch how I did one exercise and try to copy it.'

David had never before been used as an example for his contemporaries to follow, and he thoroughly enjoyed the experience. 'It was the first time a teacher had ever said anything like that to me. That was a big turning point for me, because I thought if I can do that in gymnastics, why can't I do it in History or Geography or whatever?

'I was never very good at Maths but at English and Science I began to creep up the scale because I realised that if I could do something well physically, it gave me a spur. Before then, I believe that deep down I had subconsciously given up. I always used to feel the lessons were so complicated and I would just give up before I started so I was always bottom of the class. But Mr Joy proved that I could do something well. That gave me enormous confidence and it opened the door for me. I was a natural gymnast and it has been with me ever since.

'He started me reading a lot and helped me in every way. I worked at Science and got an award, and I went on to become a prefect, and captain of the football and swimming teams. I owe that man a lot.' David deliberately avoided pointing out that his improvement at school exactly coincided with his discovery that he was a surviving twin. He prefers not to delve into the psychology of loss but it seems clear that his new-found purpose and sense of awareness had at least some connection with the surprising new knowledge that he was living while his brother was dead.

Maureen Wanders was another teacher who treated young David more sensitively. She spotted his flair for entertaining and recalls, 'He was a natural performer who always made the other children laugh. He seemed to stop growing when he was 13 or 14 and I think he was quite self-conscious about being short. But he was high-spirited and very popular. He brought the house down in one play we put on.

'And in class he could always be relied upon to liven things up. He wasn't naughty — just great fun, and with a great sense of humour. David shone at English, but Drama was where his real talent lay. You could not miss his natural flair.'

David frankly recalled, 'At school I was a well-known joker and the reason why was because I was very small and very slight and in order to survive I started clowning. I think this is true of a lot of people who are in comedy.

'In my case, I knew that if you're little you tend to get beaten up by the bigger lads so in order to defend myself as I was not very well-built I decided to make them laugh. It was no help being a coward. They kicked cowards. You had to use your brains. And all bullies need a court jester. I couldn't fight them with my fists so I fought them with my wits. I didn't want to get kicked to death so I made them laugh. I really worked at it so if there was any problem I could get them so busy laughing that they forgot about beating me up.'

David was always able to laugh off his lack of inches but just sometimes he did yearn to be tall. He often looked smaller than he was because he was swallowed by clothes provided just a little too big to give long-lasting value. 'We never had much money in our family,' he said. 'Everything I owned my mother would say, "He'll grow into it," so I had jackets with sleeves that were too long and shoes that were too big. And one Christmas when I was 10 or 11, the thing I wanted more than anything was a bike. Come Christmas morning and there it was — but my feet wouldn't reach the pedals.

'As usual, my mother had bought me a full-sized model "to grow into". My father had to put wooden blocks on the pedals and even then my toes only just touched them. My street cred really plummeted after that.' David's mother always had great hopes for her children. She was pleased that David's schoolwork was improving but still anxious to help. She frequently sent David, and any other youngsters she could dragoon, up to the local library in Finchley to listen to worthy self-improving lectures as an addition to their schoolwork.

A third youngster, called Brian Barneycoat and known as Bodgy for short, became friendly with the young pair and the trio became great pals for many years. Even as a young boy, the most noticeable thing about David was his sharp sense of humour. He led the threesome on a trip into Central London to see his radio heroes The Goons. Peter Sellers was David's childhood idol. He played his Goons records over and over again on the record player in the White front room and marvelled at the hilarious Sellers mimicry and range of voices. David was addicted to the Goons and thoroughly enjoyed watching one episode being recorded. He said, 'They broke all the rules and, of course, the older generation did not understand what on earth we were all going on about. They were so off the wall.'

David gradually realised that he had a talent to amuse, even if it did embarrass his friends sometimes. A favourite early comic stunt was to alarm the occupants of a crowded Tube train by pretending to sew his fingers together. 'He would pull a hair from his head and then go to thread it through a needle,' recalls Mike Weedon. 'He would start with his little finger and work round them all and then pass through the palm of his hand. Then he would pull it and automatically the fingers of his hands would close. He would take about ten minutes for it all to happen and people would be fascinated. We would be cringing, it was so embarrassing. We all thought he was crazy. But I suppose he was only acting.'

Not all young David's attempts at humour were quite so subtle. A hapless window cleaner, widely considered by David and his young pals in Lodge Lane to be something of a dirty old man, experienced a rather smellier and more slapstick comedy routine. In those days, when horse-drawn carts were still a familiar feature of the North London traffic, the window cleaner always carried buckets to scoop up the horse droppings to sell as manure to some of the enthusiastic rose growers of the community. This meant his barrow was usually laden with not just ladders but buckets of steaming natural fertiliser.

David thoughtfully inserted two bangers deep into one bucket, lit the fuse and made a run for it. The resulting explosion left the poor window cleaner and a couple of innocent passers-by simply covered in horse muck.

Ernie's younger sister Julie Pressland was a good friend from childhood. She remembers the incident clearly. 'We all thought the window cleaner was a pervert so no one was very sorry for him,' she says. 'It was a real mess. There was horse shit everywhere. The window cleaner was really mad and, kids being kids, someone told him David was responsible. But by then, David was long gone.

'That was pretty typical of David. He was full of devilment but he never did anyone any real harm. It was just for a joke. He loved to make people laugh even in those days. I remember he had an air gun and he filled another neighbour's tin bath full of holes.

'Another time we had some washing strung out on a line in the back yard and my mum kept looking out and saying, "There's a funny wind — it's only blowing the knickers." David was hanging out of his back window taking pot shots at our underwear with his toy gun! There were five women in our family so there were always plenty of drawers on the line for him to aim at.'

David did later become an accomplished cook, but one of his early efforts looked distinctly unpalatable. His mother was baking and young David came out into the yard with some pastry that he said he wanted to make into pies. He mixed it up with leaves, mud and sugar and baked it. Then, when he had cooked the alarming mixture he sat down and ate it. And with characteristically convincing dramatic style he pretended he was munching on a chocolate eclair!

Julie says, 'He was always very funny. And even when we were young he could walk into a room and make people laugh. It was never unkind, cruel humour but always gentle, taking the mickey out of himself instead of other people. He would make a joke about his lack of height and get everyone laughing at him. We lived on the poor side of the street. The houses on the other side were more expensive and we always used to call that the posh side.'

Julie and David spent hours just chatting in the rickety lean-to which separated their tiny back gardens. 'He was always good to be with because he was such a laugh. His imagination would always conjure up stories and jokes. But he did have a serious side. I remember once he planted this tree at the bottom of his garden. It was really more a yard than a garden. There were no flowers or greenery at all and he wanted to make it look nicer. He really nurtured this tree. He watered it and really tried to look after it. I think he was a sort of premature "green". It got to be about 6ft tall and he was really proud of it. Then the man whose garden backed on to David's chopped it down one day when we were at school. He said it cut out his light. David was absolutely gutted. Really upset.'

Julie's older sister Maureen was impressed by David's ability to mimic a wide range of different voices. 'I'll never forget David coming outside into the yard at the back on a warm summer's night and putting on a really posh voice, "Would you care to take the air on the veranda?" he said and then he laughed. He had the kind of laugh which meant you just had to laugh with him.'

David was by now above average at his lessons but rarely excelled. He saved his efforts for more worthwhile causes, like arguing passionately with his pals that Elvis Presley should most certainly make that much talked about but never realised tour of Britain. And at that stage, David was completely unaware that he had a genuine link with Presley through the death of a twin sibling.

★   ★   ★

Acting entered young David's life in school plays. Mike Weedon remembers acting with him in an early play called *The Ostler*. 'He had a singing part and really shone. Even as a boy he had a real charisma about him on stage.'

David had his own room at home where he spent hours listening to the radio. His favourite show was the science-fiction adventure series *Journey into Space* and he sent off for a picture of the crew of the Discovery. He was delighted when it arrived, complete with autographs on the back.

David's house was usually the base for the youngsters and Mike Weedon recalls it was generally Olwen who took an interest in their youthful games and ambitions. 'His dad was an old sour-puss, old Arthur. David's mum was fun. But Arthur had a very bad gait and would limp and that might have been part of his bad moods. He kept out of the way and we kept out of his way. Although his dad always had an eye out that we didn't really get into trouble.'

What Mike Weedon never knew was that Arthur senior was wracked with pain from crippling arthritis. David was often deeply upset when he saw his father in agony. It left a lasting impression on him and in later life he frequently took time out quietly to help arthritis charities.

The intrepid threesome all shared a lack of inches. They were all very short for their age all the way through school but were never unduly worried. 'We used to call ourselves The Shorthouses,' laughed Mike Weedon. 'I got picked on a couple of times because of my size but David was so funny and well liked I don't think he ever got picked on.'

But perhaps the event which really shaped the future came when David was 14, just after his mother had broken the news to him about his dead twin. The school play had a problem when a young actor dropped out with measles and Headmaster Hackett was looking around for a replacement. David remembers, 'For some reason he decided I could do this part. I can still hear him saying, "White, I want a word with you." I thought, Oh Gawd, what have I done now? This is it. I must be in trouble again.'

But in fact the Head carried the news that the boy's illness would keep him out of the production and cheeky young David White was his choice as a replacement. 'I want you to take over,' he told David. Perhaps surprisingly, the suggestion was not then a welcome one. David might have enjoyed dressing up and larking about at home but doing it in public before the critical eyes of his pals was quite another thing. 'I wasn't very keen at all,' he says. 'I thought acting and plays were girls' things. When you're in a working-class school, being in a play seems like playing girls' games. You don't fancy doing it because it's all a bit girlish and I most definitely wanted to be seen as one of the lads.'

But the Headmaster insisted. 'I think you would be absolutely right and you are the only one I can think of to do this part,' he said firmly. The expression on David's face told its own reluctant tale so the Head added cryptically, 'Let me put it this way. Don't ask me to tell you to do it.'

With that, he left young David White to cogitate on his first troublesome casting problem. 'I was standing there for about five minutes trying to work out what he had said,' remembered David. 'Of course, I worked out that I was going to do it anyway. The difference was that he was asking me to do it. I slowly realised that if I said "No" he was going to tell me to do it. That was it. It was a *fait accompli*, really. I had no choice, I did it under duress.'

The play was a one-act production called *Wayside War*, set during the time of the Cromwellian Wars. David embarked on the new experience with a heavy heart: 'I was playing a cavalier and dressing up in all those funny clothes made it even worse. But something happened to me when I started to do it. It was somehow amazing. It was fun. It worked. After all that pressure to take part, I found to my complete surprise that I was actually enjoying myself.

'It was a spy story, based on real events which had actually happened which really intrigued me. There was a spy in Bridgewater who was giving all this information to the other side. This cavalier stayed at this inn and he knew someone in the area was giving all the secrets away but he did not know who. There was a wonderful woman in this hostelry and they met and spent the evening, and later the night, together. Of course, during this he discovers that she was the spy.

'But he sort of falls in love with her and the next morning she is going off and he knows that he has got to arrest her because she is putting his side in danger. But he lets her go. Obviously he should never have done that, but he did. Because it was all based on actual happenings, for the first time it made history come alive for me. And being on stage was an amazing experience for me.

'We did it for three nights. Our parents and friends all came and it went down really well. Then they said we were going to do it in a drama festival. That was something completely new to me, I didn't know what a drama festival was. But I found out that all these amateur groups and schools put in their shows and then over about two weeks they all get performed. And you go and watch a lot of the other plays and then on the last night the four plays selected by the adjudicator are performed. Our play was chosen in the last four, and then after we did it we found out that we had won the trophy. It bowled me over. Suddenly there was a competitive thing in my life and I met all these people who were enthusiastic about acting. Just being in the play was amazing. I can remember the audience laughing and it occurred to me that I was really, really enjoying it. It was a way of being clever and a success, and I'd never been much of either in school.'

David's mother was impressed. She said, 'We knew he had something special. He had this quick way with him that could lift people in the audience. I think it comes from our family. Back in Wales, our family would always provide their own entertainment.

Everyone stood up and did a turn, going back generations. Something of that went straight through to David. But not just to him, to all my children. Arthur and June had it, too, and it made me think of the baby that died. I told David and he gave me one of his looks.'

The stage success gave young David confidence but he still had no thought of acting becoming a career. 'I don't think I gave a second thought to taking it that seriously,' said David. 'I was much too busy having a good time.'

The teenage trio of David, Mike Weedon and Brian Barneycoat enjoyed their own company and after school would rush off on their bicycles on trips into the green countryside on the very edge of London. At weekends, they would cycle to Broxbourne to secret dens they made on the banks of the River Lea.

Next-door neighbour Ernie Pressland was called up for National Service at 18 and sold his bicycle to David who was four years younger. It was a flash model with 'Tour de France' handlebars and the price was £2. 'I was ripped off and not for the first time,' reflected David bleakly. Even so, the trio would think nothing of round trips of 50 miles or more and all have memories of long, sun-filled idyllic days. Mike Weedon remembers, 'We were three loners really, I suppose. We didn't get into girls' company much. We really liked our bikes.'

David was unquestionably the leader of the little gang and usually the inspiration of their escapades. Mike Weedon recalls fondly, 'David organised so many pranks that it became commonplace for him to do it. If he didn't lark about then you knew he must be in a really bad mood. He would play around all the time. He was really a fairly good student but he never stood out.'

But baiting teachers with practical jokes and at all costs avoiding taking schoolwork too seriously did not endear the trio to the school authorities. Headmaster Hackett was concerned, as the boys approached 15, that their childish pranks could turn into more serious teenage trouble-making and wisely decided that perhaps they needed a more creative outlet for their energy and mischief. Recognising David's considerable dramatic skill and potential ability to act more than the goat, he sent the two young lads with another problem boy to Douglas Weatherhead, then the drama instructor for Middlesex who was running an evening drama group attached to the local amateur Incognito Theatre Group.

'I've got three boys here and if they don't find themselves something to do they're going to get themselves into trouble,' said the Headmaster to the amiable Mr Weatherhead, who was still a stalwart of the Incognitos some 35 years on but sadly passed away in 1996. He welcomed the three nervous youngsters and introduced them to the Incognito Theatre, an old soda siphon factory converted by the enthusiastic amateurs with seats from a blitzed cinema, which remains their headquarters to this day.

Douglas Weatherhead recalls fondly, 'Right from the start I could see that David was quite obviously a winner. Mike Weedon was quite reasonable but David, you could see from the start, was simply exceptional. He picked up accents and intonations beautifully. He would have been a very good serious actor, but of course his lack of height went against him. In those days, you had to be the classic tall and good-looking Laurence Olivier type to get anywhere. I can't remember the third boy's name but we lost him quite quickly. David and Mike, who were real pals, stayed.'

David recalls that his initial euphoria at acting with the Incognitos was not totally based upon dramatic ambition. 'We went down there for the first time one Monday night because we were now inflamed with the success of *Wayside War*. And we found that there were 22 girls there and one bloke. We thought, Yeah, we'll have some of that. That was our first picture of the

Incognitos. I think that is what coloured our enthusiasm really.

'They had a proper senior amateur group and they also had this fabulous training group for young people as well. It was marvellous. They had their own little theatre. They trained lots of people to act. It was very good, it was a way of getting young people involved with the theatre. It was like a social group, of course, but there was also the chance to take parts in the senior group. They taught me so many of the skills of the theatre.

'We used to go on Mondays and Wednesdays and it quickly became much more than a hobby for me. It gradually became more and more fascinating and more and more interesting. The more I found out about acting, the more interesting it became.

'The more new doors I opened up the more I realised there was to acting. It got steadily more difficult and because it got more difficult I always wanted more and more to get over the next hurdle to learn the new technique or understand the next new idea. I wanted to succeed as an actor so much and I was desperate to improve my skills. But every level I reached seemed to open up new levels to aim at. The more deep and the more complex the whole business of acting became the more involved I became. I was there for ten years and in that time I went and acted with other amateur groups as well. As I was given more and more important roles to play, the challenge became greater.

'I never found acting an easy thing to do. It was difficult, very difficult. But because it was so difficult it became a question of developing dedication and application to try to keep improving and developing my skills. And I learned early on that the only person who can really do all that is yourself. I tried to learn and absorb from people who knew more than me, from teachers, directors, actors or anyone, and I tried to apply that knowledge in every way I could.'

Part of David's initial audition for the Incognitos was to pretend to be much older, first 45 and then 85. Most youngsters of his age would scarcely have appreciated the difference and been inclined to bend every joint stiff to simulate either stage of life. But David, observers recall, was able apparently to suggest effortlessly the difference between middle age and great age.

'David was a natural,' says Douglas Weatherhead. 'He took to acting like a duck to water. Mike was a great friend of David's and he was quite good but, of course, David was so much better that he always got the big parts while Mike was left with the small parts.

'David was also a great joker. He had a marvellous sense of humour and used to tease Mike that he was forever trying to pad out his parts. On one occasion, when Mike was supposed to have suffered a small cut on his cheek in a Drayton and Hare farce, David joked that he would no doubt finish up as a number-one accident case.

'David always kept us in fits of laughter. Whenever we took a break for coffee, he kept the whole thing going. I never did find out what sort of trouble the Headmaster thought he was heading for, but once he found an outlet in acting there was no sign of any trouble from him. That was it. He was wide-eyed with enthusiasm when he arrived.

'I remember that, like most of the young lads at the time, he never had much money. And once we were rehearsing a play with David taking a leading role when one of our rather stuffier senior members remarked rather pointedly that David had still not stumped up his annual membership subscription. I think it was half a crown at the time. I was so indignant at this and so impressed by David's talent that I said if the lad didn't pay it, I would pay it myself. And I would have done — it would have been a very worthwhile investment, don't you think?'

Despite their lack of academic dedication, both David and Mike Weedon became prefects in their final year at Northside. Their authority in handing out lines and detention to their juniors was hardly helped by their lack of inches. Both were just 5ft 4in tall when they left school. We did shoot up a bit afterwards,' says Mike. 'And we both finished at 5ft 6in.'

The final act of leaving school was quite a traumatic experience for them. Mike remembers, 'We had always been saying that we couldn't wait to leave school, but on the last day I know we all really didn't want to go. It was a very emotional experience for all of us. We all had to go up on stage in turn and there was this great big guy called John Smith who went up and just burst out crying he was so upset. There were tears streaming down his face and I know it affected us all. David was highly strung and a very sensitive young man. After all our big talk about the future, we were really surprised at how choked we all felt.'

The diminutive trio remained good friends long after they left school and, as soon as they were 16, they all exchanged their faithful pushbikes for much more exciting motorbikes which instantly enlarged the scope of their adventures. David's first motorbike was an aged 350cc BSA on which he lavished hours of tender loving care.

His mother was never too keen on her precious son's new obsession, fearing the dangers of David revving around the country on the powerful machine. She was even less enthusiastic when he took the bike to pieces in her tiny hallway. Bitterly cold weather meant that this was the only place to service the bike but Olwen gave David a fierce telling off every time a drop of oil found its way on to her carpet.

The motorbikes changed the lives of the youngsters. Their horizons were suddenly limitless. All of a sudden, from being limited to within a few hours' pedalling distance of their homes, they could now explore the whole country. First on the list was the Lake District.

With David leading the way on his powerful 350cc machine, with Brian Barneycoat — or 'Bodgy' as he was known — riding pillion and Mike following on his smaller 250cc bike, they set out to explore the beauties of the Lakes. Unfortunately, the bargain basement accommodation turned out to be not even worth the small sum they paid for it. 'When we got there, we found it was a terrible little caravan on the banks of Lake Windermere,' said Mike Weedon. 'We only got it cheap because it was falling to bits. It was parked right on the side of the lake and it was pretty miserable really, especially when I ended up getting left behind when my bike packed up.'

Despite his enthusiasm for high speed, David was usually a careful motorcyclist, yet he did come close to losing his life on his motorbike when he was racing back from Clacton, with Mike Weedon riding pillion. It was a busy summer evening with the main roads so clogged with traffic that inventive David had picked a favourite personal short-cut winding round a sequence of back roads. As dusk fell, the two youngsters thrilled to the speedy journey and leaned energetically into every bend, until they reached a particularly sharp corner when David yelled to his passenger, 'There's too much gravel, I'm going to lose it.'

To Mike's horror, David pulled out of the bend, straightened the screaming machine and went straight ahead over the bank at the side of the road. With enormous good fortune, they crashed violently through the undergrowth and found the road again on the other side. They hit the bank and the bike just took off. When they landed again, they were remarkably lucky to hit the road facing straight ahead and carried on unscathed. Mike breathlessly yelled to his daring driver, 'Dave, Dave, stop. Let's have a fag.'

But the daredevil young man on his flying machine was seriously scared himself. He yelled back grimly, 'If I stop now, I'll lose my nerve,' and just kept on heading for home.

David's love of speed was undimmed by the experience. He later exchanged his trusty 350cc BSA for a much more powerful

500cc Shooting Star which could comfortably exceed the magical 'ton'. Mike Weedon recalls, 'He really cherished that 500. He did the ton more than once. He loved high speed. He used to get quite excited about having gone more than 100mph. We had no farings to make us more streamlined in those days, so David would lie down as flat as he could on the bike to get up to those sorts of speeds. He loved it.

'We used to race each other up the A1 and back down the Watford by-pass, but it was nothing really serious. We just enjoyed racing for the fun of it and hoped the police didn't manage to spot us.'

David plays down his high-speed youth and insists, 'We were never real tearaways on the bikes, we were gentleman motorcyclists. There were the rockers, but me and my mates had flat caps and goggles and we weren't into all the Teddy Boy thing either. We were very shy and found it very difficult to talk to the ladies and we didn't succeed in that department at all. So we concentrated on our motorbikes. I suppose that is what young lads do — find other ways to expend their energy. We used to strip them down, heat them up, and rebuild them.

'I was so into motorbikes that in our outside toilet on the toilet roll holder was carved something like "While You Sit Here You Will Have All Your Best Dreams". And I wrote underneath "Or A Super Road Rocket". At the time, that was the Mercedes Benz of motorbiking.

'Today I drive a Jaguar XJS. In those days, a Super Road Rocket was as far away as the moon or an XJS because they cost about £750 then. We were earning £12 a week then. If I really pushed myself, I could save £2 a week which I did.'

The three lads also spent a few weeks with Bodgy's grandfather down in Cornwall where they were all bedded down in the same room on a huge straw mattress for the night. Mike remembers, 'It was in a little place called Mylor where there was a creek which led to Falmouth Bay. We all went out on a fishing trip in this rowing boat and tried to catch some mackerel.

'Then the tide turned and we had to suddenly start trying to row in against the tide. For a long time we didn't seem to be getting anywhere but finally we managed to get back into the creek and back to Bodgy's grandfather's place only to be told that the mackerel were out of season. We had been wasting our time.'

Mike and Bodgy finished the day drowning their sorrows with a few beers in the local, The Pandora Inn. On the way home, they had to climb a 1:4 hill. A combination of disappointment and alcohol had dimmed their concentration and they lost control and completed a difficult day by finishing up in a ditch. But David missed out on this final disaster because he had chatted up a young lady down by the seaside and had taken her out for the evening. He was starting to realise that laughter was a great way of breaking the ice with a girls. 'I could never impress a girl by being cool or sophisticated,' said David, 'even if I wanted to. But if I could make them laugh, they seemed to become more friendly.'

David was the first of the trio to take much of an interest in the opposite sex, although he was always careful to make sure that girls never came between him and his motorbike. He was always close to girl next door, Julie Pressland, who was just three years younger.

'Julie was always sweet on David,' remembers Mike Weedon. 'But I don't think there was ever any reciprocation there. We were just young guys and girls never really came into our lives that much at the time, even David's.'

Julie insists she and David were only ever very good friends. 'I was never his girlfriend, or in love with him, or any of the other nonsense that has been suggested. I know he did have girlfriends but to me he was always so single-minded that what he wanted to do was to make it as an actor, and I don't think there was ever any room for a serious romance or marriage. As long ago as I can remember, he was so dedicated to making it that nothing was going to get in his way. I think he always thought, deep down, that you could either have a normal family life, a marriage and children and all that or you could be a successful actor. He just didn't believe you could do both. He felt if you tried to carry a wife and children along as an actor they would somehow fall by the wayside.'

Julie was perceptive enough to know that the real and enduring love of David's life was to be his acting. Certainly he enjoyed passing flirtations with girls quick enough to follow his sharp sense of humour but he never had the obsession for the opposite sex that drove so many young men to devote their lives to the pursuit. David reflected later, 'When I was 16, the only thing my mates were interested in was the pub, the dance hall and girls. The last thing they were interested in was acting. You had to have guts to run against the tide.'

★   ★   ★

David Jason and Nicholas Lyndhurst may have become household names through the same TV show but their routes to fame could hardly have been more different.

David was an enthusiastic amateur for many years before turning professional, whereas Nicholas was essentially groomed for a career in showbusiness from boyhood.

Born in Emsworth, Hampshire, on 20 April 1961, Nicholas from an early age constantly pestered his mother to send him off to stage school. He went on about it so much that eventually she gave in and managed to scrape enough money together for him to become a weekly boarder for half a term at the prestigious Corona Academy in London. She was sure that would get the acting bug out of his system, but Nicholas was soon earning his own money from commercials which helped him to pay his stage school fees.

'I was a sweet-faced little boy with blond hair and I immediately got work in TV commercials for sweets and toys,' he says.

It was, as he has always recognised, a superb grounding. 'At the Corona Academy we were taught from day one that it was not a star factory and that 80 per cent of your colleagues, most of whom were much better than you, were unemployed,' he says. 'That was drilled into us from an early age. But it was a perfect foundation. There is a popular belief that at stage school it's all tutus and ringlets and everyone singing "The Sun'll Come Out Tomorrow" but it's not like that at all. I can't speak for any of the others, but we were taught the hardships first and then the techniques. We were always advised on how tough it is.'

Nicholas Lyndhurst was unfortunate that his parents' marriage was not as happy and long-lasting as that of his friend and co-star David Jason. Nicholas' father Joe has been a largely absent figure in his life ever since he was a baby.

Joe was already married to his wife Yvonne when he fell for Nicholas's mother Liz, who was a 17-year-old dancer at his father's holiday camp in Sussex.

Liz said, 'I was young and stupid. He was the boss's son and very handsome. When I was off touring with the shows, he used to follow me around and turn up at the stage door. It was very flattering. I became pregnant and more or less told him by letter I was going to have the baby. He told me it was my decision and he'd help as much as he could. I was alone throughout my pregnancy because he still lived with his wife. But I still hoped we'd live together as a family.'

Liz gave birth to Nicholas in a nursing home, not wanting her lover to be at the birth because of the stigma of being an unmarried mother. 'I decided to give him Joe's surname. But I left the space for his father's name on his birth certificate blank because he was still a secret.'

Joe first saw Nicholas ten days after the birth. Afterwards, he moved in with Liz and their baby in a seaside bungalow. But he only stayed a few weeks before telling Liz he wanted to return to his wife. Liz said, 'I found out he told her he'd been on holiday. All along, he'd left the door open so he could go back to her. I was very upset. But I just looked at him and said, "Well, you'd better go then".'

Liz never considered putting Nicholas up for adoption. She said, 'I desperately wanted a baby — a boy — because my own relationship with my mother had not been very happy. I'd given Nick a lousy father. So I couldn't be a lousy mum.'

In the years to come, bringing Nicholas up alone was a struggle. Liz even had to sell her clothes and jewellery to put food on the table. Joe did give her some money and sometimes handed presents to his son, but gradually the contact dwindled.

Nick's first acting appearance was at the age of four — as a donkey in a school play. By eight, he had set his heart on becoming an actor. Two years later, he landed his first TV commercial.

Nicholas was still at school when he appeared as an orphan in the BBC's *Anne of Avonlea*, the sequel to *Anne of Green Gables*, in *Heidi* and in the dual role of Tom Canty and Prince Edward in *The Prince and the Pauper*. It was no mean achievement for a 14-year-old boy. 'They let me go away to jobs then back to class,' he remembers. 'I think it's a good method — it certainly worked for me.'

But then Nicholas hit a sticky patch. He was growing fast and, like many developing kids, he became somewhat spotty and no producer wanted a spotty youngster promoting sweets and chocolate. Instead, he applied himself to his studies and looked forward to the day when he left school and became a fully-fledged professional actor.

Like David Jason, Nicholas owes his break into comedy to Ronnie Barker. He was given a small role in six episodes of *Going Straight*, a sitcom sequel to the brilliant *Porridge* which followed Barker's newly released former prison inmate Norman Stanley Fletcher on his adventures once he was back on the outside.

'I played his dense son Raymond who came in maybe once every other episode and said a ridiculous line like "steel tape measure" apropos of nothing,' says Nicholas. 'And it brought the house down. That was a wonderful introduction for me into situation comedy. And if you can't learn anything from Ronnie Barker, then you don't deserve to be in comedy. It was an excellent training ground in light entertainment. I was introduced to it gently and I had some great lines.'

From there he jumped straight into Carla Lane's brilliant family sitcom *Butterflies* playing Wendy Craig's younger son Adam. It was a huge success with audiences and critics alike and brought Nicholas to the attention of a wide TV audience for the first time. The series ran for four years and Nicholas remembers it fondly.

'That was wonderful,' he says. 'We really were like a family.'

One night in 1980 when Nicholas was 19, a BBC messenger pushed six new scripts through his letterbox accompanied by an urgent note from the producer asking whether he could read through them that very night and meet him the next morning.

Nicholas was about to go out with a group of friends and he didn't want to let them down so he left the package on a table and resolved he would read them when he got back that night.

He returned home quite late after a few drinks and sat down to read the scripts for a new sitcom called *Only Fools and Horses*. 'They were brilliant,' he says simply. The part they wanted him to play was that of a young lad called Rodney Trotter.

Nicholas Lyndhurst was only 19 when he landed the role of

Rodney and he still hadn't passed his driving test. This was a problem because the script in an early episode called for Rodney to drive a car at high speed and almost run Del over. Producer Ray Butt found a safe place, off the public road, for Nick to drive and soon found out that, even though he didn't have a full licence, he was still a fine driver. Ray said, 'I told Nick not to go too fast but he came round the corner with tyres squealing and did the drive brilliantly.'

But Nick always loved to throw himself whole-heartedly into the show. He and David bravely set sail on the Thames for one short scene in the second series. Nick recalled, 'It was high tide and it was very rough out there. David had to row hard to keep up with it and we were nearly swamped. I doubt they would let us do it these days.'

Nicholas Lyndhurst has the kind of face that makes complete strangers walk up to him in the street and say, 'Cheer up, Rodders.' He thinks that's rather rude but it's a cross he has had to bear thanks to a natural expression bordering on the melancholic and the fact that millions know him as Rodney Trotter from *Only Fools and Horses*.

'I loved doing every programme,' he says. 'I never once didn't want to come into work and every day was sheer pleasure. The only drag has been the fame.'

Like David, Nicholas has found the constant recognition hard to bear at times. A fan wanting his autograph once brazenly walked up to him and shoved a condom packet under his nose and said, 'Sign that.'

'Most fans are fine,' he says, 'but there's a minority who are so rude and aggressive, shoving bits of paper under your face, demanding autographs.'

Nicholas has frequently had to suffer the shouts of 'Rodney, you plonker' at totally unexpected moments from complete strangers. One driver who had stopped to give Nicholas that greeting was so convulsed by his own wit that he then drove into the back of the lorry in front.

Nicholas' mother, Liz, is his biggest fan and, despite the financial hardships early on, she now lives in a smart, modern bungalow just a few miles from Nicholas' home in Sussex and was one of the proudest people in the studio audience when they came to film the very last episode of *Only Fools and Horses*.

Liz taught Nicholas all the right values when he was growing up and when success and the accompanying financial rewards came along, he adjusted to it all without going off the rails. In his first few years of *Only Fools and Horses* fame, just about the only luxury Nicholas allowed himself was a CD player. He didn't drive, preferred to walk whenever he could, and would roller-skate down to the shops to get food for his beloved cat.

Modestly, Nicholas puts some of his success down to sheer luck and concedes that his tall, slim frame may have had something to do with it. 'Tall people are funny,' he says. 'It's very easy for them to accentuate body movement

'Being tall and skinny I had to be realistic that I was not going to play a commando in a war film. I've always been slim and I'm 6ft 2in. It's very easy to accentuate gawkiness when you are tall. Your limbs and posture are bigger than anyone else's anyway.

'When they were casting *Only Fools and Horses*, I was cast first and they felt initially there was no way David and I would match up. The only thing we had going for us was vaguely the same colour eyes and that was it. David was not very tall, but stocky, quite a chunky character and there was a lot of rubbing of foreheads behind executive desks. It was only when Lennard Pearce was cast and we all started reading together that the powers-that-be said, "Yeah, let's give it a shot."'

During his run of TV sitcom successes which include *The Piglet Files*, in which he played a spy, and his most recent success in *Goodnight Sweetheart*, Nicholas has regularly returned to the stage to prove to himself and to the world that he is not just a comic actor. His stage appearances have always won praise from critics and public alike as well as admiration from fellow cast members for his dedication. But it says much about him when he lists gaining his pilot's licence as his best achievement.

'It may sound terribly ungrateful but I'm probably more proud of earning that precious brown licence than anything else I've done in my life,' he says.

3

A Proper Job

The acting bug had bitten David for real and all his efforts were channelled into making his appearances with the Incognitos as professional as possible.

When he left school, David was wary of leaping straight in and following his brother into the precarious existence of struggling to make his way as a would-be actor. Arthur was first persuaded by their parents to take a 'sensible job' as an apprentice butcher but, like David, he knew he really wanted to act and launched boldly into the competitive world of weekly rep. David was happy and enjoying his amateur performances with the Incognitos and agreed to follow his parents' considered advice that he should get a trade behind him first. His forceful mother Olwen typically insisted, 'Actin'? That's not respectable. You need a job. You need a trade.'

David's first job was as an apprentice garage mechanic but he did not take to that, later recalling unhappily that his initial attempt at a sensible career consisted largely of 'lying under cars in mid-winter, this stuff dropping on you, the wind whistling up your bum'.

He left after a year and decided to train as an electrician, while still pursuing his acting interests on an unpaid basis, and joined the London Electricity Board as an apprentice but the Board made him redundant. 'I was 20 when I was made redundant by the LEB,' he recalls. 'It was an awful thing but it was not the end of the world. It was difficult for me. I had spent my life being employed by people. So my mate and I started our own business.'

David decided if no one else would employ him, he would have to work for himself and with a friend called Bob Bevil he set up B and W Installations, after Bevil and White. But David sums up in one word his efforts to become a businessman: 'Pathetic. As an amateur, I was acting every night of the week in those days. I formed my own electrical business so that I could be more of a free agent. But I was doing so much acting, I was always having to take time off from work to get home, get changed, learn lines. I was packing up work at about four in the afternoon to get ready for an amateur performance at eight.

'I was getting more and more unhappy at work. I was really only happy when I was acting. We did not want to sit around and blame the Government. We were very disappointed and unhappy and we had to earn our wages as we were living at home but still needed money. We cleaned cars, did decorating, anything.

'Then one day I got an offer to go to drama school. I was about 21 and well into amateur dramatics. I was spending every night of the week in the theatre. I was working during the day and more or less every night I would be down at the theatre rehearsing and acting, rehearsing plays seemed to be what I did the entire time. As an amateur you did it for nothing.

'Then I won this award and the adjudicator — I think it was Anthony Von Gyseghem, a very well-respected man — said, "I would never recommend anyone to take up the theatre but there is one man who has a possibility of making a career out of it," and he named me. My head was so big I couldn't get out of the room. I was absolutely over the moon.

'But at the time, I was sort of engaged to this girl. My young lady lived in Lee Green, the other side of Lewisham, which is the other side of London from my home in North Finchley. It was a long way late at night in the rain. I used to take her home on my motorbike so you can tell how besotted I was, and then I had to turn round and come back home.

'I had not bought her a ring but we were unofficially engaged. We were just waiting for her 18th birthday to announce it. On the journey to her house that night of the award, I was full of it and I said to her, "What do you think? Perhaps I could become an actor."

'There was no reply at first and then she said, "Look, if you want to be an actor, you go and be an actor, but don't think you are going to marry me. You're not. That is not what I want out of life. I want a man who is going to come home and spend a certain amount of time there. I want a husband, a two-up and two-down house, a steady income and a family. I want a reliable chap with a steady income, a car, a couple of kids."

'So much for love,' said David. 'Anyway, I was so terribly in love with this girl that I didn't want to go to drama school because I wanted to get married to her.

'At that point, I gave up the idea of becoming a professional actor. I was more interested in her at the time. But that sowed the seed and because I was totally involved as an amateur actor and no one was going to take that away from me, I went back to being a happy amateur. Within a year we had a terrible row, and we split up. I have never seen her since. I only know from a friend of mine that she did eventually get married many, many years ago. Really the split was not over what she said, exactly, but she was a catalyst.

'By the time I was 23, I knew I was no longer going to get married. I would get close to girls and then have this fear of being tied down. It gradually became more apparent to me that I could have a go at acting and if I wasn't really any good I could go back to being an electrician. I couldn't bear the thought of reaching 35 without having had a shot at what I really wanted. I started to think, Right — this is the time. I have no ties. I must have a go at being an actor. If I didn't, I knew I would never forgive myself.'

But the rejection really hurt. A former workmate said, 'David was really gutted to be knocked back like that. He was not really ever a great womaniser but women liked his lively sense of humour and he always seemed to be the one in charge of the relationships. Suddenly the girl, and she was only very young, gave him the elbow and he really didn't like it. I thought he was always strange and a bit more remote with girls after that.'

Both Douglas and his wife Peggy Weatherhead were impressed by the youngster's enthusiasm and eagerness to learn. And they noted his cheeky sense of humour, too. Douglas remembers, 'I think it was mainly at his mother's insistence that he got his trade as an electrician. She wasn't having two sons who were both in this acting business. David was always a laugh. We were doing this play all about Greek and Roman senators for one of the youth festivals and David was playing a character called Didimus Hippocrates.

'At the same time, we bought a new washing machine which was being plumbed in and we asked an electrician friend to wire it in for us. We did not know that it was to be David who was working for our friend who actually did the job. That is, we didn't until we got home and found a big notice on the wall which read "Didimus Hippocrates worked and slept here".'

Douglas and Peggy roared with laughter. She remembers that, 'David was a very dedicated lad. He wasn't really interested in anything else but acting. But he was full of fun. He used to pull funny faces and lark about all over the place until it was time to go on stage when he would be as good as gold. He wasn't particularly interested in girlfriends at all.'

David has always loved to leave his mark. Colin Williams, a

fellow Incognito member from those days, also worked at the same trade as David for another North London electrical firm. He recalls, 'We often met through work. I remember going to one of our friend's houses where they were having an extension done to the kitchen. David had chased all the walls and put the cables in and then he couldn't get back there so he called me in. When I went into the kitchen the first thing I saw, in David's handwriting "Kildare was here" scrawled right across the wall. The room was to be redecorated so it didn't matter, I suppose.

'I know he wouldn't mind me saying that he was always a much better actor than an electrician, so I am not surprised that is why he is so successful.'

It was certainly good training at putting on the show with a minimum of backing, working with the Incognitos. The energetic Douglas Weatherhead had his young team travelling all over London by public transport just for the chance of competing in as many drama festivals as possible. 'David never minded hard work,' says Douglas. 'Once we had to take all our props to the other side of London on the bus. I remember David and I struggling up the narrow and awkward spiral staircase on to the top deck of a double-decker with a Welsh dresser. We just laughed about it all.'

David was always desperately eager to get on stage and one evening in his enthusiasm he walked into a jagged piece of corrugated iron on one of the ramshackle buildings outside. He staggered into the tiny theatre with blood pouring from his head and said, 'I've had a bit of a bang.'

Amateur actress Vera Neck said, 'David would never walk if he could run anywhere. He came in bleeding from this nasty gash on his forehead and he dripped blood all over the stage for the rest of the evening. We all felt he should go and have stitches in the injury but he wasn't going to let a little thing like that make him miss his rehearsals. He was always supremely careless about his appearance so blood gushing down his shirt was nothing out of the ordinary.'

David would often race to rehearsals straight from work and sometimes his grubby clothes raised eyebrows among the more senior and established members of the Incognitos. Vera Neck says, 'He sometimes turned up in dirty, grubby things. I remember being shocked at the colour of his underpants when we were rehearsing one of those *Sailor Beware* things and he had to drop his trousers.

'There were all these elderly ladies among the cast — I suppose he was about 20 and we were 30-something — who went "Tut-tut-tut-tut". His pants were every colour of the rainbow but you could see an underlying grey. And he couldn't blame his mum. But I'll never forget those grubby underpants.

'The play had a bit of rough and tumble and he disappeared over the back of a couch with his bum in the air. We matronly types all went, "Dear, dear, dear, dear!"'

Vera Neck lived in Torrington Park, Friern Barnet, and Olwen used to clean for her for three hours every week. 'She was lovely,' remembers Vera, 'very concerned for her family and very particular about her job.' They had many conversations about David's dramatic ambitions. With his older brother Arthur, who had got into acting while doing his National Service in the Army, already struggling in the uncertain world of repertory theatre, Olwen worried greatly about her second son following. Vera suggested that he might get his dramatic ambitions right out of his system by acting with the amateur group. Olwen readily agreed.

David loved the atmosphere of earnest enthusiasm among all the members of the Incognitos and it was not long before he was snapping up some of the prime parts. He said, 'I was encouraged to act at school. I was a natural at playing the fool. I loved it with the Incognitos. I wasn't showing off, it was about entering a Walter Mitty sort of world where you could do anything, be absolutely anybody.'

He was still just 15 years old in July 1955 when noted local critic Bill Gelder from the *Barnet and Finchley Press* warmly praised his performance in *Robert's Wife* by St John Ervine. Gelder wrote and David deeply appreciated, 'David White did well as a young chap wanting to do the "right" thing by a girl.'

But it was in a guest appearance for the nearby Manor Players that Bill Gelder hinted publicly that the youngster might one day earn his living from his acting. Gelder wrote, '... the extraordinarily precocious schoolboy David White, looking like a young James Cagney and playing, though only 16, with the ease of a born actor ... possibly the highlight of the evening which was bright enough in all conscience.' The acclaim delighted David. He carefully cut out the review and made sure his parents did not miss out on his notice.

His mother, who still considered that one son risking his future in such a chancey profession was more than enough, proudly noted the critic's perceptive opinion but was still insistent that David persevere with his electrical qualifications.

'It was very nice to get praise from Bill Gelder,' says David. 'He was always considered the best drama critic of the lot. If you got a good review from him, it counted. Most of the local press tend to praise the whole cast for fear of offending someone. I suppose they can't say so-and-so is a load of rubbish, but Bill Gelder could be quite hard and quite cutting and he was always respected.'

Not that David took life too seriously in those days. Julie Pressland remembers a young man who was always terrific fun to be with. 'It was great to be in David's company,' she says. 'I used to love to go around with him. He had determination. We all enrolled for some evening classes or other but most of us dropped out soon afterwards. But David was very single-minded, he carried on with his amateur dramatics. He went for it. David always believed that you should decide whatever you want to do and then go for it.

'But he was a laugh as well. It was in 1962 when David took

me for my first Chinese meal. I had never had Chinese food before but he talked me into it. He said it was delicious and really raved about it. I remember I had a new suit for the evening and when we got to the restaurant and the food arrived I thought it was the most dreadful slop I had ever seen in my life. The first time you see Chinese food it can look disgusting. I kept saying, "It's very nice, it's very nice," because I didn't want to offend David.

'When I got home, I was sick all over this new suit and I never touched Chinese food again for about 15 years after that. I will never forget that night. I pretended all evening that I liked the food as much as he did. Then at the end he said, "Oh, we must finish off with some jasmine tea." I thought, My God, that will certainly finish me off. I told David the next day that I had brought up his Chinese all over my new suit and he just burst out laughing. He thought it was hilarious.'

But he was also honest enough to admit later that during those early stages of his amateur career, 'I really didn't think I had the ability to turn professional. Most people who become actors are so confident. They know for certain that they are right and everybody else is wrong. I was the opposite. I was very, very insecure — mind you, I think I'm still insecure but I'm not as bad as I was.'

In fact, the black moods of frustration that would sometimes descend on the generally perky young man do date right back to his youth. A workmate said, 'David was a great guy to go out with because normally he was a laugh a minute. But he could suddenly turn.

'One night we were in a pub in Finchley and he had been working hard at chatting up this very pretty young girl. Then an old boyfriend of hers arrived, a very well-spoken chap dressed in a smart blazer and cavalry twills. I think he was home from the Army. All of a sudden, she just turned away from David and started talking to this posh bloke. David was livid. He hardly said another word all night. When I mentioned it the next day he gave me a really menacing look and said, "I hate those stuck-up bastards. They think they own the world." I was surprised because he was still seething with anger. He wasn't that keen on the girl, it was just the way he had been dropped. He couldn't bear that.'

The ability to get laughs that he had displayed so often at school was swiftly transferred to the stage. He had enormous straight acting talent but always preferred comedy. Vera Neck says, 'He did do quite a variety of straight roles but if there was a chance to drop a tray, sit on his bottom or drop his trousers, he was there.'

She is a statuesque lady of 5ft 7in which caused some amusing moments when they were cast as lovers in a Spanish play. 'We had to devise ways of making me look a bit shorter than David,' recalls Vera. 'I sat at his feet rather a lot. We didn't have many love scenes because we were physically so ill-matched. On the few occasions it did happen, we just had to cheat it.

'I found him quite affectionate. We had tremendous warmth and rapport on stage. He had it with everyone. He is such a lovely actor. We chanced on a time in our group when there must have been half-a-dozen people who could in ordinary circumstances have earned their living as actors, had they been temperamentally suited to it. I wasn't, I had the talent but not the temperament. But the feeling that flowed between those few people who were there at that time was wonderful.

'David was the leading light. We loved him. He used to come to all the parties and he was always the life and soul in a muck-about way. He was a clown. He just liked mucking about.'

Another of David's regular leading ladies was Barbara Dunks. Again, she was an inch or so taller than he was, so a fair amount of knee-bending and sitting down was called for. Barbara became another firm friend and devoted fan of the poverty-stricken young hopeful. She remembers, 'He was such a callow, gangling youth when I first saw him but I knew straight away that he had that magical something that all actors yearn for ... presence.

'He was so full of life and even at 15 you knew he was special. But he was such a monkey at making you laugh at all the wrong moments. When you were in the middle of a terribly serious interchange in rehearsals he could just look at you and you would just break up. He just had that twinkle. The producer would be going mad but there was nothing you could do about it. He was always very serious and proper when we were doing it for real but in rehearsals you could never be sure he wasn't going to produce a piece of mischief.

'It was so sad, though, that it seemed he could never take the hero's part because he was so short. Instead, he was automatically put into the comedy parts which he was brilliant at. But other boys, who frequently did not possess a millionth of his talent so often became the tall hero. I always felt that the height thing did bother him. Knowing David, he would say it didn't but I have seen him watch a play with the hero or leading man in a scene and I just knew that he would have loved that part.

'The trouble was that, even in amateur things, you get typecast, people start to forget you might be able to do anything but comedy. If ever there was a funny part they would think, Oh, we'll get David to do that and 6ft Henry to do the hero. Sometimes it was simply the wrong way round. You could see it was.'

Barbara recognised that David had decided he did not want to get involved with any girls. 'He was friendly with the girls in the club but he did not seem to want to get serious about anybody. He used to come down to the theatre in his little van. We used to pull his leg about being an electrician, say he was enough to give anyone a shock.

'We were in a revue together, early on in his time with the Incognitos and we had to sing "Bye, Bye Blackbird". I remember we were in hysterics in the wings because it was so bad. Well, *we* thought it was bad but in fact the audience loved it because they knew us all from the serious plays and thought for us all to be in this light-hearted revue singing this silly song not very well was great fun.

'It was a real joke for all of us and although we were all supposed to behave ourselves we thought it was a huge joke. We were all togged up ready to sing this bloomin' song, but in all the giggling and larking about in the wings just as we were supposed to dance on I happened to stand on poor old David's bootlace and he rolled on to the stage in a heap. Being David, of course, he carried the mistake off brilliantly, he could always do that, and I'm sure the audience thought it was supposed to be all part of the show.

'There was no one better for getting you out of a mess than David. He had a mind like lightning for thinking things out whenever we went wrong. There was this scene when we were together in *The Glass Menagerie*. We had this dreadful old wind-up gramophone and at one point I had to wind it up and put the needle down to play a record.

'But something went wrong and instead of lovely music we just got this horrible scratching sound. David came in to the centre of the stage and just took control. He picked up the needle and made a remark that fitted in and cut out the need for the music and we carried on as though nothing had happened.

'But it meant through David's guidance we started in the middle of the scene and we went to the end and then back to the beginning. We were all terribly muddled but David was so brilliant that nobody even knew we had gone wrong. Apart, that is, from poor Vera Neck who was the prompter that night. She was so flustered at the end that she rushed on and said, "I've had four pingers in five fages. What's happening?" She was in such a state she didn't know where we were. David was never flustered. He just used to say, "Pick it up and keep carrying on."

'His brother Arthur was acting professionally by then and I

always got the feeling with David that, although I knew he would love to become an actor, there was always this feeling of caution and reticence about him, especially at the beginning because, deep down, he did not really know whether he would be good enough. We all knew he would, but he didn't.

'He was so good and it all came so naturally to him. The technicalities of the stage never bothered him. Offstage he was just a very nice boy, always cracking jokes, always cheerful. But I think he was concerned about not having his share of serious roles. It was Brian Babb who first cast him in a leading, non-comedy role in *Next Time I'll Sing to You* and, of course, he did it beautifully. People realised from then on that he could be a serious actor. The trouble was that all of the four or five leading ladies at that time were taller than David, so it was always difficult with us.'

David's 21st birthday party was an occasion for the White family to really push the boat out. In order to cram in as many guests on David's big day they took off all the downstairs doors to make more space. David prepared much of the sumptuous spread himself and the music of Johnny Tillotson, Elvis Presley and the Everly Brothers rang out down Lodge Lane. 'It was a wonderful party,' remembers Julie Pressland. 'We all thought it was great having an open-plan house.

'I went to David's house a lot at that time. Me and David and his partner Bob Bevil and my friend Carol Haddock used to go to our local dance hall, the Atheneum in Muswell Hill or up to Alexandra Palace for a drink and then come back to David's.

'We'd sit in his front room and talk and talk for hours on end. He had such plans and ambitions for the future, he just loved everything about acting and drama, he was so very determined to be good at every part he had. We were a foursome for a time but David and I never had a romance. I did have a crush on David but that was when I was five or six. He was literally the boy next door, a great pal.

'That was when I began to notice a more serious side. He was still great fun and often he would be larking about of course, just like before. But also he would sometimes recite long bits of poetry or quotations from Shakespeare. He was becoming very well read and getting more and more into his acting. It seemed to dominate his whole life. He loved Richard Burton and his recording of *Under Milk Wood* in that wonderful voice. David could copy that voice brilliantly and the Welsh in him really seemed to come out. We all knew then that he had an amazing God-given talent.

'David had all the typical motorbike leather gear but when he went out in the evening in his suit and tie he always looked impeccable. He had this gorgeous, thick wavy hair and that cheeky grin. But even more he had this remarkable personality where he could walk into a pub and just make everyone laugh.

'It seemed so effortless. He could instantly have people eating out of his hand. It was obvious to me that he was going to do much more with his life than mend fuses. He always made jokes about not being very tall. I remember once he couldn't get served in our local, The Torrington at the end of Lodge Lane, so he stood on the bar rail and just held his money out for a giggle. He didn't mind everyone laughing at him being small, he stood up there to make us all laugh.'

Not quite everyone was captivated by the David White charisma. When the Lodge Lane off-licence, just one door away from the White household, was modernised, young David was in his early 20s and less than impressed by the sudden wind of change. He walked in to find that the old beer pumps had been swept away in a major revamp. The elegant, polished wood serving counters had been replaced by gleaming new plastic affairs. The old-fashioned off-licence had been turned into a modern mini-market.

Julie and David called in for an inspection. Julie recalls, 'I asked David what he thought of the new look and he took one look round and said, "I think it's awful." He hated it and the way that all the tradition of the place had been swept away and walked straight out. The man who had done all the revamping looked crestfallen and said to me, "He's a bit of an upstart, isn't he?"'

Julie herself got a shock the night David came home rather late from another hugely successful night with the Incognitos. She recalls, 'I was 22 at the time and he gave me the fright of my life. I used to sleep in our front bedroom and I was woken up at about three o'clock one morning by what I thought was the sound of someone trying to break into one of the houses. I looked out and it was David standing all forlorn with his toolbag. I opened the window as quietly as I could and he said that he was very late home from doing a play and his mum had locked him out.

'I went downstairs and brought him through our house so he could climb over the fence and get in the back way. I was frightened because I was in my nightie and my mum and dad were asleep. I kept telling him to be quiet and he kept giggling and larking about. Then when I got him outside he got on top of the fence and of all things he started reciting the balcony scene from *Romeo and Juliet*. I was really panicking by then because I knew if my mum came downstairs and found David there with me in my nightclothes she would never believe that I was just helping him to get home. I said, "For God's sake shut up, if my mum and dad hear you, we'll both be dead." But that was so typical of his humour, he always had a tremendous amount of fun in him.

'We got on very well together and we were always amazed that our mothers also got on really well. Because while David's mum was very broad Welsh, my mum was just as broad Irish. They both had really strong accents and they used to have these incredible conversations. David used to say that the only reason they never rowed with each other was because they did not have a clue what the other one was saying.

'In our growing-up years, everybody liked David. He was

always very funny with a natural gentle humour that was never directed at anyone but himself. I know they say most people who are very funny are usually manic depressives, but David never was. You never saw him depressed or down. He just had a naturally sunny good nature.'

David was always very generous. He was one of the first of his contemporaries in Lodge Lane to get a car, a little Mini van that he and Bob used for their business. He was always ready to use it to help people out. When Ernie Pressland's baby daughter Sarah was suddenly taken ill with a racing heart, David rushed her and Ernie's wife Claire to hospital. Ernie is still grateful: 'Even in those days they were homing in on potential cot deaths. My mother knew there was something wrong with Sarah because she had had two youngsters die herself. I was at work at the time and David took the wife and the baby up to Whittington Hospital. They wanted to get her there as fast as possible and it was just as well David was around to help.

'It turned out Sarah was born with two little pace-makers in her heart instead of one. Every so often something will trigger off the second one and her heart would go ten to the dozen and she got a loss of blood pressure. She is fine now and has a baby son of her own called Daniel. We will always be grateful to David.'

David was in action again with his makeshift ambulance when Ernie's and Julie's sister Maureen needed rushing to hospital to have her baby. And to complete the job, he took Maureen's husband Rob to bring her and the baby home.

Yet on arriving for the return trip, David could not resist a joke. As Maureen was coming out of the ward with the nurse who was holding the baby, David and Rob were approaching down a long corridor. Suddenly David brushed past Rob and shouted, 'Now we'll see whose baby this is!'

It took Maureen and Rob a moment but they did quickly realise this was a typical David White laugh. The nurse was not so experienced in this curiously quirky sense of humour and almost dropped the baby.

Only Fools and Horses hero Derek Trotter would have been deeply ashamed of David White if he had been around to see the young electrician buy his first car. He already had a share in the Mini van of course, a symbol of the struggling business partnership, but that did not quite fit the bill for the particular purpose the enthusiastic amateur actor had in mind for his motor.

'I was desperate to get into cars,' said David, 'because I knew it was the only way to pull the birds. You can't do it with your motorbike. So I went down to Colindale and bought a great, gleaming Ford Zephyr Six. It looked a lovely car but I was really, really ripped off. It was the most clapped-out thing in the world. My real passion was for motorbikes and I sold my bike for £60 to buy the car and I got really ripped off on that as well.

'I think I must be the most ripped-off person in the world. The car salesman was a typical Boycie. He must have seen me coming a mile off. I fell in love with the Zephyr as soon as I saw it which must have been my first mistake. It looked fabulous and it would be worth a fortune now. It was a lovely car except that, of course, it was completely clapped out. But when you are getting your first car you know how it is. You're so keen to get behind the wheel you don't spend long enough looking underneath the bonnet.

'But I soon learned an important and very expensive lesson. The gearbox was full of sawdust and so was the back axle, and the engine was totally knackered. I seemed to spend my entire life under the bonnet tinkering with the engine trying to get the blasted thing to go. I don't think I ever had time to try to pick up any girls in the car. It never went for long enough without grinding to a halt.'

Gradually the Incognitos all came to realise that their little amateur group was witnessing some highly professional performances from young David White. In his early 20s, David was reaching remarkable heights in the world of North London amateur dramatics. David was 24 when he produced what many contemporaries agree was his finest dramatic performance, in *Winter Journey* by Clifford Odets. It was not his usual comic turn but the highly charged role of a tough New York theatrical director forcing one more decent role out of a crumpled and drunken actor.

David's director Christopher Webb recalls, 'The part was played in the West End by Michael Redgrave. It called for David to really put this poor actor through it. The guy is really on his beam ends when David's character blasts him once more into action. We worked very closely together on it for many nights. I pushed him very hard over and over again because I knew he had a fine performance in him. There was a real clash of wills. There is nothing like actors having a bit of hatred for their director to inspire that bit extra from them.

'We used to rehearse in empty schoolrooms and I would allow a small number of people to come and watch. I convinced David that he had to be really worked up when the scene started. I got him working on his breathing and really pumping himself up before we even started. One particular night there was a real excitement in the air and when he launched into his tirade against this other actor the atmosphere was absolutely electric.

'The scene was quite spell-binding. One or two of the girls in the tiny audience were in tears as David generated such force and will power it was almost overwhelming. It was amazing, quite brilliant. I think that was when he really decided he had it in him to make a career of acting. But the scene was never as marvellous again. It was good on the night but never that good.'

Local critic Bill Gelder was impressed enough to announce to the readers of Finchley and Barnet, 'So far as the acting was concerned, there were three performances good enough to be judged by the highest amateur standards. Indeed, that by David

White might be said without flattery to be in a professional class, it was done with such verve and explosive force. Mr White made his reputation with the Incognitos and is one of the comparatively few amateurs whom I could conscientiously recommend for the professional theatre.

'He has a brother there already (it must run in the family) but chooses instead, and perhaps wisely, to earn a steady living as an electrical engineer, devoting any surplus high-voltage energy to the interests of the local stage. Without pushing the electrical metaphor too hard, he gave a dynamic performance as the producer of the play within the play.'

By the time he was 25, David had produced many memorable performances for the Incognitos. 'I was playing all the heavies,' he says, 'even with my height slightly against me I played all the weighty roles — *Look Back in Anger*, *Epitaph for George Dillon*, all the Arthur Miller plays. I naturally considered myself a dramatic actor. I thought I could do anything.

'I did not realise that my height would be so very much against me when I joined Rep where all the leading ladies would be 5ft 6in or 5ft 7in tall and leading men always had to be taller than leading ladies. It was a sort of unwritten law. Nowadays it is different and I don't think you have that if you think of all the people like Al Pacino and so on. They are all midgets running around with big roles and they are the most powerful actors. It is all right on screen, but it's not so easy on stage.'

Shortly after his success in *Winter Journey*, David had a crucial piece of good fortune. The push that he needed to turn professional came courtesy of his brother Arthur, who had landed a role in the Noel Coward play *South Sea Bubble* at Bromley. Arthur was working with director Simon Oates, an old friend, and was busy rehearsing the small but potentially amusing role of a comical butler. At the last minute, Arthur was offered a much sought-after television job with the BBC's trail-blazing crime series *Z-Cars* and he begged his pal to be released from the agreement.

Simon Oates recalls, 'Arthur told me, "My brother wants to be an actor" so I went to see David at the Manor Players in Finchley playing Paul of Tarsus in *A Man Born to Be King*. It wasn't much to do with comedy but I could see right away that he was stunningly talented.'

Afterwards, Simon approached David and said, 'I hear you want to turn pro.'

'Yes, I do,' answered David immediately.

'Well make your mind up,' said the director.

David did not need any time to consider the offer. It was the chance he had been waiting for. He made his mind up there and then.

In spite of his mother's woeful warnings, he gave his share of the ailing electrical business to his partner in exchange for the company's Mini van and joined Bromley Rep. 'I said "Yes" to the offer, of course,' said David. 'But I was terrified. There are certain moments in your life — like the first time you have sex, I suppose — which you can never re-create. You can't breathe with the excitement of it. I was being paid fifteen quid a week and I couldn't believe they were giving me money for something I would have done for nothing.'

Simon Oates recalls, 'He had to put a bit of brown make-up on for the part as he was supposed to be a South Sea Islander. It wasn't a large part but you could see his comic potential. He was just naturally funny. There was a great big talent there waiting to be honed.'

David might have been a little disgruntled to be playing yet another type of servant: 'I was always playing bloody waiters,' he grumbled. But, as David noted afterwards, 'Simon Oates has got one of those terribly evil senses of humour. He could see that I could do things and he became sort of fascinated with this during the course of rehearsals.

'*South Sea Bubble* was really quite a sophisticated Noel Coward comedy and he realised that he had in me this little rough diamond type and he could get me to do things that were slightly more bold, slightly louder, because he had this wonderful sense of humour. He just kept on getting me to do little bits of things to make himself laugh.

'The other actors did not like it at all. I didn't realise at the time they were bothered, I didn't know then that you could upset people or tread on people's toes. I just thought, Yeah, I'll do that, great, and get a laugh. The other actors were coming up to me and saying, "That's not in the play," or "This is supposed to be Noel Coward, you know." But the director said, "Go on." That was the beginning of the end of any straight parts for me. So I never had much of a chance really. It would be, "Oh no, we can't have him. He'll dive through a hatch or something."'

Perhaps David was not quite as far from the humorous aspirations of the great Noel Coward as he feared, as *The Bromley and Kentish Times* recorded solemnly at the time, 'A small, but well acted, part is that of David White as the native butler of the governor.' Director Oates was delighted with his find. 'He made me cry with laughter.'

The date of that first paid performance was 5 April 1965. A remarkable comedy career had begun. Oates says, 'He did go back to Bromley after the week-long run of the play. I suggested he should be taken on by the company and he was.'

David might have landed his first paid engagement but he still did not possess that essential actor's accessory — an agent. His brother Arthur was asked by old friend Malcolm Taylor, an actor who was trying to move into production, to take a part in a new run of *Under Milk Wood* which was to be staged at the Vanbrugh Theatre, the London headquarters of the famous Royal Academy of Dramatic Art. Arthur turned the job down saying he was not available, but he suggested his younger brother. Malcolm Taylor was not too impressed by the thought. He said, 'Well, it's very kind of you, Arthur, but I don't really want amateurs.'

David had done only the one paid job by then but, despite his obvious lack of experience, Malcolm Taylor agreed to see him. Taylor recalls, 'I relented in the end and thought it wouldn't do any harm to give Arthur's brother an audition. He came round to my flat in Maida Vale and I will always remember him sitting, shaking with fear, on my sofa. But as soon as he opened his mouth to do the part, I knew that he had real talent. He got the job.'

David and Arthur even tried working together between jobs as an imaginative ventriloquist act. Naturally, being the younger brother David played the dummy and often complained about Arthur's cold hand going up his jumper. It led eventually to the brothers being summoned for an audition for a custard commercial. Arthur said, 'There were a whole lot of proper ventriloquists there but we got the job. We did the advertisement but I don't think the executives liked it much because David stuffed custard into his ear instead of his mouth!' The brothers clowned around relentlessly in this unlikely double act and even trawled the clubs to try to get work.

David recalls, 'I had no work at the time. I would have done anything if it was in the theatre. This bloke asked me to go down and audition, which I did, and he gave me the part. We played for four weeks in the Vanbrugh for something like £5 a week and split the box office. At the end of four weeks, I think we all earned about £30 which wasn't as bad as it sounds in those days when you haven't got a family or any responsibilities, and you haven't got a car and you're living at home. And it was a wonderful opportunity.'

It most certainly was, because in the audience on one evening early in the run was an eager young agent called Ann Callender, a junior partner with the Richard Stone organisation. Ann was there with her actor-turned-writer husband David Croft, a multitalented man destined to become the BBC's comedy stalwart with a string of successes including *Dad's Army, Are you Being Served?, It 'Ain't 'Alf 'Ot, Mum, Hi de Hi* and *'Allo, 'Allo.*

Perhaps as well as anyone in British television, David Croft can spot talent when he sees it. He remembers his first experience of David White in action: 'I can claim to have really discovered David,' says David Croft. 'I went to a reading at RADA with Ann of *Under Milk Wood* and a bloke who was going to read one of the parts did not turn up. David stepped in and he was hilarious. Every time he opened his mouth he got a huge laugh.'

'My wife Ann was a very junior executive at the time and she was not really allowed to take people on. But David was simply so very exceptional.'

Ann Callender remembers, 'I had been there to see another artist, an actor called Patrick Tull, but I was completely taken by this young man who seemed unbelievably talented and really rather exceptional. My David was right, of course, David White was just so funny I had to try to sign him up.

'I was very nervous about it, though, because as a very junior partner I certainly was not allowed to approach artists. We used to get hundreds of letters from would-be actors. It was a very leading agency. Ruth Llewellyn, who became Ruth Madoc, was in the class and the producer was a man called Malcolm Taylor. Afterwards, I went round backstage and said to Malcolm, "That chap is very, very talented. Has he got an agent?" I got a rather old-fashioned look and he said to me, "Why don't you ask him?"

'By then, David was busily helping himself to food from the buffet and I went up to him and said, "I thought you were awfully good this evening. Have you got an agent?"

'He looked at me and said, "No." I took a deep breath because technically speaking I was not supposed to sign anyone up. I said, "Well, would you like to come and see me on Monday?"'

The response was scarcely what Ann Callender expected.

'No, not really,' said David White sharply, and walked off.

Ann Callender went puce in the face with equal measures of anger and embarrassment. 'I was risking my job and my future,' said Ann. 'I just could not believe he had been so rude. I stormed back to the producer. He asked me what the matter was, as I was still shaking with a sort of frustrated fury. I said, "I don't know who that young man is but he is very rude." Malcolm Taylor replied that the man in question was not at all rude normally.'

A few minutes later, a subdued David White approached Ann Callender and said, 'Hello, how are you? I'm sorry I was a bit rude.'

She was relieved. 'Shall we start again? You haven't got an agent, what have you done before?'

He paused for a moment to collect his thoughts and said, 'Nothing, really.'

Ann Callender insisted, 'You must have done something.'

But David explained, 'Well, no. I'm the stage electrician.'

He explained that he had stepped into the production at the last minute and that, like so many hopeful actors, he had desperately tried to get himself an agent.

David said later, 'I told her I had tried to get an agent like everybody else does. I had written about 5,000 letters to anyone and everyone in the business just by going through all the addresses I found in *Spotlight*. I wrote to every producer and every director I could find, just like poor struggling actors have always done. I used to sit down and write out ten a day by hand and send them all hopefully off. I suppose they finished up in the waste paper bin with all the rest. It's tragic the way they don't even get looked at but I didn't know that then.

'I was abashed when Ann approached me. I don't think I could believe it. I told her I had tried to get an agent but nobody wanted me. I was still working as an electrician on and off. You don't just walk into this business, get one job and it goes on for ever. Only a very few people get that. I mean, I was even out of work for six months after *Under Milk Wood*.'

Ann Callender was not at all put off by her rebuff. She had remarked to Malcolm Taylor that very first evening that she knew David was going to be a very big star. 'That first encounter did not bother me too much when he was so rude because I realised he was just shy,' she said.

'He was, and indeed, still is, an exceptionally shy person. You might have thought that was just the approach he had been yearning for but he had just done a performance, a semi-professional performance, and I think he was a little taken aback. Afterwards, I spent a lot of time with him and found out a lot about him. I think he was introverted, he thought a great deal, always gave a great deal of study to everything and I think he was very frightened of the outside world.

'I don't say he was frightened of being manipulated because he has quite a strong character so it would not be exactly that, but he was determined to get on with what he wanted to get on with. If the money came along with the fame then that was terrific, but it really came very, very second.'

On the following Monday, David did have his appointment with Ann Callender in the impressive offices of the Richard Stone agency. She remembers, 'There was no question about his talent. Everyone who saw him in *Under Milk Wood* must have noticed it. He was absolutely brilliant. He came and saw me and we had a long chat and I did, in fact, become his agent. Mind you, I had to put up with a lot of teasing. Richard Stone kept saying, "What on earth are you doing taking on the stage electrician? We don't handle electricians."'

David's second play at Bromley was *Diplomatic Baggage* and if his new reputation for getting laughs was not already irrevocably established at the end of his first production, it most certainly was by the close of the second.

David remembers his formative moments in precise detail. '*Diplomatic Baggage* was a farce, a good old typically British farce,' he recalls. 'I was a waiter again and there was this important scene where I had to come into this hotel room where there was a bloke with two girls in a state of undress.

'The bloke orders a meal and, as the waiter, I deliver his food on this trolley with a tablecloth right down to the ground. "Leave the meal," says the bloke and I leave. Then he finds out that his wife is coming so he is desperate to find somewhere to hide the girls. He gets the two girls to hide in the bottom of the trolley, hidden by the tablecloth. Then he calls the waiter back to take away this trolley.

'Now, my waiter had been messed about all day and by this time he was pretty fed-up. So he comes in and grabs the trolley and has to pull it away thinking it was the same weight as before when he has pushed it in. The audience knows, of course, that it is much heavier with the weight of the girls. I went to walk away pulling the trolley.

'The stage directions were what you might call, pretty minimal. They just said, "*The trolley is now much heavier and he falls over.*" My idea for conveying that sort of grew from rehearsals but when it came to it with all the excitement of the first night, I just really went for it much bigger than I would normally have done.

'As I pulled the trolley, I did an exaggerated version of what I thought would really happen, my feet went from under me and I flew up into the air up to being horizontal and then fell straight down on the floor. It doesn't sound that much when you describe it in words but when it happened the audience went hysterical. It brought the house down. Being physically adept it was not that difficult for me, I thought it was quite natural. But the audience went on laughing and clapping for about five minutes afterwards.

'And I went further. I had the waiter get up, not understanding why the trolley would not move. I walked round the trolley and stared at it suspiciously. On top was a huge silver dish with a big lid. I quickly whipped it off as if suspecting there was some incredibly heavy food under there. The audience found what they thought was going through the waiter's head really amusing and they just kept laughing and laughing.

'By then, everybody in the rest of the cast was looking at me. We've been stopped now for maybe ten minutes and the audience is still laughing fit to bust.

'I was just a little unknown and I was just doing what came naturally. I did a little bit more and then eventually I thought, Blimey, I'll have to take this trolley off sometime, and I made my much delayed exit.

'Afterwards, the director came up to me and I thought I was going to get this almighty bollocking but instead he just kept saying, "Wonderful, brilliant, fantastic. That's your job from now on. You are the comedy man now." And from that moment on I never got a straight role in that Rep for nine months, which became a cause of great chagrin to me. In a way that has haunted me ever since. I always feel a slight disappointment that people are pigeon-holed. That you are not considered an actor, or any good as an actor just because you are a funny man. That has always been a thorn in my side.'

David was taken on at Bromley Rep as their last contracted artist. After he was signed, they changed the system and employed actors simply on a four-week basis. He was delighted because it meant regular work at long last. He remembers, 'And it was hard work as well. We would start at ten o'clock in the morning and finish at ten o'clock at night. You would start rehearsing one play in the morning and finish at half-past four in the afternoon. Then at seven o'clock you were in the theatre getting your make-up on for another play. So always as you worked on one play you were rehearsing another.

'There again came the hard work and dedication because I

spent my entire time either learning words or rehearsing or doing a show. I was living, breathing, eating, sleeping, talking, thinking a show. The theatre completely took over my life and I loved it.

'That was what life was all about for me. It was terribly exciting and terribly rewarding for someone from my background with no training to be involved with real actors. They had all been to drama school and had much more experience than me. Some had been in the business a long time. I was absorbing everything they could give me. It was wonderful. Absolutely wonderful.

'I don't think there is anything wrong with that. I think that that is exactly the way it should be. And I would have been quite happy to have continued in that way at Bromley for ever. I thought it would be like that for ever. Of course, we all had dreams and we would sometimes sit around, people in the same situation, and we would constantly audition all the time. We would joke, of course, "Oh, you'll never be in my series" or "When I make a film you won't be in that either". We all used to talk that nonsense but we never actually believed that any of it would come true.

'I was more concerned with doing whatever job I had got right so that I would get another job. I was always very worried about that, always very keen to impress. I never wanted to upset people in case they said I didn't do a very good job, because that could mean you were out of work. So I felt it was in your own interests to be as good and as dedicated as you could be because that meant continuity of work. If you really only wanted to be an actor then that is all the criteria there was.

'If you wanted to be famous and all that then you could stand up to directors but I could never do that because I did not want to get a bad reputation. I just concentrated on what I was doing because I was so interested in the theatre. I was slowly gathering knowledge.'

The doubtful pleasures of Rep and summer seasons followed and David learned how to live on his enthusiasm and precious little in the way of wages. 'I spent a long time in the wilderness,' said David. 'And that is how I expected to spend the rest of my life — just fooling about on the end of some pier or other.

'I was really poor. I must have played every major town in this country, and stayed in some of the worst digs imaginable. I had to learn a lot of tricks to survive.'

David was always more worried about his acting than his wage packet and he raised his grievance about being pushed into a comedy slot with the boss of his agency, Richard Stone. David recalls, 'Richard said to me, "You must never swim against the tide. Go with it. Go with the current. There will come a point at some time in the future when you come into still water. But don't start by trying to swim upstream when you have got something going for you. Go with it." I listened to his advice and that is what I did. I faithfully took what came along and it was always comedy.'

Following his brother into the acting business was a decision that far from delighted his parents. David said afterwards, 'The day we told Dad we wanted to become actors he was shattered. "Why give up worthwhile trades and waste your lives?"'

David knew he would always regret it if he did not take his big chance. He was unhappy as an electrician and believed he had it in him to become a professional actor. But at the ripe old age of 25 he was still cautious enough to decide, 'I gave myself a time limit. If I wasn't earning a good living by 30 I would return to my old trade. They were terrible years but by then I was besotted with the stage.'

Now he had a new career, David White found he needed a new name. He said, 'When I got my job in the theatre, I got three Equity members to sign my contract so that I could join Equity and sent the form off. But they phoned me up and said I couldn't have the name David White as there was already another actor registered with Equity with that name. They don't allow two actors to use the same name as it would be confusing.

'They said they could send the forms back but I was only in the job for a month and I knew that if there was any delay I might miss my chance to get in. The woman from Equity said she could do the change over the phone, so I was on the spot, I had to decide on a new name there and then. First of all I said I'll just extend my name and become David Whitehead. She said "No", that name was already being used as well.

'She said, "Is there any other name?" What popped into my mind was Jason. I suggested David Jason and she went away and then came back and said, "That's all right." All of a sudden I was David Jason. At the time, I had no idea where the name came from,' said David with an anxious eye on keeping a painful family secret out of public scrutiny.

But David's mother was adamant that Jason was the name of his dead brother and that she was delighted when David chose it to keep the memory of his twin alive. 'He did what was right,' she said. 'You should never forget the death of a child. I had four children and I love them all equally and I want them all to be equally remembered. Not just the one.'

David finds this sort of personal revelation difficult to say the least. When pressed by the authors on the point, he said quietly, 'My mother was a bit confused.'

In fact, feisty Olwen appeared anything but confused as she talked about her children, sitting in her tiny cluttered flat not far from Lodge Lane, crammed with its knick-knacks and with David's picture on the cover of *TV Times* next to the television set. She insisted, 'David's father wanted him to become a fish porter like him but I encouraged him to try something different. I encouraged all of them. June was very good in a school play. I think that made Arthur and David take notice. She could have been an actress, I'm sure. But Jason should not be forgotten. Never, ever forgotten.'

David has always chosen not to confront his mother's

memories. Before she died, he said in explanation, 'I discovered afterwards where the name came from when I thought about it. I had no idea when I picked it where Jason came from. But when I really began to puzzle it out I remembered my primary school days and a lovely teacher called Mrs Kent who made sure we had storytime once a week. She started to relate the story of *The Odyssey* and she told us stories of *Jason and the Argonauts*.

'The thing that captured my imagination, and she was a marvellous storyteller, was *Jason and the Golden Fleece*. I was really impressed by this hero from mythology battling to win the Golden Fleece. It was a brilliant story, brilliantly told.'

But a young actress who was very close to David at the time said, 'He only once ever talked about being a twin. It was very late one night when we had both had rather too much to drink. He was upset and he said something about it being a funny feeling losing a twin brother you never knew. He said he used to feel it made every birthday sad as well as happy and that sometimes he even felt guilty. He said he never talked to his mother about it. David was like that. If there was something he didn't want to think about he could block it right out. I saw him do it with people. He didn't yell or argue. If he took against someone he would simply behave as though they did not exist. It was a bit creepy, really.'

Ann Callender set about finding work for her young hopeful in earnest but she was not helped by David's shy disposition. 'He was never a very social man and he did not like turning up at agency parties or things like that. This made my job more difficult because in those days you used to invite all your mates who were producers and directors and all your actor clients who were looking for a good job to a party and hope that something would gel somewhere.

'But David was never a socialite, he did not like being paraded and he was not very keen on anything about that traditional slave market that an agency used to be. We got on terribly well and had loads of meetings about his career but there weren't many social occasions.

'He was very shy with girls. He spent a long time with Michelle Dotrice and, in fact, I thought he would probably end up marrying her, but in the end it did not come to anything.'

But David was learning about the business perhaps faster than his agent realised. Today, top comedian Bob Monkhouse is a friend and a fan of David Jason but he recalls the time when the young wannabee was a handful to work with. Bob Monkhouse cheerfully recalled, 'It was back in 1971 when I met him. I had never heard of David Jason and I went to see a show called *She's Done It Again!* with Brian Rix playing the part of a vicar whose wife has just had sextuplets. It was a very old farce, written for Robertson Hare. I was to take over from Brian. I met David during rehearsal and loved him on sight. I didn't really see anything of David apart from his own sort of self-mockery and modesty on show. I didn't know he was an arrogant little sod!

'We opened at the Playhouse, Weston-super-Mare with this thing. And, for me, it was like being hit between the eyes with a sledgehammer. I went out there to get laughs and there was no way anyone could get laughs apart from David. He was hysterical. He was acrobatic. He was wearing this white wig, with a white moustache and beard. He looked like a little old man. Everything about him was 70, except these incredible acrobatics, and falls and amazing bits of business which all appeared on the night.

'We had never seen it at rehearsals but, on the night, suddenly his foot was jammed between the cushions on the couch and he couldn't get it out and there was five minutes of hysterical laughter and the other foot went in. He was just wonderful. He tumbled everywhere and the people adored him. And who was best at the end of the show? When we walked down, he walked down before me and the roof lifted off. Then I walked down as the star of the thing and everyone went quiet.

'He got a huge roar every night from the audience. Then I started doing a curtain speech at the end of the show before I introduced the rest of the cast. David always got a huge ovation, much more than me or anyone else. So, after about a month of our five-month run I said to the cast, "Look, you don't want to have to stay all in make-up until after my curtain speech. Get cleaned up and I'll say, 'Here's our cast as they would appear on the streets of Weston-super-Mare.'" They said, "Thanks, Bob, that means we'll have time to get a meal after the show."

'But when David came down without his white wig, his white moustache and his white beard, nobody knew who he was. So he didn't get much of a round. Wonderful, I stepped into the middle and got the big applause. Everybody wondered where the little old guy had gone. And, do you know, David didn't twig it until the last week. Somebody pointed it out to him and he came to see me, but he took it well because we had been exchanging insults and signs all the way through.

'He used to crack me up. There was one scene where he had to come to me with the sixth and final baby in a crib. He had to come running in and give it to me. Well, the things he put in that crib that the audience couldn't see. First of all there was the baby, then he had a horror mask on the baby, horrible lolling eyes and tongue hanging out all bloody. Then he started doing obscene things with the baby. I won't go into details but it involved the use of a frankfurter sausage and a lot of ketchup. Eventually I used to dread this crib coming out for fear of what he had put in it. He even put all my underwear in it one time. And I still had to look in and say, "What a beautiful baby."

'So I started cracking him up. There was a scene where he was on stage with another actor and he had to look out of the window, which the audience couldn't see through. I used to stand behind it and do things of which I am now deeply ashamed. It was wonderful to see his eyes go. because nobody laughs like David.

When he goes, the bones turn to jelly and he just collapses with laughter. The eyes seem as if they're going to explode in his head. I think it was the funniest, happiest summer season, because of Jason, that I have ever had.

'Because we got on so well I asked him to do my radio show, *Mostly Monkhouse*, which ran for three series. He was my sidekick in 1972, 1973 and 1974 and the show did very big figures. I wrote all these insults for him to say and perform a script like I knew he could do and he was absolutely marvellous. I'm happy to say it helped him to become established.

'We don't live very far from each other and he comes over a couple of times a year for dinner. But we never did do the one dream that both of us had, a silent movie which I wrote and was going to direct. I remember when I bought my house in June 1975 we walked all round the garden and worked out the plot of the movie. But we never got it off the ground.'

David's agent could see her bashful young client needed a television chance and she turned to rising young comedy producer Humphrey Barclay as the man to provide it. She wrote to Barclay just at the time he was moving from radio to join the London ITV station Rediffusion to begin working on a completely new comedy strand.

Barclay recalls, 'I had just left radio and landed this job in television and for the first time I was actually a television producer. I was very new and very nervous and I was charged with putting together a children's comedy show. We had already got Eric Idle, Michael Palin and Terry Jones who were fine but they were all very cerebral and university-like. I was looking for someone who could provide some contrast.

'I approached Malcolm Taylor. He auditioned and was very jolly and good fun but he said, "You don't want me, you want my friend David Jason."'

To this day, Malcolm Taylor finds it hard to explain this

remarkable act of unselfishness. He said, 'Humphrey just explained to me that his new show was a revue-style comedy and he wanted a young actor to take part in the sketches and perhaps contribute a bit to the writing.

'I just straight away thought that David Jason would be a natural for the show and to my astonishment I heard myself suggesting David. I still don't know why I did it. So I suppose I was responsible for helping David to get a start in theatre and television in as much as anyone with that much comedy talent needs help. I have certainly never done anything so unselfish since then. I must have been mad.'

David is still grateful. Malcolm did become a very close friend of his but in this cut-throat business where good television chances are savagely competed for, this was a singularly selfless act. David said, 'It was a fantastically generous thing for Malcolm to do. People think that sort of kindness doesn't occur in our business but Malcolm proved it does happen. He knew Humphrey was after a little comedy actor with a great range and was kind enough to think of me. He explained to Humphrey that I was working on the end of the pier in Bournemouth with Dick Emery and because of that recommendation, because Malcolm suggested me instead of saying "I can play that part" himself, I got the chance.

'Humphrey Barclay telephoned me and said could he come down and see the show. I said, "Wonderful." I was doing very small parts in two plays back to back and one of them was doing absolutely nothing. The better one was *Chase Me Comrade*, another typical old English farce.'

David did not make his big entrance until mid-way through the second half and Barclay, the thoughtful former classics graduate from Trinity College, Cambridge, sat surrounded by guffawing holidaymakers who were thoroughly enjoying Dick Emery cavorting about the stage in drag. As the evening wore on and

David Jason's absence continued, Barclay was beginning to gaze longingly at the exit.

Eventually, the moment arrived. It was a crucial time in David Jason's young life and he recalls, 'For the first time in my career, I went "anti" the director. I really just followed my own instincts. My character, Bobby Hargreaves the next-door neighbour who has just moved in, had to come on stage at a point in the play when everyone else has disappeared. The others are all chasing this guy dressed up as this Russian ballerina or whatever, and I am trying to find out if there is anybody in the house.

'At the bottom of the stairs there is a ship's bell. I have the entire stage to myself and I have to ring the bell which is the signal for everyone else to rush back on stage. Every time I cross the stage in my search I run past the bell and look at it significantly. I think about ringing it and I even make as if to ring it. This begins to wind up the audience and they start yelling, "Go on, ring the bell. Ring it. Ring it." But I make them wait and I drag it out as they are shouting and it started to drive that audience mad.'

In the audience, Humphrey Barclay, the mild-mannered former head boy of Harrow School and one-time Cambridge Footlights director, a master of all the most sophisticated aspects of humour, had completely forgotten all thoughts of leaving early. He was yelling and shouting with the rest of the audience, 'Ring the bell, Ring the bell.'

At last, David Jason relented and rang the bell. 'Then they really went bananas,' said the young actor. 'They knew what I was going to do. But, you see, in comedy often it is not what you do but when you do it. This is the Laurel and Hardy message. If you watch Laurel and Hardy who have always been one of my faves, you find yourself going, "I know what you're going to do. But when are you going to do it?" I had learned that.

'Humphrey met me afterwards, and he told me, "I really must say that I was thinking of leaving because it was not exactly my scene. But when you came on and did that business with the bell, I have never seen anything like it in my life. You drove that audience to distraction. Even I was yelling, "Ring it, ring it."'

David's ploy worked with the producer, but again it was not quite so popular with some of his fellow cast members. David said, 'It drove the rest of the cast crazy because no one could come back on stage until I rang the bell. A lot of people interpreted it as me hogging the limelight and I can understand how they could interpret it like that, but I was totally innocent of that. I honestly don't believe it was ever anything other than wanting to serve the audience to the best of my ability. That was my job and my joy.'

Certainly Humphrey Barclay was convinced. 'He was just so funny,' says Barclay. 'I can still remember that first entrance very clearly. The business with the bell and his little face with those big eyes just convulsed the audience.

'I went back into his dressing room and we chatted and he was very down to earth. I swanked about being a television producer and admitted I hadn't done it for long. He said he hadn't long given up being an electrician. And I just knew for sure that he had this magical ability to make people laugh. A very funny man.

'I asked him if he would be in this TV show I was planning called *Do Not Adjust Your Set*. It sounded an awful phoney cliché but happily I was trustworthy and truthful because he was in it and he was very, very good. It was the start of a long and happy association. He was always wonderful to work with because he just communicates humour and he worked very, very hard at learning.

'I'll always remember he was so good at falling over in *Do Not Adjust Your Set*. I mentioned that one day and Terry Jones said, "I can fall over and all that," but I said, "Yes, but not as well as David."'

The young comedy actress Denise Coffey completed the team and *Do Not Adjust Your Set* became an innovative and successful show. But it did have a most peculiar start. David said, 'There was

Nicholas Lyndhurst with *Goodnight Sweetheart* co-star Michelle Holmes and (*inset*) with Janet Dibley from the hit comedy series *The Two of Us*.

**The Dream Team share a laugh on
the set of** *Only Fools and Horses.*

Top: David with Welsh beauty and Hollywood star Catherine Zeta-Jones, who co-starred in *The Darling Buds of May*.

Below: With Gillian Hinchcliffe, with whom he has found new happiness.

Top: Uncle Albert, Rodders and Del Boy together again for a special short, in aid of *Comic Relief*. Buster Merryfield (Uncle Albert) sadly died from a brain tumour in June 1999.

Bottom left: Nic with his *Gulliver's Travels* co-star, Warwick Davies.

Bottom right: An unhappy day as Nicholas Lyndhurst and Ken Macdonald (Mike, the Nag's Head landlord) attend the funeral of the much-loved Buster Merryfield.

Nic accepts the Most Popular Advertisement Award at the National Television
Awards, 1997.

A young David Jason in *Do Not Adjust Your Set*, pictured here with Michael Palin, Terry Jones and Eric Idle.

David and Myfanwy Talog, with whom he shared his life for so long. Sadly, she died of cancer at the age of 49.

this wonderful moment when we all met and they told us, "This is a really major opportunity, an amazingly huge project. We want you to do six half-hour revue-type television programmes for kids. It's never been done before. We want you to be more or less adult." The attitude Humphrey Barclay and the other guys had was to treat the audience as we would ourselves. It was quite revolutionary at the time.

'Right at the start, Humphrey announced he had to prove to all the powers-that-be at the station that we were really worth this great investment. He took us all out to lunch and said that we had to go back that afternoon and prove ourselves to be funny.

'He said he had a studio booked and that we had to go in there and be funny. That is the hardest thing on earth with no script or direction or preparation. "How do we do it?" we asked. Humphrey said, "You've got to do it, because your future relies upon it." We protested that nobody had prepared anything and Humphrey said, "Yes, that's the idea."

'I thought then that I had walked into a lunatic asylum. I thought, This is crazy. We all thought it was mad, and Michael Palin freaked out completely.

Anyway, we all filed into the studio at Kingsway and we just went ... silly. We just went daft. Terry Jones kept on throwing himself backwards off his chair. Every time anybody spoke Terry Jones threw himself off his chair.

'That was all he did and I thought, I wish I had thought of that. So I threw myself off my chair and then everybody threw themselves off their chairs. So we were all doing it. Then we thought, we can't all do that. That piece of tape would probably be worth a fortune today because we were pathetic. We were rubbish. We had no form and no content. They just said go out there and be funny and we weren't. What we did not know at the time was that the company was so committed to the show, so far down the road with the Humphrey Barclay idea, that we would have gone ahead anyway.'

Do Not Adjust Your Set, launched on Boxing Day 1967, was an instant hit with its young audience and plenty of parents tried to get home early enough to join in the zany humour. David recalled, 'It grabbed people with its anarchic humour. Adults would say, "I don't know what you're watching this bloody rubbish for," but the kids loved it.' One of the highlights of each show was David Jason's appearance as Special Agent Captain Fantastic in a running superhero serial that was deeply absurd. David appeared with Denise Coffey in an unlikely double act and the pair also wrote the scripts.

It was very popular and David's agent Ann Callender found herself in receipt of staggering offers to develop the item into a series of its own. 'Captain Fantastic really took off in popularity,' she said. 'There was this idea to turn it into a show of its own but David suddenly decided that under no circumstances did he want to be typecast or get involved in anything like that so early in his career.

'He felt it would prevent him from widening his scope. So, much to a lot of people's disappointment, mine included because there was a great deal of money involved, he decided not to go ahead.

'He was quite brilliant in Captain Fantastic, especially in the way he used a lot of his remarkable tumbling abilities. And to reject a lot of money and instant fame, as television could bring in those days, took guts and determination on his part. At that stage, I have to say that I thought David had it within him to become another Tony Hancock-style figure rather than the actor he became.

'I think it was sheer dedication to his craft as an actor which led him to reject the offers to develop Captain Fantastic. He felt that to have jumped towards fame so soon would mean that he would burn himself out. I remember him saying, "I would like to be a star, but I don't want to be a shooting star."'

Quite why he was so adamant about Captain Fantastic still remains a trifle unclear to David. 'It is a fact that on odd occasions in my life I have been extremely dogmatic. I have made decisions that flew against everything I thought was the way to succeed and totally turned my own argument on its head. There have been two or three occasions and this was certainly one of them.

'With Captain Fantastic we loved messing about on film, using all sorts of strange techniques and being as inventive as possible, using lots of old silent movie stunts, pinching some sketches and dreaming up other ones, with loads of visual gags and the formula worked. Colour television was just coming and they said what we want to do is a half-hour series of Captain Fantastic in colour.

'I said, "Great, and it will all be on film, won't it?"

'"No," they said. "It will not sustain half-an-hour on film. We'll do it in the studio with ten minutes of film inserts."

'I was being offered this amazing deal. I'm not talking about money, but this amazing opportunity to have my own series. It was a huge chance for someone in my position. I had enjoyed being in a popular show but I was just one little individual part of the group.

'And yet although the idea of having my own series as Captain Fantastic appealed enormously, I said that unless we could do it all on film, I didn't want to do it. No one could believe I had said that at the time. But I did not want to carry on in those terrible cardboard cut out sets that we had got so used to working in in those days. I knew it would take the essence of the character away because he was a film character.

'We were using all sorts of trick photography and clever film techniques. These days I suppose it would seem crude, but at the time I felt we were doing wonderful stuff. In the studio it would have been just like everything else. I don't think I have ever been as begged and badgered to do anything in my life. I was coerced, I was blackmailed, I was really pushed towards doing it and I just said, "No." I didn't want to do it because I just knew that if you took the filming away and put Captain Fantastic into a studio it would so weaken the character that he would no longer be worth playing. It would just be nothing, or just like everything else.

'It was a great offer and I suppose in a way Ann Callender was right, I should have done it. But with luck and hindsight you can think anything.'

David always felt a little apart from the three other male stars of *Do Not Adjust Your Set*. After three hugely successful series, Messrs Jones, Palin and Idle began a campaign to move the show to a less restricting late-night slot. David said, 'We wanted to do an adult version of *Do Not Adjust Your Set* but the powers that be said, "No way. It's the most successful children's series we have ever had. It's obviously children's material, you guys don't know what you're talking about."

'The three of them said we want to make a late-night series with this format because our material is being so choked by the editors who keep saying, "You can't do that because it's for children." They got more and more frustrated.

'The upshot was that because they weren't allowed to turn our series into a late show they went away and came back a couple or three years later with John Cleese and Graham Chapman and it was called *Monty Python's Flying Circus*. Need I say more?'

The last episode of *Do Not Adjust Your Set* went out on 14 May 1969 and, having been part of such a successful team, David was understandably upset at being excluded from the future comedy plans of Jones, Idle and Palin. Though he wasn't to know it at the time, David posed for a promotional photograph for *Do Not Adjust Your Set* which was to prove painfully prophetic. David and the other three were pictured standing behind a television set which bore the caption 'Ouch!'. David's natural antipathy towards the upper-crust public school and university end of the business was already well established.

David did, however, work with Graham Chapman seven years later in the film *The Odd-Job Man*. Chapman played an insurance executive deserted by his wife and on the brink of suicide. Losing the nerve to kill himself, he hires a weird little odd-job man, played by David, to do it for him. But in view of the way Chapman and the other soon-to-be Pythons left David behind, it was somewhat ironic, too, that, in *The Odd-Job Man*, David had a scene where he held a gun to Chapman's head.

'Yes, I did feel disappointed,' says David of his parting from Idle, Jones and Palin. 'I certainly was not doing so many things at that time that I couldn't have been a part of that. But Denise and I were more actors coming from an acting background and the other guys were all from an academic world of Cambridge and the Footlights. They had done a marvellous show, where Humphrey had got to know them, called *Cambridge Circus*.

'Their way of applying their use of the language to make things funny was brilliant. They had marvellous command of language which obviously I did not have because I had come up a very different way. And they already knew each other when we started so they were always a bit of a team and a club. So they went away and they did not include Denise and I. We were actors and they preferred to link up with people of similar intellectual weight like John Cleese who was quite brilliant.

'That is what happened and I think they were right, you see. Had the people in charge at the time given them their head, then perhaps I would have gone along with them and that would have changed my career totally. I am not at all bitter. Because I didn't go with them I went in a totally different direction.'

That was the public reaction. Privately, he was devastated. A friend with whom David stayed at the time recalls, 'He liked Terry Jones and Michael Palin particularly as people but he felt very unhappy to be excluded. He felt used, as some of the ideas they had talked about later seemed to take shape in the success of

Python. He used to come back to my flat and throw himself on the floor and beat the carpet some nights when some sneering intellectual reference had gone over his head and he had caught an exchanged glance that he thought was putting him down.

'David knew he was just as good as any of them but he didn't have their background and connections. He felt vulnerable and out of his depth when they started talking about paintings or films and sometimes he was sure they did it just to wind him up.

'One night after a bit of aggro in the studio, he came home raving about the "Condescending c★★ts" and I think ever since then David has been very suspicious of that sort of Establishment background. He tends to lump it all together. If he meets someone who talks about when he was at Cambridge or drops the name of his old school or even regiment, David is quickly on his guard. He definitely didn't like being left out of the gang.

'One particular night he came home just shuddering with anger. I've never seen anything like it. It wasn't the fame and it wasn't the money. It was just there was this great talented gang of them and he had been left out. He knew they were brilliant and he knew they would succeed. He so wanted to be part of it all and for no reason at all it was taken away from him. It must have been very hard for him to bear. For days you could scarcely talk to him.'

While the embryonic Pythons set off on their first steps to international stardom, David headed in a distinctly different direction, to the mythical Midlands motel that was for so long the setting for the interminable ITV soap opera *Crossroads*.

To say he was underwhelmed is an understatement. After all, *Crossroads* was the show where characters could walk behind the freezer in the kitchen or across the garage for a spanner and disappear for six months. Comedians used to joke that actors who remembered their lines would be sacked on the spot. Even his best friend couldn't call it a good career move.

Ann Callender remembers, 'It was hysterical, because David

did not really want to do it, but at the same time he wanted to learn the television technique for fast turnaround drama. He went into the programme, made up in Birmingham by ATV, as a rather silly gardener type and he was up there for quite a few weeks in spite of his persistent efforts to escape.

'At first he used to say in our frequent telephone conversations that he had been given a rather dull and tedious person to play. He said the gardener was a very boring character but he accepted that it was very good experience although it was not a very large or interesting role.

'Then after three weeks up there I suddenly had a very angry David on the telephone. He said, "Have you seen the scripts?" I said, "No," most play scripts were sent to me but hardly *Crossroads*. He said, "I just can't do this any more. It is completely ridiculous." I did not understand what was going on, I said, "Calm down, David, and tell me what is wrong."

'He said, "You know that nice boring little gardener chap I was playing?" I said, "Yes, David." He paused and then almost spat down the telephone, "Well, he has suddenly turned into some sort of psychopathic killer." He was incandescent with rage.

'What had happened, of course, as was usual in *Crossroads*, was that the writers had switched over and the new writer was taking the story off in a new direction. I did not tell David that, instead I said, "I don't know what you can do about it because you have not got much time. I think you have got to realise that perhaps the silly little gardening character was just a front and this man was, in fact, schizophrenic and the bad side is just starting to come out now."'

Propriety prevents Ann Callender from recalling David Jason's precise response. 'I won't tell you exactly what he said, but I can say that he just was not terribly receptive to that idea,' she recalls. 'In the end I said, "Come on, David. You're a professional," and he accepted the situation and said, "Yeah, I'll just get on with it."

'Two or three weeks went by and I did not exactly see the

programme every day. It was on while I was still at work and in those days agents did not run to television sets in the office. Then he came on the phone again and my heart sank wondering what was the new problem. He was not earning a great deal of money and he was very punctilious about everything.

'He said, "You won't believe this. I have just had the scripts for the next couple of weeks." I said, "What has happened this time? Are they going to catch you and send you to prison for some dreadful crime?" He said, "No, I'm back being a stupid gardener again." He came out of *Crossroads* not very long after that, having learned a very great deal.'

David made such an impact on life at King's Oak that Jane Rossington, the only ever-present member of the cast, completely missed it. 'I know he was in *Crossroads*, but I'm ashamed to say I never noticed him.'

After *Crossroads*, David did some work in the theatre including a memorable portrayal of Bob Acres in *The Rivals* in the West End which led to his taking over from Michael Crawford in the long-running *No Sex Please — We're British* at the Strand Theatre and then a star role in another comedy, *Look No Hans!*, at the same theatre.

Malcolm Taylor directed *The Rivals* which opened on 1 May 1972 and earned David a notice in the *Daily Telegraph*'s review to the effect that his Acres was 'quite good fun'. Malcolm Taylor goes much further. 'He was brilliant in it,' he said, 'and I am sure it was his performance there that gave him the chance to take over in *No Sex Please*. He was a fantastic comic actor even then. And, of course, he loved all the tumbling. He could certainly do anything that Michael Crawford did.'

Like Crawford, David also suffered his fair share of knocks while throwing himself energetically into his stage role. And, like Crawford, he decided to have regular consultations with osteopath Paul Johnson, although he was reluctant to do so at first.

'I thought it was all a bit gobbledygook,' says David, 'but I made up my mind to go and see Paul when I found I was doing myself so much body damage and I was starting to get myself all twisted up. Once I put my shoulder out, and I was constantly pulling muscles and tendons. Michael Crawford used to have Paul on contract for treatment three times a week, but I had to pay for him myself.

'Paul was absolutely brilliant and used to tweak me out. I also spent a lot of time talking to him and I became a great believer in him. I got to learn a lot about body problems and I soon learned that if I didn't do warm-up exercises then I was going to do myself some damage. I learned, too, a lot about referred pain — the fact that your body can hurt somewhere but the damage is actually somewhere else on your body. I learned a good deal while I was doing all that falling about and it means I can now go to an osteopath and get the problem isolated and sorted out much quicker.'

At one point in the run of *No Sex Please — We're British*, David spent two weeks going through the strenuous routines with a dislocated toe. 'I didn't know I'd dislocated it,' he says. 'I thought I'd just sprained it. It was all right while I rested my foot during the day but by the time I got to the theatre, I was in a lot of pain.'

Humphrey Barclay who had television plans for David found himself advising David on his theatre approach. He said, 'It was difficult for him when he took over from Michael Crawford because he had to do Michael Crawford's marvellous bit of comic business and then develop his own. I remember one night in my flat when we worked out a routine with a parcel that he was supposed to be wrapping and he ended up tripping over and doing his brilliant tumbling act. His face lit up with delight when he eventually got it right.'

But, again, David Jason's style of professionalism and dedication did not endear him to all members of the cast. David said, 'I remember when I was in *No Sex Please* I used to have this long piece of business which would really get the audience going and this other actor used to say, "Oh, God, here comes the milkman."

'I said, "What do you mean 'the milkman'?" He said, "Let's be fair, old boy, we have all got trains to catch. You milked some scenes so much you have made us miss them some nights taking so long." I said, "That's what I'm paid for, that's what we're here for. The audience doesn't know about trains. You can't apologise afterwards and say, 'I'm sorry you didn't all have a good laugh tonight but we do have a train to catch.' When the audience buys a ticket they buy me and they expect to get value for money. I'll walk home if that's what it takes."'

David also learned a financial lesson from *No Sex Please*. He took over Michael Crawford's role for £100 a week. He found out later that Crawford, on the strength of his television comedy hit with *Some Mothers Do 'Ave 'Em,* had been paid much more as he was on 9 per cent of the box office. 'They made a lot of money out of me,' said David darkly.

In *Darling Mr London*, he provided Ann Callender with her favourite stage moment. 'David could be a genius of a comic, especially when he was doing physical stunts. One scene involved one of the sofas that turns into a put-you-up bed, which had been put up for obvious reasons. When the husband comes home early, David had to dive into this bed which then turned back into a sofa and folded up with him inside. It was a most dangerous and complicated piece of business but David did it brilliantly.'

Her husband David Croft was producing *Hugh and I* with Hugh Lloyd and he happily included David in guest appearances. Croft recalls, 'I gave him a couple of early jobs and he was very funny. He really was such a good tumbler and faller-over. I used him for that first of all. He was supposed to be a little man with the laundry and eventually, of course, he had to leap into the basket just before the lid slammed shut. He was so very good, I remember that Terry Scott wasn't at all pleased.

'The most important thing about David is that he is funny. The audience laughs at him, there is never any mistaking that, he has a natural sense of fun. You can't teach people that sense of comedy and how to be funny. We developed his sense of humour but he was not particularly funny off screen; the funniest people rarely are.'

David Jason's opportunities for carving out a career with David Croft's long successful comedy television repertory company were curtailed by BBC procedures. Ann Callender said, 'David [Croft] was then a BBC producer and when you have an agent and you have a husband in that position there was a most humiliating process that you have to go through whereby your husband had to write a letter saying that under no circumstances will your artists get preferential treatment.'

In any case, David made his early television start with ITV but David Croft is still sorry that, having spotted that comic talent in its infancy in *Under Milk Wood*, he has not been able to harness it more frequently. Croft said, 'The sad thing is that one way and another I have never been able to use him again. He used to say to me, "After all these years you've never used me, what's the matter?" But he is a super performer, a lovely performer. The trouble is that David is too famous now to fit into my sort of show. There is no real place for a star in a team show and I have always preferred teams.'

David recalls that he did, in fact, almost become a member of one of those teams. He said, 'I've been up for lots of parts in this business and some of them would surely have changed my whole life and career. There is quite a bit of luck to our game.

'When I was playing all these old men I got an interview to read for a character in *Dad's Army*. It was for Corporal Jones that Clive Dunn was supposed to play. Clive wanted the part but he was in the Spike Milligan show at the time and David Croft and his co-writer Jimmy Perry were disappointed but looking round for someone else.

'I went in in the morning and read for them at ten o'clock and at half-past twelve my agent rang to say I had got the job. It was wonderful, a marvellous break to get in on the start of a new series. It was a lovely script and even though I did not know who else was in it that didn't matter to me.

'But at three in the afternoon my agent phoned again to tell me bad news; that part in *Dad's Army*, I hadn't got it after all. Apparently during lunchtime at the BBC they had gone into the bar and Bill Cotton, one of the bosses then, had said to Clive Dunn that he was sorry they were not doing any more Spike Milligan's but at least he had the new *Dad's Army* role. This was all unknown to Croft who had already cast me. Bill Cotton went to David Croft and said, "It's all right, you've got Clive Dunn for that part."'

David is philosophical about missing out. He said, 'If I had gone into *Dad's Army* then the whole of the rest of my career would have been different. I would probably never have done *Open All Hours* or *Only Fools and Horses*.'

After Malcolm Taylor's generous act of recommendation, his friendship with David Jason grew. So much so, that in 1968 when Taylor married actress Anne Rutter, who had appeared with David in *The Rivals*, he asked David to be Best Man. It was an invitation that guaranteed laughter all the way.

Taylor recalls, 'The night before the wedding, we all went out for a Chinese meal in the Edgware Road and then back to my flat after a very good night out with plenty to drink all round. In the morning, I was anxious to make sure everything was ready and I carefully cleaned my shoes. A little later I was surprised that David insisted on cleaning them again, though I thought he was just being helpful so I did not protest.

'I did not find out what he was up to until later. It was a top hats and morning suits do in Beaconsfield. We all got very smartly to the church and, as I knelt down at the front at the beginning of the ceremony, I could hear all this barely suppressed laughter burbling behind me.

'Of course, the bastard had only written HE on the sole of my left shoe and LP! on the sole of the right shoe, so when I knelt down I was screaming for help. That was the first thing. Then when we moved into our frightfully middle-class reception on a marquee on the lawn David stood up to make his speech. There was a sprinkling of theatricals there, Sheila Hancock was a guest and so was Frank Windsor as I was directing *Softly, Softly* at the time.

'David got to his feet. Then he stood on a chair so we could all see him clearly. He tipped his hat back and said in a loud, clear voice, "Balls ..." I thought, My God, he's flipped! He is going to lay into the whole ceremony. What on earth is he going to say next? And one of Anne's older relations started to walk out fearing a tirade of abuse.

'But before she got very far, he went on, "Balls ... weddings and christenings are great fun." And we all breathed a huge collective sigh of relief. He went on in such hilarious style from there my real regret is that I did not think of recording his speech. It was a marvellous comedy routine.

'And as if that was not enough, David actually joined us on our honeymoon! We went for a fortnight to Corfu and after the first week David came out on his own and joined us. We were delighted to have him because he was such fun. He loved taking off the Greek waiters doing a whole serving routine in his peculiar version of the Greek language which nobody else could quite understand. The waiters loved it and so did we.'

Corfu was always one of David's favourite holiday haunts. And often he would accompany Malcolm Taylor and Anne Rutter and their friend writer Richard Harris and his wife. Richard Harris recalls, 'We used to have great fun. The three of us had this joke where we would refer to each other by our initials. Malcolm Taylor was known as MT, David was DJ and I was RH. We would say, "Oh hello, MT, I've just had lunch with DJ." It was just a laugh. David was obviously very talented and a great laugh. We were very young then, David had just finished working as an electrician. He usually came on his own, he never had a steady girlfriend when I knew him. He was as ambitious as any young actor and certainly he used to get frustrated. He was always a pretty solitary chap, but great fun in those days.'

4

Shooting to Stardom

Even in the fairytale world of movie-making it is very nearly asking the impossible of a film director to make a full-length comedy feature film in just three weeks, especially when those three weeks are spanning Easter, when the sets are constantly being unexpectedly dismantled and irretrievably taken away as shooting progresses, and when an unscheduled sex scene has to be shot as an afterthought to spice up the movie.

Yet amazingly, *Albert's Follies*, which was burdened with all these handicaps and more, was the film which was intended to launch David Jason to stardom. In the end, it was a disaster movie with most of the disasters happening behind the scenes. In its own way, *Albert's Follies*, or *White Cargo* as the film was eventually re-titled, was truly a miracle of movie-making and director Ray Selfe looks back on it all with a mixture of pride, pain, pleasure, laughter and disbelief.

The miracle is that the film was ever made at all. Time was so tight that Selfe admits to being forced to use several takes in the finished movie in which his star, David Jason, was not giving his performance for the camera but was simply filmed in rehearsal. 'We'd rehearse David with the camera rolling and use that take,' Selfe recalls. 'There just wasn't the time to do it properly and I was under terrible pressure to get it all done in three weeks. The production manager was continually pressurising me and I had to turn in somewhere around six or seven minutes of material every day.'

As if he didn't have enough problems to worry about, Selfe's efforts to deliver a light, entertaining comedy film were further complicated when, after the cameras had been rolling for four days, a request came through to give *Albert's Follies* a different flavour. At the outset, Selfe had perceived *Albert's Follies* as an old-fashioned comedy with the well-meaning idiot getting himself into tricky situations and chasing a girl who is much stronger than he is and who isn't destined for him anyway. So Selfe was surprised when the order to 'tart it up a bit' came from his producers as he struggled to combat the mounting difficulties he was already facing.

'They'd first of all wanted an X-certificate film and then they'd realised it would limit their market so they asked me to go for a U-certificate,' says Selfe. 'Then half-way through the fifth day of shooting they changed their minds and said would I make it an X-certificate. I said "No, not at this stage because it would change the whole slant of the movie."'

Instead, Selfe chose to continue with his already tight schedule at Twickenham Studios and then shoot one additional scene elsewhere. And so it came about that the film which had started out with such high hopes for David Jason finished production in the most unlikely circumstances — in a specially hired room at the Westminster Hotel in London where Selfe, acting as both cameraman and lighting man as well as director in order to save money, shot an extra scene with 6ft 6in tall actor Dave Prowse being ordered to romp in bed with a topless blonde.

Albert's Follies, produced by Border Film Productions (nothing to do with Border TV), started out as a fairly harmless, knockabout comic tale of a boring, pen-pushing civil servant called Albert who dreams of playing out James Bond-style heroics of rescuing girls in distress. The original, ambitious plan was to incorporate 3D sequences when Albert stepped into his James Bond guise. But lack of time and money put paid to that innovation. By the time it was ready for release, the film had ended up not as *Albert's Follies*, but with the new title of *White Cargo*, a reference to part of the plot about a sex slave trade whereby English strippers are shipped off to harems in the East.

Selfe, who had made literally hundreds of films without ever interesting the people who hand out the Oscar nominations, was entrusted with the job of bringing the movie in within its three-week allotted schedule and within its £80,000 budget. That was a low figure by movie production standards even in 1973. But that year the film *American Graffiti*, made for the then minuscule Hollywood budget of £350,000, was showing movie-makers that you didn't necessarily need millions to produce a winner at the box office. That film's return was 50 times the investment.

Given the huge time and financial restrictions and other pressures imposed upon him by the producers of *Albert's Follies*, Selfe nevertheless had all the credentials to deliver. His track record included making a film about Kenny Ball and his Jazzmen in a single day and that speed of work certainly impressed the backers.

Ian Lavender was originally in the frame to play hapless Albert. Lavender had made a name for himself as Private Pike in the hugely popular BBC situation comedy *Dad's Army* about the antics of the Home Guard. But his impact on television audiences worked against him. Selfe considered Lavender's TV image as Pike would simply be too strong and would therefore be a hindrance to the movie rather than a help.

Lavender's name might have helped attract a cinema audience but Selfe thought he was too readily identifiable. Selfe reckoned that if he was to create a brand new fool for the big screen, then he required an actor who was not instantly recognised by millions. When asked whom he favoured to take on the star role, Selfe instantly said it should be David Jason and dangled the carrot that David was unlikely to cost a fortune to sign although he was starting to make something of a name for himself taking over from Michael Crawford in the West End stage comedy *No Sex Please — We're British*.

Selfe had worked with David some three years before when he was a contributor to Frank Muir's TV programme *We Have Ways of Making You Laugh*. 'I used to produce a three-minute comedy film every week for that show and David was brought in to do the commentary for one he did with Terry Gilliam on the history of the whoopee cushion,' Selfe recalls. David was duly signed as Albert.

Selfe had envisaged shooting *Albert's Follies*, which he had written as a Walter Mitty-style escapade, at various locations around London but Border Film Productions decreed it should be shot in a studio. Selfe tried to negotiate with both Shepperton Studios and Pinewood Studios before a deal was struck for the film to be made at Twickenham Studios over Easter in 1973. 'Nobody wanted to go into the studios over Easter because of the four-day holiday in the middle,' Selfe observes.

On the first day of filming, Selfe was anxious as always to enthuse the crew and impress upon them his ability by not messing about. He displayed real urgency about getting the job done but the speed at which he worked caused mouths to fall open. When it came to David's very first scene, Selfe did just one take and, much to the astonishment of the crew, announced, 'Cut and print. Fine.'

'Actually,' says Selfe, 'I always believed that the first take you can cut and print. If it's not right you can go back and shoot it later.' But this audacious start astounded some of the crew, particularly a cameraman who had worked on high-budget, prestigious James Bond movies and was used to films being made with utmost care and precision and realising perhaps a handful of seconds worth of film a day if they were lucky. He immediately came over to Selfe and asked him if he was going to go for another take just as an insurance.

'No,' Selfe told him, and quickly pressed on to the next scene. 'The cameraman smoked a pipe,' Selfe recalls with a chuckle. 'Between every take he would take his pipe out and put it into his mouth. But in the three weeks of shooting that film he always managed to get the pipe into his mouth but he never ever got the time to light it! It was all first takes.

'He kept moaning to me, "Can't you take a bit longer? Can't you do another take?" My answer was always that I'd got to finish it in the time they'd given me and there was nothing I could do about it. They were only a tiny production company. It wasn't a question of them putting any more money into it. There was no more money.'

In addition to David, Selfe had cast two other comedians — Hugh Lloyd and Tim Barrett — to play bumbling men from the Ministry. David was clearly the film's number one comedy star but he generously liked to refer to this duo as 'the comic relief'. The three of them got on extremely well and one of the very rare occasions when Selfe permitted himself more than a single take involved a scene in which Lloyd and Barrett were dressed up as gas inspectors and Barrett had to give David an address.

'We had to do four takes on that,' says Selfe, 'because they kept on rolling up with laughter as Barrett changed the address every time. Even on the take I actually used, you can see a twinkle in David's eye as he's on the brink of corpsing again.' Not quite so funny for the cast and crew was the fact that they could not but fail to notice with increasing incredulity and much alarm that the sets of *Albert's Follies* were visibly diminishing as filming progressed. They would finish filming on a particular set one evening and head for home only to find part of that set had disappeared when they turned up to resume filming the following morning. The reason for these sudden disappearances, as they later discovered, was that several of the sets had been borrowed from another film at Twickenham Studios and had merely been reclaimed.

Selfe counted his blessings that he was fortunate enough to have in his production team a brilliant art director who managed to improvise with the utmost ingenuity. 'We had a manor built inside the studio from the remains of another movie, *The Ruling Class* starring Peter O'Toole, which had been shooting at Twickenham a few months previously,' says Selfe. 'We were also building another set on the outside of that one. But between each take, a piece of the set would get taken down and the area we were shooting in was getting smaller and smaller.

'Originally, we had a huge lounge with a corridor and several rooms off it, and a staircase. But as we finished shooting in the lounge they dismantled it, and when we finished shooting on the staircase they dismantled that, too. In the end we were down to just a corridor with a set of double doors at the end of it.' Inevitably a shrinking set posed no end of problems, not least when David was due to film a scene where he had to race along the corridor, vigorously twist the handles of the double doors and throw them open.

'By this time, all that was left was half the corridor,' chortles Selfe. 'And, so the set wouldn't fall down, they'd put four-by-two planks across the doors to strengthen and stabilise them and sealed the large door handles so they wouldn't open. When it came to film the scene, David being David and wanting to give his all, rushed up to the doors, grabbed the handles, gave them a vicious twist and, of course, they didn't move. He nearly broke his wrists.

He swore for four minutes after that and didn't repeat himself once.'

David was not the only one feeling pain. Dave Prowse, later to become a big screen favourite with youngsters all over the world as the evil Darth Vader in *Star Wars*, had to film a scene where he stood in a coil of rope which was eventually to curl up first round his legs, then his waist, and finally up under his arms lifting him right up in the air. But as the coil travelled up his legs, Dave felt a piercing jab of pain in a kneecap. 'The rope had caught round my kneecap and pulled it right out of joint,' he says, wincing still at the memory. 'I was in agony.'

Albert's Follies was something of a reunion for Prowse and David Jason because they had known each other for many years. Prowse had appeared in an episode of the BBC's TV police series *Softly, Softly* and the Welsh director had introduced him to a little group of Welsh actors who included Jennifer Hill, Ruth and Philip Madoc, and David Jason.

'I'm not Welsh myself but I used to hang around with this group and at that time David couldn't get work to save his life,' says Prowse. 'He was paranoid about not working. He was the most insecure little guy you could come across. He was always a very funny little man. But it was strange because at that time they were trying to get his career off the ground and nothing seemed to click for him. He was a super little guy but very, very insecure.'

Prowse originally had only a small part in *Albert's Follies* but that all changed when he met director Ray Selfe. 'He said, "We can't offer you anything as small as this. You must have a major role." The next thing I know, I'm involved in script conferences. It was really strange.'

Prowse had been striving for a breakthrough for so long. He was pleased to hear that *Albert's Follies* was a film which had elevated David to the leading role. 'But it was the worst film of all time,' he says. 'It really was. At one point, David had to get over a wall to get into some big establishment and you see him climbing up the wall when it's dark and then you see him landing on the ground in daylight! It was an absolute disaster. Everything that could possibly go wrong went wrong. They were strapped for cash and everything was done in such a rush instead of things being prepared properly. Everything was done on a shoe-string, and quick.'

With two of his main cast nursing injuries, still more complications arose for Selfe from his masters. He was told that under no circumstances was he allowed to continue filming beyond 6.00pm as there would be no overtime pay. 'We never once went over six o'clock,' he remembers. 'At one minute to six we'd get the last take in the can and then it would be cut, print and goodnight.'

That, however, suited David. He had to finish at 5.30pm every evening anyway to jump into a car to whisk him back to the West End from Twickenham through the rush-hour traffic in time to go on stage at the Strand Theatre in *No Sex Please — We're British*.

'We lost David on matinée days,' says Selfe ruefully, 'and there were days when somebody new was in the cast who had to be broken in and David couldn't make it in the afternoon because they had a rehearsal.

'David was working under terrible strain because he was doing his very action-packed version of *No Sex Please — We're British*. He must have been pretty exhausted at the end of the day.' The whole experience was a nightmare for David. He had been dazzled by the prospect of appearing in a feature film but simply appalled by the production standards.

At the Strand Theatre, David had stepped into the role created by Michael Crawford. *No Sex Please — We're British* was set in a flat above a bank, home to respectable newly-weds played by *Upstairs, Downstairs* star Simon Williams and Belinda Carroll. There, to their horror, they find they are being flooded with wholesale consignments of pornographic books, pictures and films which they try to keep hidden from a nasty mother-in-law played by Evelyn Laye, a prying policeman and a couple of important bank officials. The fun comes from the attempts of David as a sheepish bank clerk to get rid of it for them by various disastrous means, including flushing it down the lavatory and clogging up the rubbish disposal system.

As the bank clerk Brian Runnicles, Michael Crawford had set a highly energetic level of performance frantically rushing to and fro through the eight doors of an ingenious set, each door holding some bigger surprise than the last, and David was determined to be just as acrobatic. He won huge admiration from packed houses and terrific respect from his peers for his high-octane performance.

'They took a risk with me but I stayed 18 successful months,' he was able to say later. When the curtain came down each night, David would travel the mercifully short distance home to the tiny rented flat he had moved into just off Oxford Street and fall into bed thoroughly drained. He was hardly encouraged in his efforts to get a good night's sleep by the knowledge that he had to be at Twickenham early the following morning ready to give his all in front of the film cameras for *Albert's Follies* and yet somehow remain fresh enough in the evening to reproduce his astonishing agility in *No Sex Please — We're British*.

Tired and exhausted as he was and aching from his physical exertions on stage, David never let Selfe down for one moment. Selfe recalls David gave everything to the film. 'He was absolutely excellent and contributed more than 100 per cent,' he says. 'It wasn't my first movie although it may have looked it. But it certainly didn't look like David's first movie. I remember one scene where he had to fall out of a wagon and although he had pads on his elbows and his knees, it was a helluva fall and it required some very agile work from him. He did it so brilliantly the crew gave him a round of applause. David always had such fantastic enthusiasm and a great sense of fun. Although it was all terribly hard work, we fell about at some of the things that happened.'

One of the more spicy scenes in the film called for David to turn up at a strip club and sit in the front row of the audience while glamorous, buxom blonde Sue Bond, a curvy Benny Hill girl, performed a striptease. From his front-row seat, David's character sees the heroine of the film (played by Imogen Hassall, who later tragically committed suicide) being assaulted by Dave Prowse.

In his Walter Mitty state, David leaps up on stage and rescues her. But as the bungling loser Albert, the script called for David to leap on stage, slip up on Sue's discarded silk underwear and, in the act of reaching out a hand to stop himself falling, to pull down Sue's G-string. The scene was only made possible at all by hastily transforming a carpet showroom set from the previous day's filming and dressing it to double as a strip club. But it was all in vain as the scene eventually ended up on the cutting-room floor. Selfe was at that time working to his U-certificate brief but he says, 'I knew I would have to make some compromises afterwards when they said, "Could you put something in to tart it up a little bit."'

Selfe needed to think and act fast and soon worked out the solution. Part of the plot involved a scenario about white slave trafficking in which strippers from London's West End clubs are abducted and sold off to harems. Dave Prowse's character is entrusted with the task of making up a consignment of strippers and decides, at the last moment, to put his own girlfriend in among them. But not before snatching one last night of love with her.

Selfe had already shot a scene in which Prowse and screen girlfriend Sue Bond were seen going out of a room to grab their last night of passion together. He had planned for their subsequent lovemaking to be left entirely to the audience's imagination. He had merely filmed them heading off together. So now, Selfe reasoned, all he had to do was to follow that scenario through to its obvious conclusion and film some bed scenes with the couple to 'tart it up'.

And so the movie, intended as a major launchpad to stardom for David Jason, ended with Dave Prowse and Sue Bond being summoned to a hired room at the Westminster Hotel to film a sex scene together.

Dave Prowse looks back with understandable bewilderment. 'They suddenly needed Sue and me for some sexy scenes but they didn't have any money and couldn't go back to the studios so they hired a West End hotel. With Ray Selfe as director and cameraman they had Sue and me romping around in bed trying to be sexy as part of this terrible, terrible film.'

Selfe had given Sue a start in movies by frequently using her in the short ice cream commercials he had made for the Classic cinema chains because he liked her fresh, thoroughly English wholesome look. He recalls, 'The funny thing about Sue was that she said to me when we were about to shoot this sex scene in *Albert's Follies*, "Have I really got to go topless in this one, Ray?"

'I said, "I'm afraid so," and she said, "I've never been in a feature film yet where I've not shown my tits and I told my father this was going to be the first one. Here's another film he can't see."'

White Cargo was never going to win any Oscars but Selfe had done his job in the most trying of circumstances. He had brought the movie in on time and on budget. 'It went out as a support movie to another film, it got a circuit release, the producers recovered their money, and it got sold to television,' he says.

But, as Prowse is quick to point out, it did nothing for David's career. 'They were trying to groom David Jason for stardom,' says Prowse, 'and *Albert's Follies* was going to get him off the ground. Unfortunately, I think it buried him even deeper than he was before.'

Ray Selfe is commendably honest when it comes to assessing the movie. 'It gets a one-star review as being terrible but shooting a comedy is not the easiest thing to do when you have the sort of restrictions we had,' he says. 'What people don't understand is the incredible pressures we were under when making it. I don't know what David thought of it.'

David knows exactly what he thinks about it. 'It was the kiss of death,' he reflects. 'It was meant to launch me in a big way but at that time I was very green and here was an opportunity to try to do something which seemed like a good idea and everybody seemed to believe in. I believed that other people knew more than I did and I relied on them. I thought they would make it good so I worked very hard for them. I trusted more people then than I trust now. The weight of responsibility has become much more on my shoulders. It's now my decision.

'To have cameras rolling when you are rehearsing was quite horrendous. It was my first experience of filming and it certainly made me think about taking a leading part.' Interestingly, there was rarely a mention of *Albert's Follies* or *White Cargo* on the David Jason list of acting credits in years to come.

'But I did another film after that called *The Odd-Job Man*. I first did it with Ronnie Barker as a half-hour television comedy and it was wonderful. But when they did it as a movie they changed the whole premise to move it up-market. But it went right away from the original story and it was total rubbish.

'Every time I got involved in a film for no money it always turned into a disaster. I couldn't do anything in a film to save my life. At one stage in my career I was really moving backwards at a rate of knots.'

The bad memories of *Albert's Follies* stayed with David and clouded his view of British film-making. Years later when the *Carry On* team got back together to make *Carry On Columbus*, top TV comedians like Rik Mayall, Julian Clary, Alexei Sayle and

Richard Wilson fell over themselves to take roles in the movie. But not David. Asked whether he wanted more of a movie career, he replied acidly, 'I don't think there is one in this country. Do you think I want to be up Columbus's jacksey with Julian Clary? No thank you!'

All through his career, David has been prepared to take the bumps and the bruises when called upon to turn in a very physical performance. But it was while he was making *The Odd-Job Man* that he suffered a horrific accident which left his entire body seized up. 'I had to be thrown over a settee,' he recalls, 'and I ended up between the settee and a chair and landed on my head with the whole weight of my body on top of my head. I was trapped.'

Fellow cast members were shocked to find David prone on the floor clearly dazed and there were great sighs of relief when he came round and appeared none the worse for the fall. But two days later, David was alarmed to find his body seizing up. 'I seized up so totally that I couldn't turn my head,' he says. 'I couldn't even get my arm up to scratch the back of my head. My arm wouldn't work and my hand wouldn't work either — I couldn't close my fingers into a fist.'

David immediately sought the help of Paul Johnson, the osteopath who had worked wonders for him during his run in *No Sex Please — We're British*. 'When Paul put me on the table, he discovered I'd put my neck out at the shoulder joint. I'd pulled the tendon so badly that the joints hadn't gone back and were grating against each other. I was in agony but Paul managed to sort it all out in the end. I've taken some knocks over the years but this was by far the worst.'

Fortunately for David, Humphrey Barclay's plans for his television future were rather more professional. Barclay teamed David Jason very early on with Ronnie Barker, the man who was to become a real comedy mentor and a firm friend in later years.

Barclay remembers, 'He played an aged 100-year-old gardener called Dithers in an early Ronnie Barker series called *Hark at Barker*. David was very convincing at adding on the years. You would never have guessed how old he was. And, of course, he was very funny as always.

'But the first major solo idea we came up with for him was *The Top-Secret Life of Edgar Briggs*, a spy spoof written by Bernard McKenna and Richard Laing. I still think it was one of the funniest shows I have ever been involved with.'

The Top-Secret Life of Edgar Briggs cast David as hapless no-hoper Edgar who, by a clerical error, is transferred to Counter Espionage at the Ministry of Defence. Appointed Assistant to the Commander (Noel Coleman), he manages to achieve the most remarkable results despite the fact that he is both stupid and totally unsuited to the job he has been given. David was a strange mixture of enthusiasm, apprehension and concern about the project. Before its first screening on 15 September 1974, he said, 'This is the culmination of eight years' work as an actor. I shall be on my own with Briggs. If the series flops, I'll get the blame. The responsibility of carrying the lead and wondering how viewers will react is a little worrying. It's like waiting to be executed.

'If it's a hit, anything is possible. Briggs is a super fellow. He's British and proud of it, and wholesome in the way that we Britons naturally are. He is devoted to his wife although he would love to hop into bed with his beautiful and willing colleague Cathy, played by Elizabeth Counsell. There's only one thing wrong with Briggs — he's stupid. He's also so timid he'd probably collapse if Cathy openly invited him.'

Whatever the viewers thought of *The Top-Secret Life of Edgar Briggs*, David was also nervously aware that television audiences would at least be seeing the real David Jason. 'This role makes me feel rather naked,' he said. 'Until now, I've always appeared heavily disguised in wigs, heavy make-up, funny clothes and middle-European voices.'

Beating the drum for the series, Humphrey Barclay boldly predicted, 'I think Briggs, with his amazing capacity for reaching his goal by running headlong in the wrong direction, will become something of a cult. This is a new style of television comedy — fast, dead-pan, laced with verbal nonsense and bundled together with a marvellously crazy logic all of its own.'

The first episode set the tone for old-fashioned knockabout comedy with David falling over chairs, getting soaked fully clothed in a Turkish bath, taking a nosedive over a settee and putting on a negligée without realising it. *Daily Mirror* TV writer Stan Sayer declared, 'David is a modern Buster Keaton with most of that great silent film actor's gift of timing, rhythm and skill.'

There was no doubting that David played the unfortunate espionage agent with great flair and even the *Daily Telegraph*'s TV critic Sylvia Clayton felt *The Top-Secret Life of Edgar Briggs* had 'style and panache'.

Among Edgar's long-suffering colleagues who looked upon his unlikely achievements with amusement, alarm, incredulity and jealousy was Spencer, played by that fine actor Mark Eden, later to find infamy as the beast of Weatherfield, *Coronation Street*'s Alan Bradley. Mark remembers, 'Humphrey knew David was brimming with television potential. He had just done *No Sex Please — We're British* and everyone said he was funnier than Michael Crawford. And we all really thought *Edgar Briggs* would launch David as a star. It was a very well-written series and David added in so many hilarious extra bits of comedy business.

'We immediately struck up a rapport because we both love comedy and we had a similar sense of humour. He used to think up so many funny little stunts to improve the action and he used to ring me up and say, his voice almost quivering with enthusiasm, "Can you get in a quarter-of-an-hour earlier tomorrow? I've got an idea about that scene where you come upstairs with the milk bottle," or whatever.

'And we would get in before anyone arrived and we would work it out together. He was brilliantly inventive and I just know when I watch him in series these days that a lot of that stuff is not scripted but created by him. Once, there was a scene where he had to put some things into a filing cabinet, shut it, lock it, throw the key out of the window and then find he had trapped his tie in the drawer. I had to rush over and pull and strain to get him out virtually by his throat. It wasn't really all that difficult because the tie slid out easily.

'But when we came to record the scene he put a little weight, a little piece of metal, into the bottom of his tie. This made it jam in the drawer and I had to yank really hard to get him out. At first I couldn't understand it, it wouldn't come free. David went into convulsions. He reckoned it made that scene more realistic but also he loved to make me laugh when I wasn't supposed to. He was one of the very few people who could actually break me up, make me laugh so much I could not go on. Not many people can do that.

'I went through Rep where, when people get bored, they try to make you laugh on stage and I was pretty impervious to all that. Or I thought I was until I worked with David Jason, because he used to get me every time. He was just so funny. He was also a very clever mimic. You would hear these amazing voices — John Wayne and James Mason were his favourites — and look round and it would be David.'

David Jason's flair for the physical side of being funny was given free rein in *Edgar Briggs* and he boldly grasped the challenge, insisting on doing all of his own stunts. Mark Eden said, 'Even when it involved big falls he insisted on doing it himself. He knew it would look better than using stuntmen. Once we were on the top floor of one of those big old-fashioned houses in London near the Regent's Park canal. The script called for David and I to pretend to be window cleaners and he had to get out on to a window sill.

'As he got out, he slipped and grabbed a rope and swung around a bit and then I had to grab him by this cardigan he was wearing but then he had to slip through the cardigan, which I was left holding, and crash several storeys to the ground. They were planning to use a stuntman for the final fall but David said, "No, no, I'll do it. It will look better," and of course he fell down into the pile of cardboard boxes quite brilliantly. But I wouldn't have dared to do it.

'He wanted to do everything himself. Another time we were in one of those crazy car chases and we had to go over a hump-backed bridge at high speed so fast that the car took off. They had stunt drivers ready and waiting but David insisted he wanted to do it himself and he talked me into coming along for the most terrifying ride of my life. He kept saying it would be much better because the cameras would be able to capture our faces and our expressions of fear. The expression was genuine in my case as I smashed my head against the roof when we became airborne.

'I knew then he was going to be a star. I told everyone who would listen at the time. We became good friends through the series but he was always something of a loner. If we went for a drink afterwards he would have half a pint and that would be it. And at lunchtimes he was always off on his own to the nearest greasy spoon café for a big fry-up or meat and two veg.'

David had already developed his interest in flying. He quickly qualified as a glider pilot and would use many of his spare moments to get airborne, but when the producers found out about this potentially dangerous hobby they grounded him until filming was over. David was deeply miffed. He had moved by then into the flat that is still his London base to this day, in a pre-War mansion block just off Oxford Street. 'I used to go round for a drink sometimes,' said Mark. 'Then he bought this place in Sussex to do up. It was really remote with no phone and he would arrive for work on Monday full of enthusiasm for a piece of rewiring he had done. I think he used to enjoy hard physical work as a break from the pressures of being funny.

'But more often he came round to my house for dinner. I liked him very much and my family always enjoyed his company. But he seemed so very solitary. I don't think he ever brought a girlfriend and whenever we rang to invite him he nearly always accepted.

'I think, like a lot of comedians, he was actually quite melancholy at times. It wasn't until he got going that he would start relishing it all, when he came up with a good bit of business he would hug himself with glee, he loved it. And as *Edgar Briggs* was an action series there was scope for him to do all his funny falls.

'David was very popular with everyone. You could not fail to respond to his enthusiasm and his determination to make the show absolutely as good as possible.'

In spite of all the high hopes, *The Top-Secret Life of Edgar Briggs* never quite made it in the ratings and in the world of commercial television there is rarely any prized second series for shows which don't grab instant public acclaim.

'The problem was that we went out just before *The Brothers*,' said Mark Eden. 'That was a glossy BBC soap opera about a transport firm that was just at its peak at the time. It was like putting something out against *Coronation Street*, we didn't have a chance. That was it, they scrapped the show. We all got letters from Humphrey Barclay saying he was sorry but that was the decision.'

As the star of the show, David's disappointment was acute. 'I was really upset about poor Edgar,' he reflected. 'I thought he was terrific but somehow he never caught on.' The irony of the failure in the ratings of *The Top-Secret Life of Edgar Briggs* was that the show became a worldwide hit. It became one of ITV's most successful exports and David and the other members of the cast received fan letters from all over the world for years afterwards.

Yet when ITV moved to repeat the comedy they were blocked by David Jason of all people. 'He simply said "No",' said an angry cast member. 'It was very mean of him because although he doesn't need the money lots of other people do. It would have meant a few thousand quid to me that is desperately needed. Apparently, David thought he was already over-exposed. Some of the rest of us thought that was disgraceful.'

David himself declines to discuss the blocked repeats but a friend said, '*Edgar Briggs* is history. Sure, the viewers would love it, but David knows just how raw he looked in those days and he is not at all anxious to share that with his public. Image is very important to an actor and to an insecure actor like David, it is absolutely paramount. He said "No" and he meant "No".'

★   ★   ★

While *The Top-Secret Life of Edgar Briggs* was certainly unlucky and underrated, it nevertheless fell a long way short of its objective of turning David Jason into a household name and making him ITV's answer to Michael Crawford. Crawford had given the BBC a huge comedy hit with *Some Mothers Do 'Ave 'Em*, starring as a hapless failure called Frank Spencer for whom everything always went wrong. Playing Frank with consummate skill, Crawford had also taken quite staggering risks to do his own stunts, which became a spectacular feature of the sitcom. The show had caught the public's imagination and ITV chiefs had envisaged Jason, with his flair for visual knockabout comedy, as their answer to Crawford in *The Top-Secret Life of Edgar Briggs.*

Apart from David himself, no one was more disappointed at the apparent failure than Humphrey Barclay. But, to his credit, he swallowed his disappointment, kept faith with David as a comedy actor and remained undaunted. He was convinced it was only a matter of time before David achieved a major breakthrough and the search was earnestly resumed to find him a suitable new comedy vehicle. The task fell to comedy writer Terence Frisby whose track record included netting around £300,000 in stage royalties for his highly successful sex comedy *There's a Girl in My Soup* which subsequently became a hit film starring Peter Sellers and Goldie Hawn.

Frisby had first met David Jason when David's brother Arthur had played a leading role in Frisby's first play *The Subtopians* back in 1962. In addition to being a highly promising writer, Frisby was also at that time working as an actor at Bromley Rep in Kent and he and Arthur had become friends after they had appeared in a pantomime together, Arthur playing a cannibal chief and Frisby his victim in the pot.

Frisby remembers David was often to be found hanging around the theatre. 'He'd have a few drinks with us,' Frisby recalls, 'and I got the idea that he wanted to be a theatre electrician. I didn't connect him with acting at that time.' But 13 years on, Frisby was only too delighted when Humphrey Barclay asked him to write a comedy series with David cast in the lead role.

The series Frisby came up with was *Lucky Feller* and it was culled from a film script which Frisby had written several years before for producer Jay Lewis. When Lewis suddenly died from a heart-attack, the script went straight into the bottom drawer of Frisby's desk and remained there until it was dusted off to meet Barclay's request for a new comedy series.

In essence, *Lucky Feller* was the story of the eternal triangle — but with a difference. 'It was about this innocent little man, Shorty Mepstead, trying to run his little plumbing business with his elder brother Randy who was bedding Shorty's girlfriend. In the end, Randy got her pregnant and the younger brother, Shorty, had to marry her,' is how Frisby himself encapsulates the plot.

David, naturally, was offered the role of Shorty, the gauche innocent who still lived at home in South-east London with his mother and brother Randolph, and believed he was the luckiest person in the world because he was surrounded by such ostensibly lovely people. Cheryl Hall, a bright and pretty 26-year-old actress, won the role of Kathleen, Shorty's girlfriend who gradually coaxes him out of his shyness. Peter Armitage, later to find fame in *Coronation Street*, was signed to play brother Randy after Nicky Henson had taken the role in the pilot, and Glynn Edwards, who went on famously to play the barman at The Winchester Club in *Minder*, was Kath's father.

Once the idea of *Lucky Feller* had been accepted by London Weekend Television, Frisby was despatched to share a holiday cottage in Somerset for two days to 'observe' the latent star and fashion the series to fit him. It was not an experience which overly thrilled David. 'He was just looking, listening, seeing what kind of person I was and how I behaved,' David recalled. 'Then when he'd got enough information, he just went.'

All looked extremely promising when it came to filming the first episode. One scene, in particular, at a Chinese restaurant had the studio audience in fits. 'I've never heard people laugh as much,' says Frisby. The scene involved Shorty taking girlfriend Kath out for a meal. The comic scenario had Shorty, hopelessly ignorant of Chinese cuisine, so drastically over-ordering from the menu that the waiter, played by Burt Kwouk, had to pull up another table to accommodate yet more plates piled with food.

Among the offerings were two dumplings which were to provide the audience with their cue for hysterical laughter, because Shorty had ordered prawn balls. Gazing at the spread with a puzzled expression, Kath inquired, 'Which are the prawn balls?' Frisby recalls, 'The audience laughed like you've never heard. Then David pointed at the dumplings and said, "It must be those."

Then Kath says, "Ooh, big, aren't they?" and the audience laughed for another ten minutes so that David never managed to get out the pay-off line which was, "Well, they were kingsize prawns." We did umpteen takes and the audience were collapsing and David broke up before every take. Everyone laughed so much those three lines took half-an-hour to shoot.'

No one ever accused *Lucky Feller* of overdoing the subtlety or good taste of comedy presentation but it all augured well for the series, especially as Frisby was agreeably surprised to discover that sitting in unobtrusively but attentively at the initial rehearsals every Monday was none other than LWT's chairman. 'There was always this figure at the back,' says Frisby, 'and I went over to see who it was. There was LWT's chairman John Freeman. He told me he came every Monday simply because he loved watching the show.'

LWT, for their part, had plenty of faith in the project on a production level. For one key scene where Shorty floods a supermarket there was a double set — one which could be flooded and a second, dry set for other scenes. 'We took an entire set, packed it out in the studio and flooded it,' Frisby recalls. 'It was a scene where Shorty and Randy have arrived to repair the pipes at a supermarket. At the very moment Shorty is supposed to release the cock, he discovers his brother is bedding his girl and they get into a terrible fight and all the taps are open and it floods.'

Other key moments were filmed at a launderette in West London which was literally filled from floor to ceiling with foam. 'We wore wet suits with our costumes on top and we more or less floated in the foam,' Cheryl Hall recalls. 'David and I were worried how we were going to breathe but we managed it.' David and the rest of the cast had the luxury of five days rehearsing each episode before going into the studio to film on the Saturday. Each Sunday they had the day off, much welcomed by all because the summer of 1976 turned out to be the hottest of the century.

It was truly a golden summer. All parts of the UK basked in

record hours of sunshine, temperatures soared, and it was so dry that the crowd at Lord's actually cheered when a few drops of rain stopped the cricket for 15 minutes. But rehearsing in stifling heat in a stuffy room at the Duke of York's army barracks in King's Road, Chelsea, was far from comfortable work for David and the rest of the cast. At one o'clock they broke for lunch each day and David and Cheryl would escape to an equally hot, stuffy pub to queue up for a salad and a beer while cursing the fact that thy were too late to find a seat in the popular beer garden at The Markham. By the time they got there, every seat was always taken.

Like so many of his co-stars, Cheryl took an instant liking to David and was immediately impressed by his flair for visual comedy and his meticulous approach to acting. 'He was so professional,' she reflects. 'His timing was so good, he was great with props and he taught me the importance of visual gags.

'Shorty was Mr Uncool, a man who never got anything right and we had a scene in a pub where he went to light my cigarette with his lighter. Being Shorty, of course, he activates the lighter and a huge flame shoots out and burns my entire nose. It was a tricky scene but David worked out all the angles perfectly and knew exactly where the camera should be so we could film the shooting flame then cut it so that my nose could be reddened for the next shot.

'There was one very funny moment in one of the final scenes when I was wearing a beautiful peach blouse and I had to clutch David to my bosom in a clinch. When he pulled away, my blouse was black and I couldn't understand why. I couldn't work out where this black stain had come from. The audience was laughing away about it and I noticed David looking very sheepish. Then he suddenly whispered, "It's my bald pate!" David was beginning to go bald even then and I'd never noticed because they'd blacked it out with make-up.

'David was always 100 per cent committed. He lived, ate, and breathed acting and when he wasn't acting he was always talking about the business. He had that totally focussed approach even when socialising. It wasn't just socialising, it was for an ulterior motive, a hidden agenda of who you were socialising with and whether it would do your career any good. I'd rather choose my friends by other criteria but David was always very ambitious. He very much wanted to be a star.

'He was acutely aware that at the age of 36, as he was then, he was late coming to fame. At that time I was married to the actor Robert Lindsay who was gaining recognition in another ITV comedy series called *Get Some In*. It was a show about RAF recruits doing National Service in the Fifties and, apart from Tony Selby, Bob and the other stars of *Get Some In* were all in their mid-twenties and they were all enjoying a high profile as the show became popular very quickly. David must have been looking at them and thinking, They are my contemporaries. I'm way, way too late starting out. David was running with all his might to catch the train.'

Away from *Lucky Feller*, Cheryl found David displayed distinct traits of his TV character Shorty Mepstead, especially in his attitude to women. 'He was very vulnerable off set,' she says. 'He may have been 36 but he was very naïve as far as women were concerned. Being so committed to acting, it may just be that he hadn't had the time to discover women.

'I rather took David under my wing for a while. I gave him lifts as he didn't have a car, invited him to charity football matches where I made him sign autographs as he would never play, and tried to line him up with a girlfriend. He was unattached at the time which was of constant concern to me. I remember him telling me about some girl he had nearly married when he was in his twenties and I thought he would have had her up the aisle because he said how much he'd loved her. I'd have thought David wanted and needed marriage.

'Bob Lindsay and I were very much a married couple and so we sort of adopted David. I wanted to do some match-making for him so we set up quite a few dinner parties with various girls for him at our house in Wimbledon. One particular evening we lined him up with a beautiful girl called Mondi who was also unattached and feeling vulnerable because her husband, the actor Leigh Lawson, had left her to move in with the actress Hayley Mills. At the time, Mondi was a very close friend of mine. She was stunningly beautiful — her parents were Iranian and German and she had olive skin, a lovely dark mane of hair, worked in fashion design, was always impeccably dressed and was very intelligent, too.

'I thought she and David might be good together so we had a bijou soirée for 16 people at our Wimbledon home and I told David all about Mondi. "Mondi?" he said. "That's a funny name." I told him to practise saying it and get it right for when he spoke to her. "She's a really lovely girl," I told him, "and she's unattached."

'As the evening went on, everything seemed to be going really well. Mondi was sitting in my rocking chair and David sat at her feet. But after about half-an-hour she came up to me in the kitchen and said, "Is he having me on?" I asked what the matter was because they had seemed to be getting along like a house on fire. "Well," said Mondi, "he's *so* attentive and he keeps telling me how beautiful I am." Poor David! He was trying so hard, too hard. You know women — when a man comes on to us like that you think, Hello, this guy can't be for real! If only David had played it a bit cooler he might have been all right. But he was so naïve about women.'

That naïveté was mirrored in the screen character of Shorty Mepstead and it certainly earned David the sympathy vote from viewers as the series progressed. *Lucky Feller* was launched on 2 September 1976 and earned some plaudits from the TV critics.

Sean Day-Lewis, writing in the *Daily Telegraph*, said, 'My response to David Jason as Shorty Mepstead is that he has a very characterful face and is more likeable than funny.'

The Stage, assessing the new sitcom in the wake of *The Top-Secret Life of Edgar Briggs*, remarked prophetically: 'Somewhere there is a writer whose ideas Mr Jason can execute to great effect but they have not met yet.' Terence Frisby feels *Lucky Feller's* chances of big success were blighted by short-sighted scheduling. Inexplicably, a series about a man bedding his little brother's girl behind his back was given an early evening slot. 'And the girl,' Frisby points out, 'played the most abused heroine there ever was. She was knocked out, thrown about, almost drowned, electrocuted, and screwed in the back of a car by the brother.

'Putting all that out at seven o'clock in the evening wasn't right at all. It was completely the wrong time and hardly anyone ever saw the programmes because everyone was still in their offices or going home and I was actually quite annoyed with LWT. The programmes, though, were top of London Weekend's viewing figures during a winter when LWT had a very bad time.'

There was certainly enough interest all round for LWT to invite Frisby to write a second series of *Lucky Feller*. He had wisely left the fate of Shorty and Kath in the balance at the end of the thirteenth and final programme. Followers of the series tuned in expecting to watch the series neatly rounded off by Shorty finally wedding his sweetheart Kath only to find poor Shorty being left at the altar.

'It was a really sad scene,' Cheryl Hall recalls. 'David is at the church and the scene cuts to me jumping out of a taxi and rushing on to Victoria railway station. We actually filmed at Victoria and I was wearing a complete copy of Princess Anne's wedding dress and long veil. So as not to draw attention to the fact that filming was going on, they hid a camera under one of those little arched canvas workmen's huts they'd set up outside the main entrance and the camera followed me as I ran across the concourse in my bridal gown and down the entire length of the platform.

'Kath had decided that she simply could not marry one brother and not the other so she had left them both. It was a real tear-jerker with the viewers all being prompted to pity poor David getting left at the altar. There would have been viewers all round the country sighing, "Oh, how could she leave him?"'

Followers of *Lucky Feller* never did get to see whether Shorty ever caught up with his runaway bride. LWT's request to Frisby to write a sequel fell on deaf ears, largely because LWT would not repeat the original programmes. 'I was miffed with LWT for not repeating *Lucky Feller*,' Frisby explains. 'Then when John Birt became Head of Programmes at LWT, he phoned me up and said some very complimentary things and told me he was going to repeat them all. But it was around the time that David was in *Porterhouse Blue*, and *Open All Hours* and *Only Fools and Horses* were on and David said, via an agent, that he was over-exposed and so he was able to stop them going out again. So once again I was miffed and that was the end of that. I've always called *Lucky Feller* the Unknown Comedy Series. I'd love to see those shows again. I think they'd probably stand up and I feel David was wrong to do what he did.'

David's firm reluctance to allow a second showing of *Lucky Feller* caught LWT by surprise. In 1986 they were so confident of his consent that they even sent out schedules to advertisers which clearly listed *Lucky Feller* in their programme line-up. Crucially, however, because a period of ten years had elapsed since *Lucky Feller's* original screening, the cast had power of veto if they so wished. David most certainly did.

'I want my career to go forwards, not backwards,' he stated. 'I'm on television a lot already and I don't want viewers to start saying: "Oh God, not him again," when they switch on. Because *Lucky Feller* was ten years old they had to ask my permission and I said "No" because I didn't want to be over-exposed.'

Frisby and LWT were not the only ones who were annoyed at David's stand. 'I could have done with the money I'd have got for repeats,' says Cheryl Hall. 'But quite apart from that, *Lucky Feller* was something I was proud of. It was disappointing that one of your fellow actors had said "No". Maybe he wasn't proud of *Lucky Feller*, but I don't think there was anything he could have been ashamed of.'

Aside from his grouse over the repeats, Frisby finds no fault with David's performance. 'He was fine in *Lucky Feller*,' he declares. 'But, in those days, when he didn't get a laugh the first time, he then used to say the line again. I used to say to him, "David, if they didn't laugh the first time round, they're not going to laugh the second time." But he was so determined to get a laugh that he'd say things twice.' The generally good working relationship Frisby had with David did not, however, expand into a major friendship. Frisby says, 'I don't know what he's like now but then, I think, he was very much locked into his own world. I think he was deeply insecure.'

At the end of the series, Cheryl Hall presented David with a lovely charcoal drawing of Laurel and Hardy, two comedy heroes whom David much revered. She'd noticed that on display in David's kitchen were little figures of Charlie Chaplin, Buster Keaton and Laurel and Hardy. 'Much later on, when I went round to visit David at his flat in Newman Street,' she says, 'I saw the drawing was just collecting dust propped up on his mantelpiece. "Get it framed!" I told David. But I wasn't a bit surprised really. His flat was a typical bachelor pad and I suppose in any case he was hardly ever there.'

The flat was up five flights of stairs with no elevator which somewhat deterred visitors and David, in any case, was reluctant to open it up for inspection. 'The trouble is, I haven't any taste,' he once openly moaned. 'I get neurotic about it. I get jealous when I go in other people's houses. My place is purely functional. Reasonably efficient. In other words, it's clean when I get it clean.'

One visitor who met up with David just before the launch of *Lucky Feller* was initially astounded by him at that time. He knew he was to meet the man who for five years had attracted labels like 'the new Buster Keaton' or 'the new Norman Wisdom' or even 'the new Michael Crawford'. He wasn't prepared for what he found. He said of David, 'He still lives like a bloke who might any day be re-applying for his old job as an electrician.'

Starring in a TV series had, however, done wonders for David's confidence with the opposite sex. That summer he'd walk to the nearby pub with his dark glasses on, his shirt unbuttoned and offering the greeting 'Hello, darling' to the pretty girls he encountered on the way. Almost immediately after filming finished on *Lucky Feller*, Cheryl and David went off on tour in the stage comedy *Darling Mr London* which opened at St Anne's-on-Sea on 6 September four days after *Lucky Feller* had hit the screen.

As the tour progressed, *Darling Mr London* was able to cash in on the TV exposure which Cheryl and David were getting from *Lucky Feller*. With a TV star cast to lure audiences into the theatres, *Darling Mr London* played to enthusiastic houses on its rounds of Southampton, Swansea, Wimbledon, Bradford and Bournemouth. But after working for three months together, it was a mistake for David and me to go off touring in a play,' says Cheryl. 'It was hard work. We both needed a break — but we also both needed the money. It was an uphill struggle because it wasn't a wonderful play.'

David had, in fact, toured with *Darling Mr London* the previous year on a short Spring tour which took in Billingham, Wolverhampton, Bath and Peterborough. He played the central role of a hen-pecked international telephone operator called Edward Hawkins who has sought escapism in fantasy long-distance telephone affairs with a number of foreign 'call-girls'. But when the girls arrive in England for the Miss Europhone contest, they are determined to fit a face to the voice that has been charming them so consistently and they all descend at once on his home in West Drayton.

Chaos reigns. Behind the spare room door is Monique, the Parisian *femme fatale* anxious to show Edward the thrills of a French love affair, and behind another bedroom door is Sylvana who wants to make babies with Edward's help. Waiting in the wings equally ready to get down to their underwear are the Scandinavian sexpots Britt and Ingrid.

The simple and undemanding plot unfolds in the unglamorous setting of the sitting room of Edward's semi where he has to explain the sudden invasion of pulchritude to his shocked wife Rose, played by Doreen Keogh, his ferocious brother-in-law Gordon (Derek Newark), and their drunken lodger Mark (Bob Grant) who, as a curate, of course, views such sexual shenanigans with disapproval. A set which included six doors and French windows gave David plenty of scope to produce a fast-moving performance as he rushed from one to the other.

'All the girls were stereotyped Europeans and they somehow found it necessary to take their clothes off so they were running around the stage in bikinis or bra and pants most of the time,' says Cheryl with some disdain. 'It was one of those typical British farces with lots of scantily-clad women.'

It did the box office no harm that among the nubile beauties to be found scampering across the stage in skimpy underwear each night was a voluptuous blonde Swedish actress called Lena Skoog whose colourful personal life offstage frequently earned her acres of column inches in the tabloids, usually accompanied by a revealing photograph. Also in the cast as French girl Monique was the statuesque British beauty Valerie Leon who at that time was familiar to millions of TV viewers as the predatory female in the Hai Karate aftershave advertisements.

At 5ft 10in tall in her stockinged feet, Valerie towered over

David which added to the farce. Co-starring with David was Bob Grant, the play's co-author and himself a hugely popular television actor of the moment from the sitcom *On the Buses*. All in all, *Darling Mr London* was an attractive package for anyone who liked to see television stars in person and pretty girls wearing precious little with plenty of laughs along the way. The play in general, and David in particular, garnered rave reviews.

The 'world premiére' of *Darling Mr London*, as *The Stage* grandly announced it, was at the Billingham Forum on 7 March 1975, and the local critic Robert Brayshay of the *Evening Dispatch* wrote in his review, 'It must be one of the funniest plays to be presented there. The star of the show is David Jason whose natural gift for comedy gets boundless scope. He draws as much humour from physical actions as from his lines and gives an exceptionally rewarding performance.' Another columnist noted towards the end of the play's run, 'This amusing farce had some memorable moments especially when David Jason was on stage — which was most of the time.'

At the Theatre Royal, Bath, *Darling Mr London* was given an equally warm welcome. The *Bristol Evening Post* critic Jeremy Brien labelled it 'one of the very best farces since the early Brian Rix offerings'. He wrote in his review that David was splendid in the central role and added, 'The evening is built around the talent of David Jason whose cueing in of the laughs, elaborate contortions, and brilliant command of the throw-away line are at the heart of the entertainment.' Judith Boyd of the *Bath and West Evening Chronicle* found the comedy fast and furious and said, 'Most of the energy is burnt up by David Jason as Edward and his performance never loses any of its mind-boggling vigour.' Helen Baxter of the *Peterborough Evening Telegraph* went overboard when *Darling Mr London* moved on to the Key Theatre. She said the play was brilliant and hilarious and had 'given the Key the funniest night of its life'.

As David's fame grew, so did his confidence with the opposite sex. A string of attractive young women flitted quickly in and out of the life of the rising young actor. His brother Arthur took notice when they started to arrive at his home in Brighton. Arthur said, 'Every weekend David would bring a different bird to my house. And it was never the same girl twice. My wife Joy would get totally fed up with so much crumpet coming down. She would complain, "Oh no, David, not another bird." '

As 1976 drew to a close, David could look back on a thoroughly satisfactory year. Although *Lucky Feller* had not been a resounding hit, there were plans for another series of *Open All Hours* which had been well received by critics and public alike when it had quietly opened in February on BBC 2. While the BBC looked to build on the highly promising start of *Open All Hours*, David moved to Lew Grade's ATV at Elstree for yet another sitcom. It was called *A Sharp Intake of Breath* and it turned out to be a highly significant show in the TV career of David Jason because, surprisingly, it swept him for the first time to the top of the ratings, a position he has occupied many times since.

A Sharp Intake of Breath gave David the leading role of Peter Barnes, an ordinary man battling against the perils of officialdom in assorted shapes and sizes and trying to understand and beat 'the system'. Peter's belief in freedom of choice often involved an innocent third party getting dragged into his escapades. Regular cast members included Jacqueline Clarke as Peter's wife Sheila, and Richard Wilson — now a household name as grumpy Victor Meldrew in *One Foot in the Grave* — and Alun Armstrong in a variety of roles. David's brother Arthur was asked to appear as an engineer who called to mend a broken electric heater.

Launched on 20 February 1978, two years to the day after the start of *Open All Hours*, *A Sharp Intake of Breath* swept surprisingly to number one in the ratings in its first week and stayed there. David was understandably delighted. At last, the audience figures matched the aspirations of his producers. 'I've never had so many fan letters in my life,' he beamed. 'It's almost like being a pop star. I was confident about the series but I thought it would take a little time to get it right and that audiences would take a while to catch on.'

David was quick to point out that ITV's scheduling had much to do with it. He felt the relative failure of *The Top-Secret Life of Edgar Briggs* and *Lucky Feller* could partly be blamed on the inability — or more probably the stubborn unwillingness — of the ITV companies to reach agreement on a single national time-slot for the shows. Both shows undoubtedly suffered from split-networking in terms of publicity and promotion. Televison editors on all the national newspapers were reluctant to write previews or stories about the cast when many of their readers would not be able to see the programme they were writing about. The alternative was for newspapers to tailor their TV previews to suit different editions in different areas of the country but it was far simpler for TV correspondents to write about a programme which was fully networked. They were safe in the knowledge that readers in every one of their circulation areas would be sitting down to the same programme on the same day at the same time. They could all happily write about *A Sharp Intake of Breath*.

'It certainly helped the show that everyone in Britain had the chance to see it at the same time,' said David. 'It's the first programme I've ever had fully networked and it's helped a lot. But even more than that, I think a theme of an ordinary bloke struggling against officialdom appealed right across the board. Peter Barnes, the character I play, represents the little fellow against the man in authority. Ronnie Taylor, the writer, thought of the title and we all thought it was a bit odd at first. It was based on the sound people make when they are about to be unhelpful and cause you problems. But it's a worldwide language.

'You know the sort of thing — you take your Mini to the

garage to get a new headlight bulb and find the foreman sucking in his breath between pursed lips then trying to palm you off with a new gearbox and a new back axle.'

Just as it looked as though *A Sharp Intake of Breath* had finally elevated David Jason to stardom, the show was hit by tragedy when its creator and writer Ronnie Taylor died very suddenly from a mystery virus at the age of 57. David was desperately upset. Not only had Ronnie become a good friend but together they had worked hard to build up the character of Peter Barnes as the little man always falling foul of bureaucracy. It had been a fruitful and harmonious partnership.

'For a comic actor to find a writer with whom he can work as well as Ronnie and I worked together was most unusual,' said David paying tribute. 'To find someone that compatible was very, very rare. We had six new ideas mapped out for the new series and Ronnie had written three when he got the virus.' It seemed that the death of Ronnie Taylor was to be the end of the success story for *A Sharp Intake of Breath* but David and producer-director Stuart Allen were determined to save the show.

Allen had moved over to ATV from LWT. There he had enjoyed notable success with sitcoms like *On the Buses* and *Mind Your Language*, a hilariously politically incorrect show set in a London school for foreign students, which were pulling in huge ratings. Now he had to rescue *A Sharp Intake of Breath*. 'When Ronnie died, the scripts weren't completed,' Allen recalls. 'I had to cobble together the three which Ronnie had left and I did quite a good job on them. But we obviously needed to find another writer to continue.'

By good fortune, David happened to meet comedy writer Vince Powell on an episode of the TV charades show *Give Us a Clue*. 'I suddenly realised we had the same sense of humour,' said David, 'and I persuaded him to have a go at writing *A Sharp Intake of Breath*.'

Powell was indeed a logical choice. 'Ronnie Taylor had been Powell's mentor,' says Allen. 'While at the BBC and at Granada TV, Ronnie had encouraged Powell and Powell thought a great deal of him. There was a lot of Ronnie Taylor in his early work because he admired him so much. So he was the ideal person to step in and write *A Sharp Intake of Breath*.'

A further three series were made, including one episode where David appeared with an eye-patch because of a bad attack of conjunctivitis. Throughout, David won Allen's admiration for his comedic flair. 'I always thought David Jason was immensely clever and immensely funny,' he says. 'He was such a worker, so keen on all the detail. Everything that I admired about an artist and a performer, David had and more talent and drive than anyone I've met before or since.

'He was dedicated to his work and immensely creative with his comedy. So much so that he would get a laugh where I never could have believed there was a laugh to be had. He was superb. All he needed from me was to present him. But, unfortunately, in the end it all went wrong ...' Allen was accustomed to success but even he was especially elated that *A Sharp Intake of Breath* had turned out so well. So the way it ended so abruptly came as a nasty surprise.

'I thought we'd done an awfully good job,' says Allen. 'I thought the shows were good and ATV wanted us to do another series. So an offer was made to David through his agent and the agent came back saying, "David Jason wants a younger and hungrier director."

'That wasn't very nice. We'd never had any cross words and this was a great shock to me personally because I thought we had always got on so well together and I'd admired him so immensely because of his talent. And if you're a TV director, the way to get on is to work with wonderful talent.

'I thought I'd done so well for him. I mean, he used to come to my house at Gerard's Cross in Buckinghamshire with his lovely Welsh girlfriend Myfanwy Talog with whom he seemed to have a very stable relationship and I thought he was just a great guy. So I was shocked and very disappointed by what had happened.

'The end came because Vince Powell was asked to write another series and then I rang him up and said, "Vince, they don't want me," Vince said, "That's ridiculous! You gave me the work and if they don't have you, then I shan't write it." So that was the end of that.

'I don't know what it was that David took exception to. Perhaps it was because he was jealous of my success or because he hadn't got as much then as he felt he should have had, because at that time, of course, he was only just beginning to take off. Perhaps he felt I was too admiring of him, I don't know. What I do know is that I lost David Jason and my career waned and his went up and up.

'After that, he was out of work for a while until he fell on his feet again at the BBC — but at half the salary, of course, that he would have been getting with ATV in *A Sharp Intake of Breath*.'

An actor friend of David's recalls the incident. 'There was nothing personal about it. But then there never is with David. He just thought Stuart was coasting it, which I suppose he was in a way. Who wants to push yourself to the limit all the time? Well, David Jason for one. But Stuart just believed in doing a good job and still having a life outside. The show was up there at the top of the ratings, for goodness sake. What was the point of giving yourself ulcers? David wanted someone who would be as obsessed as him. I wonder if he ever found anyone.'

When Ronnie Barker moved across from ITV to the BBC and *Hark at Barker* turned into *His Lordship Entertains*, Ronnie was keen for old Dithers to make the move as well. The aged gardener was always popular and David's ability to age up effectively led to him also taking up the role of Blanco Webb in Barker's wonderful prison comedy series *Porridge.*

Written by Dick Clement and Ian La Frenais, *Porridge* featured Barker as Norman Stanley Fletc her serving a five-year sentence in Slade prison for robbery. David played Blanco as a white-haired, doddery, short-sighted inmate for whom Fletcher always had a soft spot.

David starred in three memorable episodes: *No Peace for the Wicked* and *Happy Release* in 1975, and *Pardon Me* in 1977. In *No Peace For The Wicked*, Fletch's attempts to find some some peace and quiet on a Saturday afternoon are scuppered by constant interruptions from prison officers and cons, including a visit from Blanco proudly wheeling in a wooden mule it has taken him 15 years to make. Finally, the chaplain enters and an exasperated Fletch throws him over the balcony so he can obtain solitary confinement.

Happy Release featured Fletch and Blanco in the prison infirmary together with a nasty piece of work called Norris who is in prison for just a few days. Norris cons Blanco out of all his worldly possessions — his wireless, his silver snuff box and a musical box — by cheating at Nine Card Brag. But Fletcher, using all his native cunning, hatches a plan to have Blanco retrieve all his valuables by giving his cellmate Godber a fake map of buried treasure — a hoard of £8,000 interred in Leeds. Knowing full well that Norris will obtain the map in exchange for Blanco's goods, Fletch has the added satisfaction of Norris being incarcerated for digging up the pitch at Leeds United.

In the brilliantly conceived episode *Pardon Me*, David left Slade Prison in comic style. Blanco had been inside for 17 years for the murder of his wife, a crime he had always sworn he did not commit. He felt so angry about his unjust incarceration that, when offered parole, he refused on the grounds that it amounted to an admission of guilt.

But after Fletch had successfully raised a petition for Blanco to be pardoned, Blanco was finally absolved of the blame for his wife's death and was granted the pardon and his freedom. He had protested all along that the killer was his wife's lover. During Blanco's final farewell to Fletch, the two men shook hands and Fletch urged Blanco not to get even with the killer. 'Oh, he died long ago,' said Blanco. 'I know. It were me that did it!'

Playing Blanco as a man twice his real age, David was almost unrecognisable with wisps of grey hair, spectacles and a doddery gait. Producer Sydney Lotterby recalls, 'It was quite remarkable how David could add on the years so convincingly. It was often a problem because when you had a very old character in a large role you didn't always want a very old actor. David was simply so talented and so dedicated. Everyone knew then that he was something special. He was just so dedicated.

'Ronnie Barker was always known as "The Guv'nor" because of his towering comedy talent. He really rated David's abilities highly, so when we were looking around for a hapless nephew for the shop in Roy Clarke's *Open All Hours* we naturally did not have to look very far. David was a delight. He always used to call me "Award-winning Sydney Lotterby ..." until he started winning his own.

'We filmed *Open All Hours* up in Doncaster where a hairdressing salon called Helen's Beautique became Arkwright's corner shop. David was always known as "Little Feed" because he used to jokingly grumble that he was only there to set up the laughs for Ronnie.

'But Granville became very popular in his own right thanks to Roy Clarke's marvellous writing and David's performances. My favourite memory is the night we had Granville re-creating the famous "Singing in the Rain" number. David was so keen to get it right he must have spent hours getting it just so while providing a free cabaret for the good folk of Doncaster.'

Ronnie Barker thoroughly enjoyed the recordings as well.

'David Jason, Lynda Baron and I had great times on that series. We would be in Doncaster for three weeks doing the filmed sequences for two episodes each week. So work went on until midnight sometimes, with shouting, the noise of equipment and arc lights glaring. But nobody objected, though one chap did ask how long this would be going on for as he had to get up early for work!

'The BBC generally found an empty house for sale and that would have the canteen on the ground floor, David and myself sharing one bedroom as a dressing room and Lynda using the other. We'd put up posters and silly knick-knacks making it homelier, even though it was just for those three weeks.

'Our trio's rapport showed in the spirit of *Open All Hours*. We were three mates. On location you all get together at the end of the day, have dinner, crack a bottle or two, relax and laugh. David Jason became a good friend. What a funny man. He and I have always had such rapport, ever since we first met at London Weekend Television in a half-hour comedy called *The Odd-Job Man*.

'What a wonderful sense of timing he has, with that marvellous rubber face. What a reliable and professional man to work with. I was so thrilled when he won the British Academy award for Best Actor.'

For David Jason, Ronnie Barker was simply someone extra special. When Barker retired at the very height of his fame and popularity, David was one of the inner circle who knew all about the dramatic decision well in advance. David said, 'I first met Ronnie Barker when he asked me if I would be in *The Odd-Job Man*. It was a very funny story about a very ordinary man who lived in a council flat and loved his wife. He was the most perfect husband. In fact, he was so perfect he drove her crazy.

'His wife raved at him that she was going to leave him because he never forgot her birthday or had affairs. The guy is so depressed that he decides to top himself and the funniest part is the actual odd-job man of the title who is a really weird character called Clive who gets involved in this strange marriage.

'Ronnie Barker sent me the script and then phoned me up and said, "Will you do it?" I thought, working with Ronnie Barker, yeah! Sure I will. But I naturally thought he would want to play Clive, clearly the funniest part. But that was what he wanted me to play. I thought it was incredible. We both knew Clive was the funniest part. But he was so generous and that was the start of a long and happy association.

'Later, I was in the film version playing the same part but by then it had been rewritten and changed so much it was ruined. Graham Chapman and Diana Quick played the couple.' One reviewer helpfully observed, 'This plodding farce hammers yet another nail into the coffin of the ailing British film industry.'

David said, 'Humphrey Barclay gave me a few small parts after that in his various series. Ronnie was always keen to get people to work with who could do the job very well. Ronnie was always the same, more interested in getting the job right than in being the centre of attention.

'He is basically an actor and the best comedy actor I have ever worked with. He was my hero, helpful, considerate, a wonderful teacher. I loved his generosity but I was more affected by his ability. So much so that I always used to call him "The Guv'nor" behind his back.

'That was the word I used because there was no one better at his craft in the country. This was before *The Two Ronnies* and everything he did from then on reinforced my feelings. If Ronnie suffers from anything it's comic diarrhoea. He can't help being funny. Once we had just finished recording an episode of one show and the audience couldn't be released until the videotape had been checked through for faults. The floor manager called out to the crowd, "We're just waiting for a clear." Ronnie cracked out, "Clear? Isn't that a Chinese homosexual?" Through the years I have seen more of Ronnie Barker than most people and I know he was a very great comedy actor, the best.

'I enjoyed working with him so much because it is always a pleasure to work at the top level. And he was always so quick. The night we went out to celebrate his OBE, the restaurant was all decked out in decorations for Christmas. Ronnie took me up to the bar to buy me a drink and noticed a cluster of three balloons. One had gone down. "Ah," he said, "a pawnbrokers, and one of the partners has just died." He always made me laugh and he was great to work with. He brought my game up. It's like if you are playing tennis. If you have two good guys, their games will both improve.

'He told me some time before he retired that he was going to pull out of showbusiness. The BBC wanted to do more *Open All Hours* and more *Two Ronnies* but he was finding it extremely difficult to maintain his high standards. We had lost a few comedy men like Eric Morecambe and Tommy Cooper around then and I think he was a little sensitive to that, too. When he went, he gave me something that I will always treasure. It is a poem, one of Ronnie's witty odes, and at the end of it he says, "I now relinquish the honoured title of 'The Guv'nor' to my apprentice, the boy Granville, who is entitled herewith to call himself 'The Guv'nor'." Although the nickname started as a joke it was always a secret mark of respect from me to Ronnie and to have him return it was just amazing. I have that poem framed in my house now and it will always be one of my most prized possessions.'

In his early days as an actor, David had moved out of the family home and into a tiny rented one-bedroom flat in Newman Street, just off Oxford Street. 'The rent was £17 a week which terrified me at the time,' he said. When his television wages started to come in he felt it was time to invest in property and bought a cottage in Sussex with a view, as they say, to renovation.

David was a practical chap and planned to save money and

occupy his free time by doing much of the work himself. But the result was a good deal more amusing to the neighbours than many of his on-screen escapades to date.

David had often visited friends who lived near East Grinstead and he had spent many a pleasant weekend helping in their garden and living the country life. He became very taken with the East Sussex area and weekends soon turned from lazy days into earnest searches for a little cottage he could call his own. He looked at literally dozens after setting himself a price limit of £15,000 which would allow an extra £5,000 for renovation. 'That was my first big mistake,' he said. 'Not wanting to get saddled with too big a mortgage, I eliminated the better possibilities. I hadn't the brains to realise that by spending a little more, I would have had a better investment.'

After much deliberation, David finally picked on a nineteenth-century end-of-terrace workman's cottage in Crowborough. 'It was a charming, tiny cottage and my intention was to do it up in my spare time, pottering about as a way of relaxing between work,' he said. 'Instead, it became a monster that took over my life, a major reconstruction job.

'I have never been so miserable in my life with the strain of driving to and from the property day after day in all weathers. I was very happy with my little flat but when my career started to pick up, I thought it seemed a good idea to own a place of my own. Being single and already having a London base I didn't really want a house but I could see the sense in buying a small country cottage so that's what I set out to do. I had never owned any property before and friends told me that it was the best investment, the greatest security against inflation and all that.'

As soon as he spotted the little historic home in Crowborough he knew his search was over. It was at the end of the row of three, the garden was neat and tidy and the price was right. It needed restoration work but David knew that doing it himself would give him enormous satisfaction.

Sadly, the story did not have a happy ending. When David brought in his cousin, a builder, for some expert advice he found that the cottage needed some very expensive work, and very quickly. 'The closer we inspected the place, the worse it became,' David remembers. 'Woodworm, wet rot, dry rot — we had it all. Because I wanted to build on to an existing extension, I applied to the council for permission and had a visit from the planning officer. He told me that the original extension was illegal because it was built over a manhole. The whole lot would have to come down.'

David decided that while rebuilding the extension he might as well build another storey on top. Then an inspection of the floorboards showed serious damp and the cottage needed new flooring throughout. To add to that cheery news the main beam supporting the whole of the first floor had been cut almost through to take a pipe and there was about three-quarters of an inch of wood taking a colossal strain. Then the roof needed retiling. A relaxing way to spend his weekends had swiftly turned into a nightmare for David. Each time he visited the cottage he was greeted with mounting debris and piles of bills for the work. 'They were all big ones of £300 or £400, never small ones,' he groaned. He began to dread making the two-hour drive down to Crowborough not knowing what new disaster awaited him. Frequently he was filled with gloom when he set off on the two-hour journey back at the end of the day.

The new extension, built to replace the old one that had been taken down, posed new problems. Because it was now two storeys high, the original roof had to be extended to match. And as if he didn't have enough to worry about, David fell off the roof one day. Unable to afford scaffolding right the way round the cottage, there was nothing to break his fall but fortunately his gymnastic ability helped him to land without injury. He was less fortunate a few weeks later when he slipped while mowing the lawn with a rotary mower.

The injury sounded comical when he posed for photographers in hospital but, in fact, David almost severed the toes on one foot. He was fortunate to be saved from more serious injury by virtue of the fact he was wearing thick-soled shoes when his foot slipped under the blades. He spent a complete summer in bed with his foot suspended above him. A deep cut in David's big toe caused most concern for the doctors. David was fully aware that if he lost his big toe, it would affect his balance and he would have to learn to walk all over again. Meanwhile, bills for building materials continued to pile up in the rubble that was the inside of the house.

'There was a time when I hated the place,' he said. 'It was sapping my energy and my money and I couldn't see a way out. I remembered reading that somebody had once said that you can only build a house with love, and I couldn't find anything approaching love in the way I felt about the cottage.

'But I got over that phase. A friend came to see the cottage and, standing in the middle of the rubble, looked round and said, "Oh, this has a very good feeling about it … a warm happy feeling." Seeing the cottage through somebody else's eyes, I stopped to think. And I decided perhaps it wasn't such a bad place after all.' But he simply refused to be beaten by the project.

A girlfriend, who asked not to be identified by name, said, 'I can remember him actually crying with anger that it seemed to be taking so long. He was so angry the house became a bit of an obsession. We had quite a few rows about it because it seemed to take up all his time and money and energy. In the worst row, I accused him of using the house as an excuse for not seeing me and he just looked at me stunned and said very coldly, "I don't need excuses to do anything. I'm not married and I'm never likely to be, so I do what I want when I want. It's my life and my cottage." It was creepy really, like being slapped across the face. He just changed. Somehow in trying to organise his time I had crossed the barrier and got too close. I thought I knew David really well until then. He was always kind and considerate and our lovelife was great. But you could go so far to get close to him and then the shutters came down.

'He was funny about that and about his family. His relationship with his brother Arthur was a bit strange. Arthur had started in the business before David and was quite successful, but even then you could see David was going places. I think Arthur was a bit jealous and sometimes would put David down in conversation a bit unnecessarily. Once, David was talking about Shakespeare and he pronounced a character's name wrong and Arthur leaped on the mistake. Things like that. David would fume but he never said anything about it, even to me. His old mother used to drive them both to distraction. She was very fiery and because she was a bit deaf she used to really shout quite loud. She didn't always look after herself very well and she lived in a damp old council flat that they wanted her to move out of. But nothing they said to her had the slightest effect.

'David was a great guy to be with. No one else has ever made me laugh so much, both in bed and out. He's not like Del-Boy at all, really, but he can put on all that flashy front if he wants to. Underneath he's sensitive and thoughtful. He used to go on and on about bits of business in shows. He was always working on a part, even when everyone was telling him it was perfect. He was very impressed by Ronnie Barker. When he was invited to Ronnie's big house in the Cotswolds he came back absolutely drooling. Ronnie had the fame and still had a happy, settled home life. I think David saw that and it was what he wanted. But Ronnie could switch off from work and talk about sport or politics. David never found it easy to switch off and, of course, he never had the happy marriage. We were great together and for a time I really loved him but I never felt David really loved me or even really trusted me. He would never really let himself go. If he did get upset it was always because he was frustrated with something to do with work. He didn't just want to do well, he simply *had* to succeed. He was obsessed with the ratings and the reviews and who was getting which part and why. I've been out with a few actors and they were all on the insecure side. But David took paranoia to new heights for me. Everything was so important to him, from the position of his name on the cast list in *Radio Times* to what fans said to him in the street. If somebody said something to him about a particular scene from *Open All Hours* he would come back home and want to talk about whether he had really got every drop of humour out of it. Even if he'd recorded it years before.

'Once, a director had talked over the top of him when he was discussing something with Ronnie Barker. He was absolutely incensed. When David talked he thought everyone else should be quiet and listen. I never minded listening to him which was probably why we got on so well. In the end, we didn't fall out, we just sort of drifted apart. Then one day he asked me very formally if he could have back the key to his flat he had given me. I thought we were still going out but when he said that I realised it was over. A few years later, I saw him at the BBC. We went up in a crowded lift to the 6th floor at Television Centre together. He was talking to someone else but he saw me and his eyes flickered. I stood waiting to be introduced. He carried on his conversation and when we all got out he and this chap walked away and I was left just standing there. It was as if I did not exist. To David I'd simply become a non-person. It took me a while to get over that.'

David declines to discuss his personal relationships but he still looks back on the difficult do-it-yourself enterprise somewhat ruefully even long after he had exchanged the cottage for an expansive detached home in Wendover, near Aylesbury, Buckinghamshire, and then moved to his present home next to the

Prime Minister's estate at Chequers.

These days he is still as eager to fill his idle moments with something interesting to do but largely restricts himself to pottering about in his garden or working on his beloved motorbikes. He is still quite able to make a comedy out of an odd-job, however. 'Usually I spend my spare time either digging in the garden,' he said, 'or decorating the shed or knocking a wall down, or tinkering with my bike. Some people are totally uninterested in anything practical. Their lives are more fulfilled by sitting down a lot and reading the papers or getting in the car and going somewhere interesting.

'I prefer to be doing something all the time, whether it's painting a wall or putting some lights up, I get a lot of satisfaction out of getting a job done, then standing back and thinking, Ah! That looks better. You should have seen me not too long ago, when I was putting up a trellis on the back wall of my house. Like a comedy it was. I was on my own and I had to work out how to get this great big heavy trellis up against the wall while actually drilling and fixing it into place.'

David's answer to the poser had the stamp of amazing invention. He tied one end of a rope to the trellis then weighted another end with a brick and threw it over the wall. All he had to do then, he reasoned, was to go round to the other side of the wall, haul the trellis up into place and tie the load to a handy tree. 'See, not only talent but also brains,' said David. 'Oh yes, very clever. And very expensive. The brick landed on the roof of my car! Undeterred by this minor setback, I managed to pull the offending trellis skywards. And in the process dislodged two dozen ridge tiles of recently installed guttering!'

You feel that, of all people, Derek Trotter, David's most brilliant comic creation, would have especially appreciated that stunt. Almost as much as David appreciates Del-Boy. By 1985, *Only Fools and Horses* and *Open All Hours* had turned David Jason into hot property and his huge TV popularity was enough to earn him the star role in a new West End stage comedy *Look No Hans!* at the Strand Theatre where he had performed such acrobatics 15 years earlier in *No Sex Please — We're British.*

Look No Hans!, by John Chapman and Michael Pertwee, was a farce set in West Berlin with David cast as a British car firm sales representative called Fisher who finds himself recruited by an industrial MI5. Lynda Bellingham played his wife whose arrival in Germany sets the cat among the dolly-birds Fisher has become acquainted with. They included striking blonde Anita Graham as put-upon stripper Mitzi, and Heather Alexander, an equally striking blonde beauty, as fetching fraülein Heidi who spends much of the play in black boots and a backless maid's outfit. Much play was made of the fact that both these two beautiful, very tall girls towered over David.

David made the very most of every comic opportunity as filing cabinets banged him on the head or kicked him in the shins, safe doors threw him up in the air, and every ring of the doorbell or telephone sent him into frenzied scuttling around the stage.

Somewhat predictably, the critics did not much care for *Look No Hans!* when it opened on 4 September 1985. But almost to a man they were fulsome in their praise for David who gave his usual whole-hearted, energetic performance.

In his review for *The Daily Telegraph*, John Barber labelled David 'an athletic, rubber-faced comic resembling a pug dog doing a fandango'. He added, 'There is not much to it beyond a comedian in a perpetual dither and a room full of doors and a half-undressed girl behind each.'

Irving Wardle in *The Times* praised David's 'marvellous unbroken chain of manic acrobatics', and Milton Shulman in the *London Evening Standard* said, 'David Jason, who looks like a flyweight boxer but has the agility of an acrobatic dancer, is a natural comic. Without him I shudder to think what a quick oblivion would have awaited this rather tired farce.'

David's most glowing review came from Michael Coveney writing in the *Financial Times*. He said, 'David Jason played the compulsive joker rather like Dudley Moore on speed, and with technique. Jason's television popularity is no flash in the pan. He's a genuinely funny actor, very fast and, like Groucho Marx, close to the nerve. Athletic, too. I wish him luck when he finds a vehicle worthy of his talent.'

Only Michael Billington in *The Guardian* was less than enthusiastic about David but blamed the play itself rather than its star. 'Women,' he wrote, 'are presented until the last five minutes as entirely bird-brained and female breasts and bottoms are regarded with a leering schoolboyish curiosity.

'It is impossible to credit that a dunderheaded buffoon (the energetic David Jason) would either be employed as a car firm salesman in West Berlin or that he would have been recruited by an industrial MI5. As a result, the lunatic contortions he undergoes to pass off a couple of pouting dollies as a maid and a cook when his flat is appropriated by British security are like a whirlwind in a wind.' The critic concluded, 'Mr Jason is like a man cycling uphill into the wind.'

5

Ship of Fools

In Studio 5 at the BBC's London Television Centre, they knew it was an extra special moment. Fans of the nation's favourite comedy show were assembled to watch a historic recording. David Jason had been enchanting enormous armchair audiences for 16 years with Del Trotter's ever optimistic promise to his endlessly struggling family that 'this time next year we'll be millionaires'. As they watched, the gales of laughter were interspersed with gasps of surprise. No one ever dreamed it would come true, but now it had.

To the fortunate few who were present this was the ultimate *Only Fools and Horses* occasion. Laughter had threatened to overload the sound systems during the recording. But when the last episode of the hilarious three-part Christmas Special was completed and Peckham's popular but impoverished dodgy dealers had just won their jackpot and walked off into the sunset, rich beyond even Del's dreams, the emotion got to everyone. Paul Barber, who played Denzil who was not in the final episode, rushed out of the audience to join them and so did Patrick Murray who plays Mickey Pearce and with the rest of the cast they were all shaking hands and congratulating each other, amazed by the standing ovation they received from the delighted studio audience. But they were also aware that this just might be the last time they got together. The crying began when the bottom lip of Ken MacDonald, better known as cheery landlord Mike, began to quiver and it spread like gossip round the Nag's Head. Almost as soon as they heard the word 'Cut', just about everyone in the room was in tears.

The tears cascaded down the famous face of David Jason as he clutched co-star Nicholas Lyndhurst in an emotional embrace that was quickly supplemented by the rest of the clearly overwhelmed cast. And they ran down the faces of the studio audience as they stood and cheered at the privilege of being present when Jason, far and away Britain's best-loved actor, produced a fabulous and possibly final performance as Del, far and away Britain's best-loved comedy character. The eternal loser at last became a winner.

The applause and the emotion wasn't just for that evening, it was for 16 years of scintillating success and it was shared between stars who felt that this was possibly the last time the happy team would be gathered together. The audience felt that, too.

It was a bit of a risk trying to top their tremendous record with a final three-parter. But the stars seemed relaxed and assured when they got back together again. David Jason set the mood as he looked determined to enjoy every minute. An audience tends to bring out the clown in him and in between takes of his bed scene with Tessa Peake-Jones as Raquel, he was cheekily mouthing to the audience, 'She's got nothing on.' Before recording began, David told the assembled *Only Fools* enthusiasts, 'It's great to be back on familiar ground. There have been lots of great moments in 16 years and tonight I promise you will be no exception. We are all very emotional at the moment and if you could just bear with us we would all be very much obliged and I'm sure you're in for a treat.'

David was very nervous about how the reunion would go down but he need not have worried. More than 20 million people voted with their remote controls to make the three-parter the runaway winner of the Christmas ratings battle and almost as soon as it was in the can the pressure began for yet more adventures of Del, Rodney and Uncle Albert to hit the screen.

'Never say never,' said delighted David Jason with a huge beam on his face when later considering the future for Del. 'You never know, we might be forced to bring the bugger back.' Even with another series of his very different hit, the detective series *A Touch of Frost*, turning into 1997's top drama on ITV, his affection for the antics of Del Trotter and the sublime scripts of John Sullivan remains extra special and undimmed.

Although our favourite actor has demonstrated the breadth and versatility of his talent many times with the wide variety of his roles, his special relationship with Del and the great British public is one that nobody really wants to end. Because, although David Jason plays many parts to perfection he really *is* Del Trotter.

They have an awful lot in common. They are both fast-talking, working-class lads from London whose success in life is down to their extraordinary ability to communicate with people. They are both attractive to women but wary of commitment. And they are both unbelievably popular. And after the Christmas cracker, they are even on a par financially now that Del has caught up in the cash stakes with David. They are both millionaires several times over.

The very first episode, *Big Brother*, went out on 8 September 1981. And even in the opening scene, with Rodney and Grandad arguing over the pronunciation of Sidney Poiter's name, the relationship of the characters was revealed as Del came bustling in, glanced at the television, and said, 'Personally, I pronounce it Harry Belafonte, but you two please yourselves.' A young, energetic and distinctly slimline Jason was just brilliant as Del. He gazed into the mirror and said, '*S'il vous plaît, s'il vous plaît.* What an enigma. I get better looking every day. Can't wait for tomorrow.'

Jason was so alive, so energetic, so full of chat as Del he was simply irresistible. John Sullivan set out his stall straight away. Rodney's resentment at Del's dominance was right there at the very beginning. Del found Rodney doing his 'accounts' to try to keep a track of the figures behind the widely differing incomes. But as so often happened, Del just blew his protests away in a blast of hilarious patter.

When he hears of the figures actually being written down, Del pauses with alarm, with his sharp Austin Reed jacket only half on. 'Well, Grandad, there you are. A lot of people told me what a right dipstick I was to make my brother a partner in the business. And this only goes to prove how bloody right they were. You dozy little twonk, Rodney. This is *prima facie* evidence. The taxman gets hold of that and he'll put us away for three years.'

Del is hilariously appalled that Rodney could even consider he is a cheat, which, of course, even at this very early stage he quite obviously is. Jason is twinkling on all cylinders as he continues, jacket still only half-on, 'Cheating you??? *Cheating???* *You???* What's that rumbling noise?'

'I can't hear nothing,' replies Rodney, guilelessly taking the bait.

'Oh, it's all right,' says Del, 'it's only Mum turning in her grave.'

And he follows up with a full-frontal attack on Rodney for having the total lack of consideration to be born a full 13 years after he was. Jacket at last shrugged into place, he says, 'You have been nothing but an embarrassment to me since the day you was born. You couldn't be like any other little brother, could you? And come along a couple of years after me. Oh no, you had to wait 13 years so while all the other mods were having punch-ups down at Southend and going to The Who concerts, I was at home babysitting. I could never get your oyster milk stains out of me Ben Sherman's. I used to find rusks in me Hush Puppies.'

David Jason looked to be thoroughly enjoying himself as he revelled in Del's deliciously rich dialogue: 'Mum was 39 when she fell for you. Did you know that for the first three months of her pregnancy you was treated as an ulcer. And to this day, I sometimes think the original diagnosis was correct.'

He changes the mood with a glance, suddenly warming to appeal to Rodney's better nature. 'Come on, Rodney, what kind of a man do you think I am? Everything between you and me is split down the middle ... 60–40.' The philosophy was all spelled out at the start: 'We don't pay VAT, we don't pay income tax or National Insurance. On the other hand we don't claim dole money, social security, supplementary benefit. The Government don't give us nothink, so we don't give the government nothink!'

With Grandad glowering in front of his two strangely positioned television sets and moaning about being given a cheese burger instead of an emperor burger, the row between the brothers escalated so fast that Rodney left home, deciding to travel to Hong Kong to revive the only love in his life, with the Chinese student he had fallen for at art college in Basingstoke, just before he was expelled for smoking cannabis. Of course, he didn't get far and came back with his tail between his legs six days later.

He gazed out of the window at the view of architectural disasters and said, 'I missed that.' Del sounded as though he did not believe him, 'The only people who missed that were the Luftwaffe.'

David Jason knew from the very first moment he was on to a winner. 'There was more weight in the characters, they were so much more full-blooded and three-dimensional than anything I had played before. Because it was so well written we could go against the normal theme of things and try and make the characters more funny. I discovered when I read the script that it was so well written and the characters were so good that you could really concentrate on the other side of it and let the characters and dialogue work for you. I love all the sides to Del. He can be really clever and manipulative but he's got a heart of gold. Del is a tragi-comic figure, trapped by his background, his environment and by himself. Yet he's an eternal optimist, a rubber ball who has the ability to bounce back no matter how badly life lets him down.

'Since that time, that's what we've done. You didn't have to invest very much in it. We do know that the characters can be very funny, very silly, emotional and moving. So it was a great mixture and having accepted that was the way to play it, touch wood it's worked.

'The writing is so good that *Only Fools and Horses* does not require so much effort from me. Del was once selling lace handkerchiefs and shouting, "Made in France at Chantilly. But due to a printer's error the labels came out 'Made in Taiwan', so we can offer them to selected customers cheap." They are such fine scripts I do not interfere. In the early days, I used to encourage John to push the characters a bit further because I could see inside his writing that he was worth much more than making jokes. John is not just a joke writer, he is much more than that. He is a fine writer about people and relationships with real observations to make about life.

'The way he makes them work so beautifully is to have the family interact. Right at the beginning, we had this episode where Del finds some lead on a building site and it turns out to be an atomic air-raid shelter. Rodney then convinces Del that they should rebuild this shelter on top of the flats and as an experiment they spend a weekend inside.

'Of course, Rodney takes it seriously and goes and gets all the batteries and so on while Del comes in his silk pyjamas with his name on the top. Then there was Grandad who was the only one of us who had really been through a war, of course. The brilliance of Sullivan was that he was able to trap these three guys in a room for over half an episode. The only people who had done that before were *Steptoe and Son*, again thanks to tremendous writing.

'But what Sullivan managed to do when we were all trapped inside this shelter busy taking the mickey out of each other, but mainly Grandad, was wonderful. Rodney said, "It doesn't matter, Grandad, because in the next war we will be all right because we will be in this lead-lined shelter. We might be in here for two or three weeks." Grandad says, "Well, what happens after we get out, there won't be anything." Del says, "There'll always be a little Paki shop open somewhere."

'But then after the joke the mood changes when Grandad becomes thoughtful and says, "Yeah, that's what they said during the last war. They said they would make homes fit for heroes. All they did was make heroes fit for homes." And suddenly this old boy who we have been busy taking the mickey out of has said something profound and moving that reaches out to all generations. That got to both Rodney and Del. And to me and Nick.

'I think it was at that moment that I realised that John Sullivan had got so much more inside him than an ordinary comedy writer. Not only were his scripts very funny, full of funny characters saying lots of funny lines but he was also able to move people, to get them emotionally involved. There was real weight there. Once we'd done the first series and John Sullivan had seen the characters come to life as we portrayed them, it gave him the spur and he could see the way we were going and could write them from great strength. The guy is a genius.'

At first, the viewing public could hardly have agreed less. Although David, Ray Butt and John Sullivan all had high hopes for *Only Fools and Horses*, the first series did only moderately well. 'I think only about twelve people saw it and three of them were my family,' laughs Sullivan. He can afford to laugh now, but at the time Sullivan was desperately disappointed as both he and Butt believed so strongly in the show.

What was even more galling was that they all got the impression that the BBC was somewhat embarrassed by the series and they felt it was almost being hidden away.

Sullivan remembers going up to the BBC one day where every Monday the foyer was filled with photographs of notable successes from either the drama, the current affairs, or the comedy and light entertainment departments. When it was the turn of the comedy department's output to be displayed, there was *To The Manor Born* and other sitcoms but no sign of *Only Fools and Horses*. Sullivan also gained the impression that when it came to a second series, the BBC top brass seemed to be begging for something different, almost as if they wanted to get rid of a show that was a bit of a hassle for them. Neither John Sullivan nor Ray Butt was confident that a second series would be commissioned. They simply held their breath. Finally, they heard that the BBC was prepared to risk a second series, thus following the long-held BBC tradition of allowing a show to have 'the right to fail'.

Sullivan knew the first series had not done terribly well and had wondered whether the BBC would go for a second. But John Howard Davies was an astute and caring Head of Comedy and gave Sullivan a choice — something new or a follow-up *Only Fools and Horses*. Sullivan has always been grateful that the

BBC is so often prepared to give a second chance to shows that are not immediate hits.

The first series did not merit a repeat and the second series also failed to make a significant impact in the ratings. But to the joy of Sullivan, David and everyone who had worked so hard on the show, repeats of the second series suddenly took *Only Fools and Horses* high into the Top Ten TV ratings. *Only Fools and Horses* was born. By the end of the third series, *Only Fools and Horses* was pulling in 15 million viewers and it has proved to be a massive ratings winner ever since.

'The initial reaction was very disappointing,' said David. 'It was only during the third series that people really started tuning in. I was amazed by the reaction when it arrived. Wherever I went, people recognised me. I got mobbed in shops. At first I thought, It's fantastic, like being a pop star. I had been in the business for 18 years and for about 12 of those years I was completely in the wilderness. That was how I expected the rest of my life to be — just fooling about on the end of some pier.

'I was really poor. I must have played every major town in this country and stayed in some of the worst digs imaginable and got up to some tricks to survive that would surprise even Del. One of my dodges was to be the last down to breakfast and then to Hoover up absolutely everything. Sometimes you would be lucky, sometimes it would be a minute piece of toast and a thin rasher of bacon. Then you had to try to make that last all day until just before the show when you had a sandwich. And after the show, maybe a couple of beers and a bag of chips on the way home. We had to manage on no money at all because we spent it all on Thursday nights after pay chasing women!

'I really like playing Del because he sometimes gets the girl. When you're a character actor you rarely get to kiss the girls. It's the leading men who get the passionate bedroom scenes. But Del has love scenes, too! He just has a lot more front than I have. Del is all mouth and trousers and will go up to a girl and say "Hello, darlin'." I would never do that.

'Del is wonderful to play because he is such a gentle person underneath all the brash bravado. He has that sensational sense of humour and at the same time he is sympathetic to those who are down. He will give a couple of extra apples to an old girl but if he sees someone who can afford it he will rob them instead.

'The public seem to love him. I've had more free rides in taxis since Del came on the scene than I can remember. I always felt a special affinity, I know the world that Del comes from and sometimes I even try to offer an occasional line to John Sullivan. Once in Brighton market when I was out with my brother I heard a stallholder telling his customers to come a bit closer. He said, "At these prices, I can't afford to deliver." There is a lot of wonderful wit out there and John Sullivan's great skill is that he constantly taps into it.'

Although it was essentially a three-man show, there was no doubting that David as Del-Boy was the star. There was something incredibly infectious about his optimism and his constant promise to Rodney that this time next year they would be millionaires. The public warmed to Del's wheeling and dealing, his tremendous energy, and the fact that he was always up to something somewhere yet never really did anyone any harm.

The audience quickly cottoned on that Del would take a quid off anyone but he would never hit them over the head. And if someone was in trouble, he would be the first to try to help out. He had brought up Rodney and he respected old people which was why he looked after first Grandad and then Uncle Albert. He was the type to walk round the estate at Christmas to make sure the old folk were all right and would know where there were some Christmas puddings going a bit cheap. Del clearly cared for people. He might have a rough exterior but if you were in trouble, Del would help you out. It was the old working–class ethic — I don't have anything but half of what I have is yours, if you need it. David has always been quick to give Sullivan great credit for his Del-Boy creation and his superb scripts. But David's own contribution to the characterisation of Derek Trotter must not be underestimated.

Presented by Sullivan with the initial outline of Del, David was able to add his own stamp to the character by drawing on his memories of a builder called Derek Hockley whom he once worked for in East London during his days as an electrician.

David recalled, 'Del was described by John Sullivan in the outline of his stage notes and I thought, That reminds me of Derek — the rings and the gold. As I was reading it, I thought this is more and more like this guy. Then when we came to the camel-hair coat — Derek always wore one.

'John at that time imagined Del to be pot-bellied, a beer gut, and long hair. It was at a time when hair was very thick and full. Again, I said he should have short hair. The directors did not see him like that but Derek Hockley always had hair which was dead smart, neatly parted, and had that swagger.'

For years, David did not mention Derek Hockley by name for fear of embarrassing him. But one day Hockley's daughter wrote a letter to David after reading of David's description. She said he was in hospital and asked if David had time to drop him a line to cheer him up.

'I did, but I thought, I'll do more than that, I'll go down and see him. But he suddenly died. He had cancer. I had seen him a number of years before when he came to see me in a show. He was very proud of the fact I had modelled the character on him. Funnily enough, they never called him Del.'

Kitting out Del was a real labour of love for the BBC costume department, but as you might imagine, the jewellery was not quite as genuine as it might have been. The half-sovereign rings are definitely fake and usually replaced after each series because it's so cheap the gold paint wears off. It comes from cheap stores in London's Soho and costs only a few pence. But Del's necklace with the huge D on it is not so cheap. Costume designer Robin Stubbs had it specially made for around £70. The camel-hair coats once came from a shop near the BBC Television Centre in Shepherd's Bush, London, but it closed down and now the buyers have to venture into the West End. Del's flashier suits come from Austin Reed in Regent Street at around £200 a time. Stubbs said, 'We have to be discreet when we go in for them. If David is recognised he is mobbed.' The ties comes from Tie-Rack, his raincoat came from Dickins and Jones in Regent Street and his shirts from Austin Reed and Marks and Spencer.

Adding to David's astute portrayal of Del-Boy was John Sullivan's wonderful way with words. Into David's mouth he planted such gems as 'dipstick', 'lovely jubbly' and 'cushty', not to mention the extraordinary phrase *'bonnet de douche'* when raising a glass as a toast — words which gave Del a language almost of his own.

Sullivan claims that 'dipstick' was the only one he actually invented. The word 'plonker', he says, was used when he was a kid and 'lovely jubbly' was an advertising slogan for a triangular-shaped frozen orange drink which he suddenly remembered and decided to resurrect. Recently, Sullivan was not a little astonished to find a hairdresser innocently using the words 'lovely jubbly' while tending his wife's hair.

The generic origins of 'cushty' purport to come from soldiers in India where there was apparently a place called Cushtabar which was supposed to be the easiest place if you ever got to it. Its nickname was Cushty.

'Bonnet de douche' evolved during filming of an *Only Fools and Horses* Christmas Special in the Kent seaside resort of Margate.

Sullivan, in fact, stayed at a hotel in Ramsgate which regularly plays host to the French. In his hotel shower, Sullivan found there was a shower cap with the words '*Bonnet de Douche*' printed on it. With his keen eye for words, Sullivan seized on it and ended the evening toasting everyone with the words '*bonnet de douche*' and subsequently wrote it into Del's vocabulary.

To complete Del-Boy's portrait, Sullivan dreamed up the idea of giving Del a three-wheeled Robin Reliant van in which to drive around. Sullivan considered Del's image of rings, coat and briefcase and reckoned he would be practical enough to drive something that could carry all his gear around in. And yet he wanted it to be something that was in stark contrast to Del's image. A three-wheeled van seemed to fit the bill and the BBC chose a yellow one. Sullivan gave it the final twist by dreaming up the inscription on the side: NEW YORK — PARIS — PECKHAM.

★　　　★　　　★

Another vital ingredient to the show's success was David's remarkable relationship with Nicholas Lyndhurst. They developed a sixth sense about what the other was going to do and from the outset it has been a harmonious pairing.

There is a mutual respect and working friendship between the two stars that embraces camaraderie off the set as well. During filming of the second series at Studland Bay, Nicholas Lyndhurst reached the age of 21 but, in his own modest way, he had not told too many people that it was his 21st birthday.

When the day arrived, nobody wished him a happy birthday, there were no cards from the cast and crew and certainly no presents. Secretly, he hoped a cake might be produced at lunchtime but nothing was forthcoming. He was not too upset but merely thought that at least he could enjoy a few celebratory drinks with the film unit in the hotel bar at the end of the day.

On entering the bar, Nicholas was downcast to find it empty. The few crew members he saw wandering around the lobby declined his offer of a drink, announced they were off to Bournemouth for a meal and disappeared.

Finally, David came down from his room and a by now desperate Nicholas blurted out that it was his birthday. David expressed surprise but immediately offered to buy Nicholas a drink in the bar.

Over a drink, David suggested playing a practical joke on Lennard Pearce. Why didn't they both go down to the gym that was being used as the wardrobe room and superglue Lennard Pearce's shoes to the floor? So off they went to the gym and as they walked in Nicholas was greeted by all the cast and crew, champagne, flags, banners and presents. Nicholas was so overcome he was close to tears.

Given that David and Nicholas worked so well together and quickly established a rapport, it was vital that Lennard Pearce should dovetail in as Grandad. As it transpired, both David and Nick took an instant liking to Lennard and admired his acting ability.

If viewers had their way, *Only Fools and Horses* would run for ever. It has proved consistently popular across the widest range of viewers from Hackney to Harrods, and Her Majesty the Queen is a particular fan. She particularly loves to watch the Christmas episodes which are inclined to include a few more laughs than her own seasonal broadcast.

Nicholas Lyndhurst also discovered that Prince Edward was a fan while working one day in the theatre at Windsor doing a Peter Shaffer play. On the last night, Nicholas generously bought a couple of large bottles of whisky as a thank-you to the crew and after the curtain call he flew back to the dressing room to collect them, tucked them under each arm and went back on stage. He was threading his way through a group of people on the stage when he felt a tap on the shoulder. It was Prince Edward with a request to Nicholas to appear in the royal *It's a Knockout* programme.

Nicholas Lyndhurst certainly shares one feeling with his charismatic co-star — shyness. Neither actor enjoys the limelight. Nicholas says, 'David and I have talked about it a lot. We would both like to just do the job and go home and be left to get on with being ordinary human beings. The problem is that we seem to be ordinary human beings that everyone wants to stare at.

'This "fame" business has got to the stage where David and I both tend to wait until it's dark before we go out and do our shopping because there are fewer people about then. It shouldn't have to be like that but that is the way it has become. It's just that if you want to pop out and pick up your chicken joints and tin of cook-in sauce it's easier to do it without seven people following you round the supermarket and ten people waiting at the check-out to ask you to sign autographs and take your picture.

'People aren't particularly polite. I have got off trains before now because people make me feel like a captive. Yet there are funny moments as well. I was once walking down the road loaded down with shopping and a guy pulled alongside me in his Capri with the stereo blaring. He wound down his window and yelled, 'You plonker,' at the top of his voice. And then he roared off — smack into the back of the car in front of him. That was fun.'

But the sensitive Lyndhurst happily accepts the price of fame because he enjoys playing the part so much. 'We both have such a fantastic laugh sometimes. I think David and I both agree that the chandelier episode — when the Trotters were engaged to clean the elegant old chandeliers in a country mansion — was one of our favourites.'

The episode was called *A Touch of Glass* and John Sullivan rates it the hardest one he had to write. He said, 'I never write a script from page one onwards. I start somewhere in the middle or towards the end and I'll move backwards and forwards from that incident. *A Touch of Glass* was the hardest because I wrote it from the end when the chandelier falls because it was a true story that my dad told me. When he was an apprentice plumber they worked on this big house and it happened. He was telling me the saga to try to remind me to double check everything was all right and don't ever just trust your luck. I was laughing and the old man's telling me, "Seven men lost their jobs through that." I told David this one day and he said, "Please, please. Do it!" So I went away and wrote the end. But I had to think how did they get there? What are the Trotters doing in this big house?' Perfectionist Sullivan said, 'I have always felt with that one that the beginning didn't really work that well.'

But Nicholas Lyndhurst remembers it for a different reason. 'Even the mock-up chandeliers that were made for us were very expensive and obviously we could only do the shot where we let it crash to the floor once, so we were ordered by producer Ray Butt to be on our very best behaviour.

'David and I both have a problem with giggling from time to time and just before filming started Ray took me to one side and gave me this really stern warning. He said, "If you laugh, you've not only blown the end of the episode you've wasted hundreds of thousands of pounds so not only are you off the set, you're off the series." I was terrified. I thought, He really means it.

'When we got up the ladders and started doing the final shots, I was really determined to keep a straight face, and after the chandelier fell Ray wanted to keep filming us looking astonished for a long time. That went on for what seemed like ages and I was struggling to hold it. Then just out of the corner of my eye I saw Ray watching and he quietly put his hand in his pocket, pulled out his handkerchief and put it in his mouth to stop himself laughing. Tears were running down his face. He had only been winding me up about the threat of the sack to make sure he got the shot. I did manage to see the joke later.'

Lennard Pearce's brilliance at creating Grandad's blissful ability to do the wrong thing from the best intentions was never better illustrated. What made the smashing finale even more funny was Grandad, totally oblivious to the disaster he had just caused by being in the wrong place at the right time, asking in all innocence, 'All right, Del-Boy?'

Butt was not sure of Lennard's true age when he picked him for Grandad but in one of the early series he let slip that he had just got his bus pass. Butt also only later discovered that Lennard had been desperately ill for a long time and had thought his career was finished. In his maudlin moments Lennard would tell Butt that he had thought he would never work again and profusely thanked him. Lennard had thought at that stage he would not even be alive and yet there he was, suddenly a nationally known figure thanks to *Only Fools and Horses.*

The series has run for 16 years now but it has never come closer to ending than when Lennard suddenly had a heart-attack and died.

It happened in the winter of 1984 and John Sullivan was the first to get the grim news. Lennard's landlady telephoned him to say that he had been taken to hospital in Hampstead.

Sullivan and actress Jan Francis, who was also a good friend of Lennard's, dropped everything and went to visit him. Sullivan took with him a little pig for good luck. In the *Only Fools and Horses* production box there had been a little pig called Trotter which had been lost and Sullivan took Lennard another one, Son-of-Trotter, and left it with Lennard at the hospital.

But a day later Lennard Pearce was dead and when John broke the news to David and Nick in the make-up room they were devastated. Off-screen there was a pecking order that David and Nicholas had continued half-heartedly to play and Lennard was like a real grandfather to them.

Nick said, 'David and I followed Ray out and it started snowing really heavily just for a few minutes and I stood facing a shop window and cried my eyes out. After a while, we went back to our trailer and I remember David swearing very gently under his breath every so often. We were both very upset.'

Lennard's death had occurred two weeks into filming an episode in which Grandad kept falling down the cellars and getting compensation. Lennard had shot his last scenes on a cold snowy Sunday morning outside Kingston Crown Court and was not due to film again till the following Sunday. But when word came through he had died, everyone was too shocked to continue and filming was immediately abandoned out of respect to Lennard.

David Jason said, 'It was a great shock. He was a wonderful actor and he had become a great friend. We were devastated. Lennard was so much a part of the show that I didn't know if we would be able to go on, or even want to. It's as if we have lost our real grandad.'

Sullivan remembered an incident at the funeral which defined Jason's affinity with the Trotters. 'David was sitting in the pew in front of me when the vicar announced hymn number 187. Suddenly the pew began to shake and I could see David was having a fit of the giggles. I leaned forward and he held up the hymn book to show me that the page was missing. He gave me such a funny look. You could tell he was thinking that Del probably supplied the hymn books. It was as if we were both at a Trotter family funeral. David is Del.'

After the funeral, David Jason, Nicholas Lyndhurst, Ray Butt and John Sullivan had a meeting with new BBC comedy chief Gareth Gwenlan to decide what to do. Christmas was approaching and eventually it was decided to pick up filming in the New Year. None of them could bear the thought of another actor taking on the role of Grandad and the only alternative was to introduce a new character. David said, 'He couldn't just be replaced. In the series, we just couldn't have drafted in a lookalike so we decided that Grandad would die, just as Lennard had.

'We did what families do. We had a funeral. But the TV funeral was recorded not that long after we had been to the real funeral so it was very hard for all concerned.'

That immediately threw the burden on to John Sullivan who was finding Lennard's death very difficult to deal with. 'Writing a script without him was like trying to put my coat on with only one arm. It just didn't work any more.' But in spite of his feelings he quickly re-wrote the first two episodes to convey to viewers that Grandad had been taken into hospital although he was not seen. He also created a new character — Uncle Albert.

Butt now had the problem of casting the new hastily-written-in character of Uncle Albert but was astonished to find that news of Lennard's death had spread so quickly that within 48 hours he was inundated with letters from actors who wanted to replace him. Still desperately upset personally at Lennard's death, Butt slung them all on to a window sill and went away to Suffolk for Christmas resolving to look through them on his return from the festive break.

While he was away, Butt came up with one or two possible replacements but the established actors he contacted were reluctant to step into Lennard's shoes. They knew that Lennard was going to be a hard act to follow — not just because he was such a good character but because he was so well liked by the public.

With filming due to pick up again on 2 January, Butt drove back to London on New Year's Eve and went into the office determined to sort the problem out. He started sifting through the letters he had thrown on the windowsill and most quickly went into the bin. Then he came across a handwritten letter from a man with a beard called Buster Merryfield who included details of his life and mentioning that he was a retired bank manager and a late-comer to acting. That was certainly different.

Butt picked up the phone and rang him at his home where Buster told him that he was currently in pantomime playing Baron Stoneybroke in *Cinderella* at Windsor. He was due on stage for a matinée at 2.30pm but had time to go into the BBC to meet Butt and still make it to Windsor for his performance.

At that point, Butt had never seen a script for Uncle Albert and all he was able to do was ask Buster to read existing scripts for the character of Grandad. He was impressed and later rang David, Nicholas and Sullivan to arrange a meeting at which Buster could read with them all. They duly came in and they all sat down in a dressing room in Television Centre and read together with Buster. They all agreed Buster was in and four days later he was costumed up on set ready for filming.

Buster himself could hardly believe it. For 40 years he had worked in a bank dreaming all the while of being an actor. At 57, he had taken retirement and within a week of leaving he was performing in repertory at the Connaught Theatre in Worthing. Then suddenly he had a key role in Britain's best-loved comedy show.

Looking back at his banking days, Buster chuckles, 'We had many Dels come in, funnily enough. Chaps used to come in and want to borrow half a million and lean on the desk and light their cigars just like Del-Boy.'

While Buster was being cast, Sullivan was hard at work on the re-writes. He felt that the Trotters were like a family to the viewers as well and therefore insisted on writing in Grandad's funeral. It had to be real, he felt, and seen to happen. He did not want suddenly to say that Grandad had gone off somewhere, or that he had taken a holiday, and for him never to be seen again.

But Sullivan did not know how he was going to write an inevitably sad funeral of a much-loved character into a comedy show.

There was no way either that the series could open with Del and Rodney at the graveside. So, for only the second time, Sullivan wrote an episode without Grandad and tried to take the pain away by saying he was in hospital. Cleverly, Sullivan's re-writes also allowed newcomer Buster Merryfield to gain immediate sympathy from the viewers by having him get the gravestone for his departed brother.

Far and away Sullivan's hardest problem was how to write the actual funeral scene where Del and Rodney paid their great respects, where there was sorrow and grief, and yet he had to make it funny because it was a comedy show. Sullivan realised by the end of the scene he had to break away from the gloom and make the audience laugh with relief.

Brilliantly, he came up with the idea of Grandad's old hat being buried with him but at the very end of the scene it turned out that it was the vicar's hat which had been buried by mistake.

For David and Nicholas, filming the funeral scene was hard to bear coming so soon after Lennard's real funeral. But somehow they got through it — and *Only Fools and Horses* lived on. The actors and their writer got together in an unusual campaign to extend the length of their episodes and so give more scope to the cult series. David explains, 'We began with the traditional situation comedy time-slot of 30 minutes for *Only Fools and Horses*. But after a few series I kept finding myself in the situation where half-way through the week of a seven-day turnaround we were six minutes of material over. So we had to take six minutes out of every 30-minute script and throw it away. After two or three series it felt to me like we were cutting John Sullivan's heart out. I said, "This is just not on. We are throwing away more good material on to the cutting-room floor than most comedies have in their entire 30 minutes." So we had a discussion. I said I was fed up with it. Why didn't we make a 40-minute sitcom? So I suggested to John that we told the BBC that we wouldn't do another series unless they were 40-minute episodes. He said he would back me up.

'The BBC said that 40-minute episodes were impossible. They insisted that it only worked in exactly half-hour slots. We asked, "Why?" The consensus of their opinion was that they had never yet encountered a script that could not be cut to 30 minutes. But eventually they gave in and said, "OK, but on your heads be it. It will never work."

'Then John went away and wrote a script that lasted for 57 minutes. And Gareth Gwenlan who had taken over as Head of Comedy said, "We can't cut this. I think we can get a special out of this at 50 minutes."

'So we then had a seven-day turnaround to make 50 minutes. I nearly died. I got up at six and was learning my script until eight. Then I went to rehearsals at nine-thirty, started at ten, rehearsed until four, then came back to learn the script in the evening. And filming days were even worse. Nick and I were dead on our feet. I was at the end of my tether. I really had a lot of problems, I just could not turn off. I went away on holiday and after four or five days I was still getting up at six o'clock on automatic pilot. Slowly, I wound down. And the show was a brilliant success. We had created a precedent. Fifty minutes in seven days. Now we had a 50-minute format for *Only Fools and Horses*.'

Not surprisingly, the BBC came shrewdly back with a request for this new improved product which was still delivered using the old schedule. The actors revolted and were given 10 days to make each episode. 'But what we had done was to provide John with the vital elbow room to explore the characters,' said David. 'We found that there were wonderful scenes that we had cut in the past that suddenly came back to life. I remember Uncle Albert's marvellous story about being lookout on a ship in the middle of the Atlantic during the war and hitting an aircraft carrier that he had somehow failed to notice. That had been taken out so many times because it never had anything to do with any storyline. It was just a wonderfully evocative slice of life that John is always so brilliant at creating.'

While such a mutual admiration society exists between David, Nicholas and Sullivan, there is no reason why *Only Fools and Horses* should not run and run. The two stars say they are quite happy to continue as long as Sullivan keeps writing more scripts. Sullivan, for his part, says he will keep writing while David and Nicholas are happy to continue as Del and Rodney.

They both have so many happy memories. Nicholas Lyndhurst recalled, 'We were in Dorset filming one episode and had the afternoon off. So we went into Poole and nothing was open except a joke shop so we bought some silly jokes to play on the crew.

'I had some little capsules you put in cigarettes to make them explode. I thought they would be desperately funny.

'There was one scene where I had to smoke on camera and I lit up and then Pow! I nearly jumped out of my skin. I had picked up the wrong packet. That really backfired on me and the camera crew were very amused.

'I had to change costume and do another scene but I forgot to change the cigarette packet. Then again — Wham! Bang! The camera crew were rolling about all over the place. They thought it was very funny. That's just the sort of stupid trick that Rodney would do but when I did it ... well, I'll never live it down.

'There have been times when I've had to look away from David as I couldn't keep a straight face any longer. In a two-shot, if you cock it up by laughing you have to shoot it all again. I've still got nail marks in my thigh from one section we were filming.

'David and I have had such a lot of fun. When we are filming, the chances are we are never more than 30ft away from each other. He's really a terrific actor and we clicked right from the start.

'In one episode, Del and Rodney nearly came to a parting of the ways. It felt so real that I was very nearly in tears when we filmed it.'

'The only thing I share with Rodney is his awkwardness. He never quite knows what to do with his hands and I'd be lost if I didn't have pockets to thrust my hands into.

'I've grown up with *Only Fools and Horses* and it's been a delightful process.'

David Jason is just as happy with his partnership with Nick Lyndhurst. 'It's great we have such a tremendous rapport. Nick and I said at the very beginning we were determined we would never fall out. We had a long chat and said that if we ever felt we were upsetting each other we should talk about it otherwise we couldn't work together. We wouldn't have wanted to do the show if Nick and I hadn't enjoyed working with each other and admired each other's abilities. One reason you come back to do it is that you know you'll have a bloody good laugh with someone you like who's good fun.

'Whenever I came back to *Only Fools and Horses* I realised how much I missed it and how much I'd missed making each other laugh.

'There's no hurt and no malice when Del and Rodney get angry. It's only a superficial anger. It's funny they get angry. You don't believe it, you just enjoy them having a go at each other like a couple of old queens. It's good fun to watch them bicker.'

Nick admits, 'I owe virtually everything to *Only Fools and Horses* — it is where I learned so much. When David and I first started to think about making the last Christmas show, we were concerned it might be hard to slip back into the characters. But in the end it was very easy. It was like revisiting old friends again and terrific fun.

'When you are filming late at night in the freezing cold and you are all laughing out loud even when the cameras aren't rolling, something must be going right.'

David now likens playing Del-Boy to wearing a comfy pair of old slippers. 'You know, when people say, "What are those terrible old slippers you've got on?" And you say, "I know, but they ain't half comfortable. They fit every contour." That's how Del is. I just know him back to front now. Providing we are all fit and healthy there's no reason why it can't go on and on — unless, of course, Steven Spielberg offered me the lead in his next movie with Harrison Ford. Then I'd have to turn my back on *Only Fools and Horses*. But that's extremely unlikely!'

Del and Rodney did develop as the years went on. Del acquired a mobile phone, designer suits and, by the late '80s, even red braces. David said, 'He's now modelling himself on Gordon Gekko from the film *Wall Street*. He might not look like Michael Douglas but he reckons he's got the same style. It's fairly typical of Del to want to appear flashy. Every crooked little deal he makes is the one he thinks will make him a million, like a City slicker.'

John Sullivan had been reluctant to continue writing *Only Fools and Horses*, feeling that he should be moving on to fresh projects. But public demand and an appeal from the actors persuades him to switch his mind back to Peckham's Nelson Mandela House. David said, 'We talked him into writing one more Christmas Special and one more series and I was thrilled to bits. We always knew there was still life in *Only Fools* but without the writer's willingness it could never live on.' Sullivan fed in the changes in his skilfully imperceptible way as Rodney's relationship with Cassandra developed into a grown-up thing. David said, 'Rodney's affair will be a lot more successful than

Del's flirtation with the yuppie world. Del could never really mix with the upper-crusters.'

Actress Gwyneth Strong thought she was only going to be in a single episode when she was cast as Rodney's girlfriend Cassandra. But the screen relationship worked so well she became a regular as Cassandra and Rodney married and enjoyed a turbulent life together. She admitted later, 'I was terrified of joining such a talented and tightly-knit team. I had been a fan of *Only Fools and Horses* for years, so I was really daunted about joining. But everyone was so welcoming that they made it easier for me. And, of course, when it came to comedy I was able to learn from two of the very best — David Jason and Nicholas Lyndhurst.

'My first scenes were romantic ones with Rodney and he and Cassandra were supposed to be feeling nervous and shy. That was very fortunate because that's exactly how I felt. But Nick was so good to work with that my nerves quickly fell away. It's quite a difficult relationship between Rodney and Cassandra and he was such a wonderful help to me I'll always be grateful. I think that really good actors are a joy to work with and that's how I felt about Nick and David.

'I was so pleased the audiences seemed to take to Cassandra and I loved it when she and Rodney got married. They've had their ups and downs but the writer John Sullivan finds marvellous humour in all sorts of situations. Nick and David are terrific to work with. My favourite episode is the one where Rodney wins a painting contest that gives him and Del and Cassandra a holiday in Spain, only Del has entered Rodney in a children's competition and he has to pretend to be a young boy. Poor Rodney had to join this ghastly, "groovy" gang of young kids and he was so embarrassed. There were moments when I just wanted to cry I was laughing so much.'

Rodney and Cassandra married in February 1989 in a

brilliant landmark episode that reduced David Jason to genuine tears. 'It was a sad moment for Del and me — we cried real tears together. It was emotional because Nick and I have worked so closely together and I knew that Del realises for the first time that Rodders has grown up. It was a nostalgic moment, probably the most emotional in my life. Viewers were moved, too, as honeymoon-dazed Rodney finished his first day back at work and then returned to the grotty flat that he shared with Del and Uncle Albert. That gave Del the highly charged last words, 'You don't live here any more, you plonker!'

The episode is a personal favourite of David's. He said, 'John Sullivan approached me and said he wanted to put some music in and asked me if I had heard the record "Holding Back the Years". I'm not a great music person so he sent me the tape. He wanted to put it in at the moment Del was left alone. We constructed that moment very carefully to make it moving because we did not want to cheapen it.'

The series is treated with enormously tender loving care by just about everyone concerned. At the start of the 1990s, David Jason suggested Del's behaviour be improved a notch or two. He summed up his attitude by saying, 'You won't be seeing Del smoke, drink or swear as much as he used to. On the show we all feel that we have a social responsibility, so we decided to cut things down.

'When we were filming, the producer came up and said, "We have used the word bloody twice in one scene. Do we need it?" I said, "Yes," but I took the point. We are trying to have a collective responsibility. I might have the odd smoke but Del won't be swigging cocktails and puffing cigars like he used to.'

As the many millions of regular viewers will have noticed, at the finish of each series there is always a question mark over whether this might really be the end of *Only Fools and Horses*.

It's partly because Sullivan cleverly writes a neat conclusion which could provide a final curtain for the series if either David or Nicholas decided they no longer wanted to carry on. There was Rodney's wedding, Del's joyous moment of fatherhood, and another episode in which Del had the opportunity to go to Australia with Jumbo Mills.

Thanks to Sullivan's keen observation of people and life, Del-Boy has been able to move with the times. Del's liking for a cocktail topped off with an umbrella owes its existence to a visit Sullivan made to a pub he had not been to for many years in London's Old Kent Road.

He noticed that nearby there were cocktail bars and dropped in to find that the tough guys with calluses on their knuckles who used to like a pint were now drinking umbrella-topped cocktails.

The most important shift of emphasis for David came after Sullivan had introduced Tessa Peake-Jones as Del's new girlfriend Raquel in a Christmas Special. For much of the episode it appeared that Raquel was a resting actress until she was revealed, much to Del's humiliation, as a stripogram girl when she peeled off her police woman's uniform in front of Del and all his friends at his local.

Tessa's TV impact was immediate on her own life. When she went into her local pub shortly after the episode had been screened, they started playing 'Slow Boat to China' on the 60-year-old piano. And so much mail flowed in about Raquel that Sullivan seized an opportunity to bring her back in an episode where Del and the lads are on a boy's outing to Margate. Sullivan listens to the fans and he knew he had done the right thing when he found people coming up to him in the newsagent's and the baker's thanking him for reviving Raquel.

It was no surprise when Tessa was given an expanded role in the next series. First she moved in with Del, then became pregnant and provided Del with a son and heir.

David has always adhered to the theory that, in comedy shows in particular, if the cast all get on well together then it makes for a successful show. David and Tessa hit it off from the start. 'She's a super actress, super to work with,' he said, adding what a bonus that was for the series when Raquel moved into Del's home. 'If you're playing someone you are supposed to be in love with, you've got to be able to do things that are believable.'

One of the most difficult scenes David has ever had to play as Del-Boy was when Tessa Peake-Jones as Raquel gave birth. 'It was a very hard thing for me to do because I've never had any experience with babies and I just didn't know whether I could make it work,' he admitted.

David was so anxious to play the part convincingly that he studied childbirth videos. He certainly got it right — a staggering 18.9 million viewers tuned in to watch Del become a dad.

The scene became a television triumph. David said, 'The videos were quite an eye-opener. I have to say that Tessa was very securely dressed in that area. I think she had 14 pairs of knickers on. When I read the script I phoned John Sullivan up and told him he had out-Sullivaned Sullivan. It was the funniest, most moving, silliest, strangest, weirdest, oddest, warmest script ever. It was wonderful. I just fell about. I kept shutting the pages up and laughing and laughing. Then I couldn't wait to read the next page as I was already inventing what I was going to do. It was magical.

'I loved it after the baby was born and Del is a father he has always had this thing about his mum and he takes the baby over to the window and looks out at the stars and delivers a monologue to his son: "I'll give you what I never had 'cos I've always been a bit of a wally." Del says, "I have been a dreamer, son. You're going to have to live my dreams for me and do all the things I wanted to do. You're going to have to tell me all about them. Tell me if they were as good as I thought they would be."

'Here was this great wheeler-dealer who lays the birds really pouring his heart out in a very moving soliloquy. And it's all the more effective because Del is the sort of guy who thinks a soliloquy is a new sort of cocktail. John Sullivan knows just how to get right to an audience. He is marvellous because he is so dedicated. He worries and worries and spends hours and hours honing a script to perfection.

'You have to put credit where credit is certainly due. Without the ability of great writers, I would be nowhere. Since I have been in a position to have some control over work, I evaluate everything against John Sullivan's high standards. There are some wonderful writers in this country but I consider John Sullivan to be the best. Not only is that my opinion but it is a view shared by many writers themselves. John is very much a writer's writer. He also happens to be a lovely, genuine man which is a great bonus.

'One of the reasons I am able to keep going is that I try very hard to form teams of people to work together in which everyone gets on. I attempt not to have too much gossip, back-biting and unhappiness, I don't want that. It is very difficult to have a happy team. I like working with people who are fun, who are as committed to the programme as everyone else, and who take the mickey a lot. I don't go and shut myself away in the caravan. Most of the time I am out with the crew, behind the camera, wherever there is something interesting going on. Not only do I find it interesting but I also find it keeps people's spirits up.

'I could lock myself away in my caravan but I don't think that is very productive. I also think I can learn a lot. One day I would like to direct a television film. I would like to pass on my experience of comedy. I think *Only Fools* has lasted so long because it's not a cardboard cut-out show. It's very three dimensional. It has the range to swing from comedy to tragedy. It goes right across society now. It used to be considered rather common but everyone watches *Only Fools* now.'

David's enthusiasm for Del always springs from the scripts. 'I never tire of reading John Sullivan's writing. Sometimes it's only minutes after they have come through the letterbox that I've collapsed with laughing. I loved the moment when Buster Merryfield as Uncle Albert was telling one of his interminable Navy stories and he admitted he was on lookout when they crashed into another very large ship. Del says, "You mean that you were on watch and you actually ran into a 45,000-ton aircraft carrier. Blimey, they'd have been better off with Ray Charles in the crow's nest."'

Albert's abilities as a lookout are a frequent source of mirth. At the start of the fabulous *Jolly Boys' Outing* to Margate, Albert fails to warn Del, working like mad to sell some dodgy car radios, of the approach of the Law. Del flips: 'The entire massed band of the Metropolitan Police Force could march past singing "I Shot the Sheriff" without him noticing them.'

For Christmas 1991, the BBC really splashed out and flew Del and Rodney and the rest of the crew to Miami for a two-part adventure that was a real departure from life in drizzly Peckham. Locals were baffled by the anxiety of BBC security staff holding blankets to prevent photographers recording these two totally unknown actors at work. They headed for Florida when Rodney won a competition but ended up on the run from the Mafia as Del turned out to be the double of a deadly mobster.

Sadly, as soon as they arrived in the Sunshine State more than 15 inches of rain fell delaying filming by five days. 'We might as well have been in Margate,' said David. 'The weather was absolutely awful. It should have been stable and sunny, but it rained furiously for the first week and we found ourselves in deep water. We have had to have 5.00am starts ever since to catch up. But it was a high-class production and it was enormous fun. Mind you, the Americans in the crew kept getting confused about the script. We had to keep stopping to explain to them what a "git" was and what "lovely jubbly" meant.'

Producer Gareth Gwenlan had to deal with the complex American labour regulations and did not enjoy the process. 'We had terrible trouble with the US unions,' he said. 'But the real Mafia were fine. I would say that it wasn't that successful but Jason's performance was wonderful.'

Former BBC Head of Comedy Gwenlan took over after Ray Butt left the BBC. Always ultra-professional, he did everything he could to maintain the high standards of the show, and was not afraid to speak up when levels dropped. He felt *A Royal Flush*, the 1986 Christmas Special about the Trotters on a country weekend, was not up to scratch. 'I wanted to cut out 20 minutes. Oh God, it went on and on. It was made under the most difficult of circumstances ever. John had great difficulty writing it. It was filmed in the middle of December under the most awful weather. We only had daylight for four hours. David and Nick were both ill with 'flu. The tent scene was filmed in the middle of the night with lights to make it look like daylight. The fact that it was ever shown was a miracle, but my favourite moment is seeing Del with the pump-action shotgun.'

One of the big disappointments for Gwenlan and the rest of the team is that *Only Fools'* humour is so essentially British that it does not sell overseas. Gwenlan said, 'It doesn't sell anywhere. We've tried to sell to Australia like *Minder* which is one of the biggest sellers. It did sell a little to Scandinavia. America would never like it as it's based on an ethos that they find odd. They don't like losers.

'But if it were up to the top-brass of the BBC it would be on twice a week like a soap opera. A week does not go by when I

Detective Inspector Jack Frost.

Top left: David with Ronnie Barker.

Top right: With his coveted BAFTA award.

Below: The Trotters at the National Television Awards.

Top: A star is born: David Jason's birth certificate.

Below: David with his family, (*left to right*) his Aunt Edie, his brother Arthur, his mother Olwen and his father, Arthur.

The original Trotter line-up, with the late Lennard Pearce as Grandad.

don't get a phone call from the controller saying, "Is there going to be one this year or any chance of a series?" '

In March 1991, David Jason finally won a British 'Oscar' at the sixth attempt. After repeatedly losing out to more fashionable stars like Rowan Atkinson and Victoria Wood for the Light Entertainment gong, the *Only Fools and Horses* star was delighted and made a pledge which delighted fans of the series. He had previously taken the BAFTA best actor award for his dramatic role in *Porterhouse Blue*, but he was delighted to gatecrash the comedy clique. He said, 'We have been making the series for ten years and there is no reason why it can't go on for another ten years.' With typical generosity he singled out John Sullivan for special mention, saying simply, 'He gives me the ammunition and I fire the guns.'

Yet there was an edge of frustration in the background. The relationship between the BBC and David Jason and the rest of the show was often never quite as harmonious behind the scenes as it looked on the surface and the ten-year reference was a heavy public hint to the people in power at the BBC. David said frankly, 'No one has told me that we will be carrying on. I wish they would. There has been talk of another Christmas Special and I have discussed storylines but there has been a deafening silence from the BBC. It puts me in an embarrassing position. Del is my top priority but I do have lots of other offers of work and I need to know where I stand.'

The characters that Sullivan has introduced around David have all done their bit to help to keep *Only Fools and Horses* fresh and alive. One of the most popular is Boycie, the cigar-smoking spiv from the motor trade who is, definitely reluctantly, a pal of Del's.

Sullivan used to work in the car trade and met types like Boycie who have a bit of money, think they are superior, and talk about their houses and their pools. He particularly remembers a trader who got him to creosote his fence and when Sullivan arrived at the house he was stunned to find it had acres of land, miles of fencing, and plenty of ostentatious good living.

The role of Boycie went to John Challis whom Butt remembered from many years previously while directing an episode of *Citizen Smith*. Butt had needed an actor to play a bent copper for a courtroom episode and remembered John. It was only a small part but Challis made such a good job of it that, when Boycie was created, John got the call again.

Challis based pompous Boycie on a character he knew from his local pub. He said, 'I'm afraid he was a real figure of fun, the most sent-up person I've ever known. Yet he was always very smart, just like Boycie.

'Now I get sent up a lot particularly thanks to one brilliant line from John Sullivan where he had Del describe would-be father Boycie as a '... Jaffa. You know ... seedless ...' just because he hadn't managed to get Marlene pregnant at the time. I think that description has gone into the national consciousness.

'David and Nick and all the team are wonderful to work with and I love the show. Usually the recognition is great but it wasn't so great when I got pulled up by the police when we were down filming in Ramsgate. I think the police were just bored with driving round and thought it would be fun to breathalyse me. In the end, after a lot of messing about they realised I was well under the limit and said, "You're free to go but can we have your autograph?"

'Boycie certainly seems to have registered with people. A video company offered me £100,000 to do an advert. I thought about it but I turned it down. I'm an actor not a video salesman and in a funny way Boycie is sacred. David is quite rightly very jealous of Del's character ever being used and I feel the same about Boycie.'

Sexy Marlene did eventually have her baby, little Tyler, which was a great delight to actress Sue Holderness, who plays the part so well. 'I began as a huge fan,' she said. '*Only Fools* was my favourite show and when I got the call I was actually pregnant with my first child, so I never forget how long ago it was. Marlene was talked about a lot during the first three series but never seen until I was given this wonderful episode where she and Boycie were going on holiday and needed Del and Rodney to look after their dog.

'Thanks heavens John Sullivan liked Marlene and he has used me in every series since. It is just a joy to do. I get recognised and people are quite nice to me but David and Nick really suffer. They just can't move and sometimes people are really vile to Nick. They call him plonker and slap him on the back but he always reacts terribly well.'

Paul Barber plays gullible Denzil, who is often on the receiving end of one of Del's scams. Paul is deeply impressed by the dedication of the whole team. He was involved in the memorable scene involving a rare butterfly that he and Del inadvertently crushed by slapping their hands together. Just before they filmed the vital moment they were interrupted by rain. In a quiet moment, Paul suggested to producer Ray Butt that it would be even funnier if Denzil was roller-skating while they did it. Paul recalls, 'Ray just said, "That is a brilliant idea." But the only trouble was that we had to wait for two weeks for me to learn to roller-skate. But they took the care to do that. I think that extra loving care and attention is one of the reasons that *Only Fools* is so special. It's great working with David. I am always very nervous and I sometimes fluff my lines and he is always wonderful at quickly helping me out.'

Ken MacDonald plays cheery Mike, long-suffering landlord of the Nag's Head, and he says he loves the job so much he would almost do it for nothing. 'The guy I miss the most is dear old Lennard Pearce. He gave us one of the in-words of show.

When we read through the script and pick out the lines that will produce a real belter of a laugh we always call them a "Wendy House".

'That's out of respect for Lennard and it dates back to one of his own lines. Rodney announced he was going to move out to a place of his own. And Grandad said, "What ya gonna get, a Wendy 'ouse, then?" It brought the house down. The studio audience didn't stop laughing for 20 minutes. Lennard was a very great actor. Whenever David Jason and the rest of us meet we always talk about him.'

Pat Murray plays wideboy Mickey Pearce and he is a devoted fan of the David Jason talents. 'David is just exceptional,' says Pat. 'I love to watch him turn into Del. Sometimes when we're on a break or waiting for something technical someone will say, "Come on, David. Be Del for a minute or two," and he just changes. It's fantastic. It's a very happy show, there is a real team feeling. My most frightening time was when I cut my arm falling through a window a day or so before we started filming. I had my arm in a plaster cast and I thought I might lose the part. But John Sullivan wrote it into the script that I had been beaten up by the Driscoll brothers. Fantastic.'

But it only comes over as effortlessly funny because everyone involved with the show works incredibly hard. One of the most memorable moments over the 16 years of *Only Fools and Horses* was the time Del, by now a would-be yuppie, was on the chat-up in a wine bar and ended up flat on the floor when he leaned on a barflap not noticing that it had been lifted. Instead, he found himself leaning on air.

John Sullivan wrote the classic prat-fall into the script of the *Yuppy Love* episode after seeing a Flash Harry missing his footing one night when he went to lean on a bar. Sullivan recalls, 'The scene was not in the original script because we couldn't get Roger Lloyd-Pack for Trigger. I got a last minute phone call saying they could get Roger for one day, did I want to do anything? We had them in the wine bar and we had a bit of time because the script was a bit short and I thought I'd bring in the scene I'd seen in a wine bar in Balham. It's become a sort of classic scene but it was written in ten minutes.'

It looked an easy scene for David to do. But the natural instinct of anyone falling is to try to break the fall. David turned it into one of TV's unforgettably funny moments by toppling sideways like a log. It is one of the most memorable *Only Fools* moments but for David Jason it was another exercise in faultless comedy technique. He recalls, 'When John told me about the Flash Harry missing his footing he said that the guy had recovered himself just in time and then looked round the room to make sure nobody had seen his mistake. He did not see John looking and was delighted no one had seen him.

'I said, "It's brilliant, John. But I would have to do the whole fall." He said, "No, that's not the way I saw it." I said, "I know that's not the way you saw it but if I do it I want to do the whole fall." He said, "OK, I'll put it in."'

What became a magical moment for millions of viewers was really the result of meticulous planning. David Jason took John Sullivan's amusing idea and went to work. 'First of all, we had to have a shot of Del-Boy and Trigger with the flap going up and going down while they have their conversation. Then you had to drag the viewers' attention away over to the two girls and then have a shot of Del leaning against the bar. Then Del says, "Just act casual, Trig," as the barman comes out and leaves the flap up and we cut across to the two girls again to distract the viewers. Then we come back to Del falling.'

The result was one of the funniest moments in the show's long and happy history. But for David it was 'a good idea, a lot of work, and a lot of construction. It's a bit of science, it's a bit of experience and it's a bit of knowledge, but you have to work at it. I had a very small mattress to fall on to. And that is the bit that is extremely difficult. It is the difference between being real and comic. The problem is when you fall you go so far and then your instincts take over and your head and eyes will turn to see. Then your arm goes out, then your leg. The difficult part is not obeying your instincts and going against what is natural. It's funnier that way. Also while I was down I got somebody to give me a wine glass so that when I got up I still looked as though I had the same full wine glass. How many people noticed that I don't know. It was just another funny little joke that we put in.

'Just the other day a chap came up to me and said, "You know when you fell through the bar?" I said, "Yeeees." He said, "Tell me something because I've got money on this. Did you rehearse it or was it an accident?" How's that for professionalism? That's how high my abilities are regarded! In some ways I suppose that was a back-handed compliment. The guy meant it. People think that if it's comedy, it's only daft, whereas a great heavy piece of drama is seen as desperately artistic.'

But as David points out, it's not just remembering everything, there's the pressure of getting everything right. David has to face calls at six o'clock in the morning and may not finish till eight o'clock at night. But it is the day in the studio, he ventures, that is the heaviest.

In past series, Sunday has been the studio recording day and David has to arrive at 10.00am and be on camera from 10.30am, not finishing till 9.30pm. He rehearses all day and then at 6.00pm he has an hour off. 'Then, just when you're really at the bottom, when you're really very tired, they say, "Twinkle, twinkle, you're going to be a star."'

On recording days, the audience arrives around 7.30pm and David and the others have to perform in front of them and make them laugh, with cameras and sound to worry about, people rushing backwards and forwards, lines to remember, pauses to anticipate for the hoped-for laughs. That, he concedes, can be very stressful.

The idea that *Only Fools* is guilty of glamorising petty crime is firmly rejected by David Jason. 'We do have a responsibility. We know we do. There is always a danger of being imitated by stupid people. If we were shown jumping off the Clifton Suspension Bridge I dare say some wally would try to emulate it. We always show that Del is essentially a failure. And when it comes to the crunch, he is actually very honest. He is also very vulnerable. If he was harder and more successful there would be more danger of him glamorising cheap thiefdom.'

Over the years, the *Only Fools and Horses* cast and production teams have watched the show grow in popularity to the point now where Christmas is not Christmas unless TV viewers can sit back and watch the Trotter family in a TV special. Every year, it is the jewel in the BBC's festive TV crown. But in Christmas 1996, the three-show series amazingly capped everything that had gone before.

With David Jason and Nicholas Lyndhurst both in great demand for other projects, it took 14 months' planning just to get them together to film the ground-breaking three-parter. The story had Del and Rodney discovering they had an incredibly rare Harrison watch in an old lock-up. And with typical Sullivan brilliance, Rodney recalled from a scene in the very first 16-year-old episode exactly where the receipt was. It was as though *Only Fools and Horses* had gone full circle. The shows were simply packed with magical moments but the sight of Del and Rodney dressed as Batman and Robin still lives in most people's memories as one of the funniest sights of all time. The audiences were sensational: 21.31 million, 21.33 million and 24.35 million for the fabulous finale which had Del, Rodney and Uncle Albert wandering up the Yellow Brick Road with their £6 million fortune. There wasn't a dry eye in millions of houses when that went out on December 29.

And although it was officially intended to be the end, the success and the joy of the reunion shows had everyone considering another *Only Fools and Horses* possibly around the time of the Millennium.

But sometimes you can't please all of the people all of the time. Chris Woodhead, chief schools inspector and scourge of the teaching profession, earned himself some cheap publicity by criticising the idea of the Trotters as role models for the young.

John Sullivan sprang to the articulate defence of his characters. 'What is so wrong with Del and Rodney? Derek Trotter is a man who, through his own endeavours, brought up his kid brother Rodney after they lost both parents, cared for and fed his ageing grandfather and later his Uncle Albert. He makes no excuses for loving Raquel and their son Damien. He has worked every hour God sends to put groceries on the table. He is optimistic and resolute. Despite all the slings and arrows of outrageous fortune — and Del wrote the book on outrageous fortune — he picks himself up, smiles at the world and continues with his everlasting dream. Admittedly some of his "business arrangements" may not fare too well in a court of law, but compared with the activities of some of our politicians and captains of industry, Del is squeaky clean.

'Does Mr Woodhead honestly believe that the British public, particularly our young, are so thick that they actually ape everything they see on the screen or the stage? Does Shakespeare's *Romeo and Juliet* induce young people to commit suicide? Did Charles Dickens endorse pickpocketing as a fun career in *Oliver Twist*? Throughout the series, I have tried to emphasise the basic decency of the Trotters. They are not violent, they don't take drugs and they don't drink and drive. They respect the old and the very young. More importantly, they have strong family values, loyalty and love and the ability to laugh at themselves. If more people followed their example, Britain might be a happier place.'

Only Fools and Horses has millions of faithful followers but none more devoted than the band who have formed themselves into the official *Only Fools and Horses* Appreciation Society. Perry Aghajanoff and Andy Banks run the club from their homes in Essex. They put out a lively quarterly magazine called Hookie Street and enjoy good relationships with the cast and the BBC. Membership is growing fast and *Only Fools* followers from as far afield as Croatia and Bangkok have joined up.

6

A Touch of Genius

David Jason's heart was in his mouth at the Grosvenor House Hotel in 1988 when he waited to hear the announcement of the award for Best Actor at the British Academy of Film and Television Arts awards dinner.

For several years, David had regularly been nominated for an award in TV's Light Entertainment section for his role as Del-Boy in *Only Fools and Horses*. Somewhat mystifyingly, he had always been passed over.

But this year it was different. Now, here he was, up for a straight acting honour for his role as the wily old porter Skullion in Channel 4's marvellous production of Tom Sharpe's comic novel *Porterhouse Blue*.

Robert Knights, who directed David in *Porterhouse Blue*, remembers arriving for the dinner to find there appeared to be no clear route to the stage from the table where he and David had been placed for the evening.

His heart sank. It seemed to indicate that David was yet again destined to be passed over and would come away empty-handed.

Knights inwardly resigned himself to hearing the name of Robbie Coltrane read out as Best Actor for *Tutti Frutti*, a dryly funny series about a Fifties Glasgow pop group called The Majestics. But to a great roar of appreciation from a packed, dinner-jacketed audience, the winner was 'David Jason for *Porterhouse Blue*'.

There was no disguising David's utter delight. Knights's recollection is of David leaping four feet in the air and almost running across shoulders to get to the stage! He made it, all right, and his gratitude and respect for the others he had beaten to the most coveted of the BAFTA TV awards was evident for all to see.

It was an important award for David in every sense and it came with marvellous timing in his career. David had enjoyed tremendous success in *Only Fools and Horses* but *Porterhouse Blue* had allowed him to show he had a much wider range as an actor. The part of Skullion was exactly what David needed at that time. Anything less like *Only Fools and Horses* or *Open All Hours* was hard to imagine.

When David's name was originally put forward for Skullion there were, however, some reservations. Initially, Knights felt David might be too young to play an irascible 64-year-old porter. Knights also wanted to be sure in his own mind that David was not simply a sitcom actor who could succeed only on a certain level. Knights decided to check up on him and was pleased to hear from various people in the business that David was a real actor with a varied range.

Also in David's favour was the fact that he had played much older men in the past — Blanco in *Porridge* and Dithers in *Hark at Barker* — with great success. David, despite his star status, was humble enough and committed enough to the idea of playing Skullion, to audition for the part. Knights needed just two meetings with David to satisfy himself in his own mind that David was indeed the right choice.

Looking back, David later recalled, 'I had to audition for *Porterhouse Blue* because I had to convince them that I could do it. They were worried that they would get a sitcom performance —

over the top. Everyone was very concerned. They began to get nervous about me. I said I'd grow a moustache. "Oh no," they said. "You said a moustache? Don't do that." And I had these eyebrows made. Everyone was shaking their heads and I had to stick to my guns.'

Set in Cambridge University, the story of *Porterhouse Blue* centred around fictional Porterhouse college where oar-pulling and feasting take priority over academic achievement until a new college head, played by Ian Richardson, makes drastic changes. Women are to be allowed in, contraceptive machines installed, and finally head porter Skullion after finding it hard to adapt to change, is sacked after 45 years of service.

'Skullion attracted me because I loved the stiffness of the character,' David explained, 'an ex-Army man who has built-in discipline and a wonderful attitude of subservience. He likes being like a soldier again — do a job, do it well. I loved that character and I tried to bring all that out in him.'

When the cameras started rolling, David could not have looked more different from Del-Boy Trotter. Pushing an old bicycle up the street, David was wearing a starched collar, his tie was straight, and there was a carnation in the buttonhole of the staid three-piece suit topped off by a gold watch and chain.

In addition, David had bushy eyebrows and wore a bowler hat on top of his slicked back hair. The part called for David to age about 20 years and it took eight hours to dye his locks a whitish grey.

David had a complex scene on the first day's shoot where Skullion goes on television. 'We had meetings and discussions,' David recalled, 'then started shooting. Those first two or three days I was struggling a bit. I was very uncomfortable the first few days.' Any worries Knights may have had about David, however, completely disappeared two days into filming.

It was a night shoot in a park round the back of Waterloo which was supposed to be the back of a garden at Porterhouse College and conditions were anything but easy for actors and crew alike. Knights recalls that not only was the park flea-infested and the fleas were jumping because of the Waterloo dossers but there was a woman noisily servicing a man at regular intervals behind the bushes.

The scene to be shot was one where John Sessions as student Zipser falls into the college having climbed a wall. David, as Skullion, hears him and turns round like a stag at bay, unmistakably elated that there is a student misbehaving and he has spotted him.

On the first take Knights wondered whether David might have gone slightly over the top so they went for a second take. When Knights saw the rushes he went for the first take. From that moment, David showed Knights what he was going to do and the part became his.

Some of the dialogue in the script reminded David of his own father. 'Like Skullion, my father was a strict, self-reliant man,' he said, 'who didn't like change and couldn't understand the modern generation. It's quite uncanny and sad for me in a way because he even looks like my father.

'My father was a traditionalist. He came from a generation who believed in hard work. We were brought up to respect the law, an honest day's work for an honest day's pay.

'In a way, the part was a tribute to him. I needed a model, someone I could believe in to help the characterisation and memories of my father gave me what I needed.'

He added, 'We weren't very close and he used to be crotchety with me. But I think his distant attitude was due to the terrible pain he suffered from arthritis.'

Undoubtedly the funniest and most memorable scene of the entire *Porterhouse Blue* series was when an outraged Skullion finds Zipser disposing of hundreds of condoms by filling them with gas and pushing them up through his chimney as balloons from where they float and bob through the air coming to rest on the scrupulously manicured college lawns. Here Skullion has the job of bursting every one of them.

Two Cambridge colleges gave permission for their stately

quadrangles to be used for filming but then withdrew it when they learned the precise details of the script. Finally the scene was shot at a Jacobean mansion called Apethorpe Hall near Peterborough as only some two-and-a-half days of filming out of the ten weeks were actually able to go ahead in Cambridge.

Ideally, the scene called for a still, moonlit night where the condoms, if filled with a drop of water, would hang in the air. But, instead, Knights encountered high winds which nearly destroyed the scene. Annoyingly, the condoms kept taking off and popping in the gusts.

David had to wait patiently to perform his extraordinary condom-popping scene while the problem was sorted out. Eventually, a team of middle-aged ladies inflated the condoms from cylinders of helium and then they were attached to the grass by invisible thread.

At long last some 500 inflated condoms were in place close to the ground while others were poised for release into the wind to fly past the camera.

When all was ready, David asked Knights how he wanted the scene to be played. It was then that Knights told David to remember those Japanese soldiers who occasionally emerge from the Philippines swearing allegiance to the Emperor. 'Play it like a Japanese soldier for whom this is the last bayonet charge,' said Knights.

As the cameras rolled, David charged forward holding a broom like a bayonet. He began popping the condoms, stabbing at them while uttering demented Japanese-style cries. A pin had carefully been inserted into the broom so that the condoms would burst more easily.

Knights still laughs at the comic touch David himself added. After one or two stabs with his broom, David stopped to rub his eyes as if some horrible gob of spermicidal jelly had hit him smack in the eye. Wiping it from his face, he charged back into battle again then turned it into a sort of Fred Astaire dance where every step crushes the head of a condom. It was the classic description in

Tom Sharpe's book and David had made it a classic TV comedy scene.

'It was quite amazing,' said David. 'There were hundreds of these inflated condoms staked out on the lawn. I had to go round bursting them with anything handy. We started filming at 7.00pm and it went on until daybreak. We had quite a lot of complaints from farmers who found stray "balloons" on their land!'

Porterhouse Blue had a distinguished cast which included Ian Richardson, Griff Rhys Jones, John Sessions and Charles Gray, but it was David who always caught the eye. Winning the BAFTA award was the icing on the cake. 'That was the first time I think I was considered as an actor,' says David. 'I was reviewed in the more up-market papers. You had Ian Richardson and my character reflected his so that we were on a par and I was considered an actor of weight. I would not have been considered as such had I not been in *Porterhouse Blue* and had I not been opposite an actor like Ian Richardson.'

He has won shoals of other awards both before and since but the acting award was very special to David. Yet if he harboured dreams of the BAFTA prize leading instantly on to still greater things, then he was in for a disappointment. For a couple of weeks afterwards nothing happened and then there was an inquiry from Menahem Golan of Cannon Films as to whether David might be interested in making a film.

Not long afterwards, a large Mercedes with a uniformed driver bearing a script pulled up outside David's house in Buckinghamshire. 'I played it casual,' David later recalled, 'and opened the door after a suitable delay. Man in hat, gives me a package. I go in, tear it open and find I'm reading the part of Tom Shepherd. I look through the cast list — it's always dangerous — and I'm half-way through and the character has not appeared yet.

'Finally, about three-quarters of the way through I see him — gatekeeper. Car drives into chocolate factory. Tom Shepherd comes out. "Yes sir, good morning sir."

'"I'm here to see the managing director."

'"Up there on the left, sir."'

'I had three of those. They got smaller and smaller and in the last one Tom Shepherd got run over! My agent got on to casting and began to bawl them out. She did say there was not a hope of me doing it.'

The other offer to come David's way after his BAFTA triumph was a part in *Doctor Who*. 'Now I think *Doctor Who* is quite good,' David reflected later, 'but I was getting lower and lower. I had been nominated as Best Comedy Actor for about three years running, then to win Best Actor I was pipping them all at the post. I thought it might have meant something.'

It certainly meant a lot to David. 'I think that was the greatest accolade I've managed to receive,' he said of his BAFTA award for *Porterhouse Blue*. 'It put me into a different category from "That's the bloke who can only do funny Cockney voices."'

While making *Porterhouse Blue*, David met the author Tom Sharpe and talked about filming another of Sharpe's books *Wilt*. It eventually became a film starring Griff Rhys Jones.

'At the time, the rights had been bought by one of the famous film directors and it wasn't available,' David remembers. 'So I just went, "Oh dear!" But, of course, Griff and his company were probably a bit better informed and made more enquiries and found it had come up on offer. The one thing I wanted to do was *Wilt*, but Griff has done it, the swine!'

At one time *Porterhouse Black*, a sequel to *Porterhouse Blue*, was planned by Channel 4. But, to David's disappointment, the idea was abandoned when Channel 4 boss Jeremy Isaacs left his post.

Until *A Touch of Frost*, the variety of David's abilities was not always widely appreciated, especially when you consider some of his acting is done without ever being seen. He does not underestimate his ability to do funny voices.

For David's is the versatile voice behind the remarkably successful children's cartoon character Dangermouse, a serious hit on both sides of the Atlantic, and a string of other animated entertainments.

He was delighted with the success of *Dangermouse* and the characters which followed. 'One of the reasons I wanted to get involved with cartoon characters was that I was fascinated by them when I was a boy,' said David.

'I loved the way they broke the bounds of reality. They could blow someone up and leave the earth to go round the moon, come back, and everyone would still all be in one piece. I found that breaking the rules and being anarchic was very funny with animation. You can't do it nearly as well with live action. I just love cartoons if they're well made.

'In the days when I was growing up, there was no real television. I used to go to the pictures on Saturday mornings and it was all Disney then. My favourites were Pluto and Donald Duck. I'm a dog man so that is probably why I like Pluto.

'I really enjoy doing voices. When I was a kid at school I used to imitate the masters and terrify the other kids when they were swinging on ladders or messing about. They would freeze in their tracks, it was hysterical.

'Ever since I saw that *Goon Show* being recorded as a kid, Peter Sellers was my idol. I always followed his career very closely and tried to emulate him. But I know I would never be able to reach his dizzy heights. He was an extraordinarily talented man. I did meet him once when I was putting a couple of silly voices on one of his records. He was lovely, absolutely charming. I can't for the life of me remember which LP it was and I'm sorry about that because I would very much like to get a copy.

'We recorded it in the famous Abbey Road studios in London. We all sat round a table in the studio and I sat there in awe of the man. Then we all sent out for a Chinese takeaway. I was so impressed by Sellers I couldn't speak to him. He was just so amazingly wonderful and famous and there I was in his company. I have got practically all The Goons recordings. Sometimes when I'm in the car and I'm feeling a bit fed up, I listen. It's beautiful escapist stuff, completely mad. As long as it entertains, that's what it's all about.

'I've developed that sort of mimicry because it was all part of being an actor. I have a good ear and I listen. I did a lot of the radio series *Weekending*. I did James Callaghan, Tony Benn, James Mason, Enoch Powell and lots of others with varying degrees of success. I do some much more accurately than others and it's a vocal range that I employ in the cartoon work. People say, "You've got a brilliant ear, you must be able to sing." But I can't. I'm tone deaf.'

The cartoon career all began in the most unlikely circumstances back in 1977. Brian Cosgrove, the boss of Cosgrove Hall Productions which became the Manchester-based animation subsidiary of Thames Television, was looking for a man to be the voice and personality of Dangermouse.

But David Jason did not exactly get off on the right foot for the audition. Brian Cosgrove recalls, 'David arrived for the voice testing session in Wardour Street with his leg all bandaged up. I thought it looked a bit funny and wondered if it was some sort of joke but he said he had damaged his foot in an accident with a hover mower.

'So he was really not very comfortable and he came along with another actor who really was not very good and was drunk into the bargain. David did his best but he was a little put off by this chap who was tanked up, and by his injury. In spite of the problem, I could see the quality straight away. He searched so hard to get what he saw of the character into his performance. But David was annoyed because he felt he hadn't got the voice right and he really wanted the job. He told me he liked cartoons and this was more than just another job to him.'

David said later that they were trying to make Dangermouse really laid back, 'a Roger Moore-ish-type special agent'.

Brian said, 'He was a bit down about it but when I listened to the material his unique ability in this field was very evident to me. He was marvellous. Of course, it is well known that he is a good actor but also he can do things with his voice that help to create a whole personality in the peculiar way our medium requires. He was relieved when I told him later that the job was his. Our friendship began that day and has grown ever since.

'David is a perfectionist but not one who is painful to work with. If he has got an idea he discusses it and says, "What about this?" or "What if we did that?" He adds things to shows and inspires excitement with other people. He is very good to work with.'

Having landed the role of the suave and debonair mouse who faces all those dastardly villains, David Jason became remarkably protective of his character. Brian Cosgrove said, 'When you are using lots of writers mistakes can sometimes creep in. But David takes great care to monitor the script. If anyone had him living in Oxford Street instead of Baker Street, David would be straight on to it, pointing out the mistake and rightly insisting on accuracy.

'He does love a challenge and he is so good at creating different voices that sometimes after an audition he would be playing three or four extra characters as well as the standard one.

'Sometimes they would be quite difficult roles and he would grumble about them and say, "Look, I've got this to do or that to do." But then he would do it superbly and we would all talk about it afterwards and we would know he had thoroughly enjoyed it. Although he had complained and it had been difficult, you would know he had really enjoyed himself so it did not stop us giving him a challenge.

'David never rests upon his laurels. That is the other major thing I have noticed about him. It would have been very easy for him to have settled on the role of Del and that style of character and he could have done a variety of roles out of the same box. He has deliberately not done that. He has gone for different roles, for chancing his arm if you like. And also for searching for something that will move him on. He does not want to stay in one place. He wants to stretch himself. And David also seems to have a good feeling for the right material. He is offered a lot of scripts and he weeds them out very carefully.'

David has enormous respect for the people who create cartoons and is one of Cosgrove Hall's most faithful fans. 'Even if I am in a hurry and there is a good cartoon on, then everything has to wait until the cartoon has finished because I know they only last three, four or five minutes,' said David.

'People forget that the artists who make cartoons are very talented. They get denigrated because they are not Renoir. But they are in their own way. And they are probably seen by more people than any of the great artists and appreciated more and yet those artists are revered — I'm not belittling those artists — I'm saying we don't look at cartoons with the same critical eye.

'Early Disney and other old American cartoons are now beginning to be taken more seriously, even the actual artists behind them. And collectors are always on the lookout for them.

'The relationship with Brian worked very well. He draws a character and then asks me what I think. I try to find a voice that comes out of the drawing that looks as though it belongs and does not sound like an actor reading lines behind a moving picture.'

The partnership between Brian Cosgrove's artistic talents and David Jason's acting ability has helped to turn *Dangermouse* into an international success story. The super-cool squeaking sleuth has been sold to more than 50 countries around the world. In America, where the programme was the first British cartoon to be syndicated from coast to coast, he is particularly popular.

Marvin Kitman of the New York *Newsday* eulogised, '*Dangermouse* is not just a cartoon show. It's a way of life, a religion. Dangermouse has been elevated to the status of cult figure.'

After Brian Cosgrove became so close to David, he sometimes felt guilty about employing his pal so frequently. 'Each new project we found ourselves saying, "Oh, we can't use David again," but the most important thing is that we find the right actor. And more often than not that means turning to David yet again.

'He has been our Count Duckula. He has been our Toad in *Wind in the Willows*. He has been the giant in *BFG*, the Roald Dahl story. And he's been Hugo in our production of *Victor and Hugo*.

'But, honestly, we do not always go for him first when casting. When we were looking for someone to play the giant in *BFG* we tried a lot of fine actors, including Trevor Howard as an indication of the calibre of cast we went for. Now Trevor Howard was a lovely man and he did a nice voice, but it was Trevor Howard, not the giant.

'We had tried lots of other people and then one day I was having lunch with David, who had been too busy to test at first. He said, "Would you mind if I put a voice down?" He's like that — not grand or at all pompous. And he put this voice down and that was it.

'It was very similar when we were casting *Wind in the Willows*. We tried him out for Ratty and he did a marvellous Ratty. Then I tried out another actor for Toad who was not totally satisfactory. Again, I thought David was unavailable and we still had not found our Toad when he came up to me and asked if he could put down a Toad voice. He said, "I'm not after it or anything, I just feel that if I put something down it might help you find a bit of direction that I feel would be worthwhile."

'There was a particular aspect of Toad's personality that we were finding it impossible to capture. Toad is rather a nasty little character in some ways in Winston Grahame's original book yet there is a madness and an undisciplined quality to him as well.

'And yet he has to be likeable as well for the story to work because the other characters do have affection for him. David is a very fine actor and he managed to encapsulate exactly what we were thinking.

'We have always laid great importance upon getting the soundtrack right. We use the very best actors we can find. I like to think that we have become good friends with David over the years and that he now feels comfortable with us. There is no searching for supremacy with David, the job comes first. Mind you, he does not suffer fools gladly and he is very careful whom he works with.

'This industry can be very competitive and cut-throat but I doubt if anyone will have a bad word to say about David. He is good company and a funny fellow but he would be the first one to say that he is a comedy actor, not a stand-up comic. He couldn't just stand up and tell a string of jokes but when he is telling you an anecdote he makes you fall about.

'But he is not the type who hogs a conversation. You can come back and tell him a joke and tell him some of the things that have happened to you and he will laugh out loud at them. He is not a selfish actor.'

David's voice has earned him a fortune over the years and not just from Brian Cosgrove's carefully crafted cartoons. David is one of the kings of the commercial voice-overs. He is always in demand to put just the right voice to promote dozens of firms from Esso and the Woolwich Building Society to Alpen and the TSB. It is a lucrative sideline which is much, much better paid than even the best paid television drama work. As one of the voice-over kings, he was paid a staggering £100,000 by the Abbey National Building Society for just one day's work.

★   ★   ★

If the BBC had had the foresight to sign up their most popular star on an exclusive contract, David Jason would not have been available to take the lead in an enterprising new ITV comedy back in 1988. As he was summoned only from series to series and therefore open to offers, he was interested to hear from Yorkshire TV and their plans for a series called *A Bit of a Do*.

David Nobbs, the writer of the classic Reginald Perrin books and television series, had a new idea about a series of odd Yorkshire functions during which a series of odd Yorkshire people hurtled in and out of each other's lives with hilarious abandon.

The main character was tough-talking Ted Simcock, a garrulous businessman modelled in the author's mind upon fiery Freddie Trueman. Ted owned a foundry which made toasting forks and boot scrapers decorated with the faces of prime ministers. When Nobbs was asked to lunch to meet David Jason with a view to discussing him playing Ted, he wondered how television's Del-Boy would measure up.

'I was obviously pleased they chose David in that he is a big name and I knew he would attract a big audience,' said Nobbs. 'But sometimes you get the feeling that someone is not how you saw the character and I felt a bit of that. I tried to dismiss that because David is a very fine actor and in the end I thought he played Ted wonderfully. I thought he became Ted Simcock.

'Ironically, I was late for lunch because I had been to a bit of a do, a funeral actually. But we still got on very well and his agent rang back in the afternoon to say he had decided to take the part. I was delighted because Ted is one of the hardest characters for an actor to play. He had a very characteristic speech rhythm and David caught that perfectly. Then it all fell into shape.

'I thought he brought so much to Ted and it was so much easier to write the second series with him in my mind. I loved him when Ted was hosting his party dressed as Napoleon and his world is collapsing around him because he has been conned by a woman. He made it funny and moving at the same time. He is a fine actor to work with. A real professional.'

David enjoyed his two series of *A Bit of a Do* and said, 'I liked playing Ted but I did not like him as a man. He is so chauvinistic, so self-centred and so unbelievably arrogant. Having gone through so many areas of the character there are some times that you think, God, he really is a pain. But that is what made him interesting to play. He thinks he is irresistible to women and that attracted me as an actor. I liked him because he was so different from Del. David Nobbs is a good writer, I liked the scripts very much. I thought it was a sort of working-class *Dallas* with a sense of humour.'

David's search for more challenging roles did produce two notable one-off performances in 1990. He turned to *Open All Hours* writer Roy Clarke for a remarkable monologue in the BBC's *Single Voices* series. David played the title role in *The Chemist*. David described it as a sort of love story.

'It's about this man who adores his wife. She is promiscuous and it is driving him crazy. He has to talk to someone about it, so he finds himself telling his story to a video camera in the place where he works. It's very funny and very sad and I suppose that's what love is all about.'

David took the sensitive script and turned in a masterly, immensely moving performance with never a hint of Del-Boy. His character was Vernon Duxley, a husband opening his heart to the camera after a traumatic weekend. His cheating wife Marlene is making love with the local golf club chairman in their bed while he is making up his prescriptions.

'Vernon was a right plonker, a real wally,' said David. 'It was a marvellous part I had to get to grips with. A real challenge to be the only one on screen. It had a nice twist. Usually it's men having the affairs all over the place but this time the man was being slighted. I enjoyed the change. If you are going to play the same jokey parts all the time it can get boring. If I looked like Robert Redford, which I don't, I hasten to add, I could play romantic leads.'

There was nothing very romantic about David's other straight role as the father of a youngster facing the death penalty for drug running in Malaysia in Michael Wall's *Amongst Barbarians*. It was a powerful piece and the anti-drug message was very important to David. He confessed his own naïveté about drugs when he recalled being passed a cigarette at a showbiz party and thinking his hosts must be rather short of funds to be forced to share smokes.

A more street-wise friend explained he had just been offered a cannabis reefer. David is concerned at the dreadful damage caused by drugs, particularly to young people. He was pleased to take part in *Amongst Barbarians* and said, 'It was a story which had to be told. If it saves just one person from a drugs death, it will have done something very important.'

★ ★ ★

For David Jason, the most important aspect of the stunning success of *The Darling Buds of May* was not just the way Yorkshire Television's glossy adaptation of the HE Bates novels swept straight to the top of the television ratings and stayed there. The unprecedented audience bonanza, the international sales and the video which followed were all pleasing enough but definitely secondary to David's main focus.

'I was overwhelmed and enormously heartened that such a simple family story with no sex, no violence and no bad language could attract more viewers than all those dreadful action adventures of the time like *The A Team* or *Miami Vice* where people get blown away in just about every scene,' said David.

'Of course, when Vernon Lawrence at Yorkshire TV sent me the HE Bates books and approached me about the idea, I realised straight away that it could make a marvellous nostalgic series set in the '50s, a time of almost total innocence. I knew Pop Larkin was potentially a great character to play, and I also knew, in spite of what people might think, that he could be completely different from Del.

'*The Darling Buds of May* also appealed to me because it seemed to be the kind of television that is hardly seen any more. A series about a whole wonderful fictional family that whole real-life families could sit and enjoy together without any fear of embarrassment. Wholesome fun seems to have become sadly a little unfashionable these days and *Darling Buds* seemed to be doing something to reverse that trend.

'What stunned me was the response. Every episode going out as the most popular programme of the week ahead of *Coronation Street* and *EastEnders* was unbelievable. But maybe it meant that my views on television are not so far out of step with the public's.

'It was so refreshing that people didn't get killed or blasted to bits, women are not attacked or raped. The Larkins are actually all pretty nice people being on the whole jolly decent to each other. The books were lovely and charming and happily I think we managed to capture much of that naïve and lyrical appeal on the screen.

'They are such simple stories that I suppose I am still surprised that they became so popular. To be honest, not that much happens. In the nicest possible way there is not that much in it but maybe an enjoyable, undemanding hour that brings the family together round the telly somehow caught the national mood of the moment.

'A lot of the fans of *Darling Buds* seemed to be young people, which both delighted and surprised me. I always knew teenagers identified with Del but I got so many kids yelling, "Hey, Perfick!" at me and enthusing about Pop Larkin that I knew *Darling Buds* had clicked with them, too.'

Vernon Lawrence, Yorkshire TV's ebullient entertainment boss who co-produced *Darling Buds of May* with Richard Bates, the nephew of HE Bates, must take much of the credit for David being cast as Pop Larkin because Richard originally wanted Bob Hoskins to be the star.

A roly-poly book-keeper's son, Hoskins was indeed an obvious and good choice. His proven acting ability allied to his barrel shape and crew-cut, a pugnacious manner and a cheerful Cockney mateyness would no doubt have breathed much life into Pop Larkin. But just at the time the *Darling Buds of May* project was gathering momentum, Hoskins was riding high as a film star. Impressive roles in gangster movies was having him hailed in Hollywood circles as 'the new James Cagney'.

Hoskins had first impressed the Hollywood movie moguls in 1984 as an Irish-American loser in *The Cotton Club* then as a timid Jewish American screenwriter from Brooklyn in *Sweet Liberty*. Playing a heavy in the British gangster movie *The Long Good Friday* and *Mona Lisa* had made Hollywood further sit up and take notice.

A role in Steven Spielberg's *Who Killed Roger Rabbit?* further added to Hoskins' credentials as a movie star and by the time *Darling Buds of May* was seriously under discussion at Yorkshire TV, Hoskins was being discussed in Hollywood as a co-star in a new movie with Cher.

In principle, Vernon Lawrence had nothing against Hoskins. He felt he would make a fine Pop Larkin. But Vernon was looking ahead and could see that Hoskins' very success in the movies counted against him for this particular TV project. Vernon was looking not for just one series of *Darling Buds* but two, possibly three. With a flourishing film career and big movie offers coming in, Hoskins was thought unlikely to give Yorkshire TV more than one series.

Vernon felt David Jason was ideal for Pop Larkin. He emphasised to Richard Bates that David had attributes which Hoskins did not have. David had a loveable quality while Hoskins' image had been built on tough gangster roles.

It took Vernon five weeks but finally he brought Richard Bates round to his way of thinking. David took only ten days before making up his mind to play Pop Larkin. *Darling Buds* of May was launched on British Television on 5 April 1991 and almost 17 million viewers switched on. Vernon Lawrence breathed a sigh of relief. He had gambled £3 million of the company's cash on his hunch that the popular novels would successfully translate to the screen.

'It had nostalgia, something we all love,' said Vernon. 'It is wonderfully English. Better still, it's rural English. It's about a family who live the way we'd secretly all love to live, never paying the income tax, never bothering about modern fads like dieting.

'It's about a little man who pits himself against bureaucracy and wins, and who breaks through all the class barriers of the period — he deals in junk, but hobnobs with brigadiers and the lord of the manor. It's good clean fun. And it's got that very important ingredient, a genuine star — David Jason.'

David's remarkable popular appeal certainly transformed a promising idea into a sure-fire hit. And he threw himself enthusiastically into the production with his usual professionalism and chirpy good humour. He chose a typically individual way of establishing a good relationship with ample actress Pam Ferris who played Ma Larkin. Pam added two stone to her size 14 figure by packing in the pasta but even then had to wear rubber padding to fill the huge personality and bulk of Ma Larkin.

David knew that one of their early scenes was troubling Pam, and considering the two of them were scheduled to spend an afternoon splashing about in the bath together while eating a huge fry up, he could quite understand her concern. So he put on a set of his scuba gear including flippers, snorkel and face mask, and marched on to the set announcing, 'I'm ready for the bath scene. Are you ready, Pam?' When she had stopped laughing, Pam found that all her nerves had quite disappeared.

Recording went swimmingly, but David insisted, 'Underneath all those bubbles and water I did actually have my clothes on. I wouldn't recommend sitting in hot water for two hours. It makes your skin look like a prune.'

The partnership between the two of them was the foundation of the show's success. David chose Pam to play his wife and is convinced he made the right decision. He said, 'Pam is an excellent actress. We have a very warm relationship because she is an extremely nice person so it was easier for us to behave as lovers. I think if we hadn't got on, that warmth you feel between Ma and Pop Larkin would not have been there.

'It's something that is very difficult to fake. When you have a really deep passionate relationship it shows in your body language. What appealed to me about Pam was her warmth and her sense of fun. Like all couples who get on well together, we laugh at the same things.

'Pop Larkin loves creeping up behind her when she is reaching up into a cupboard — he sees it all there and he dives in for a big cuddle. She responds and it looks as if they are having a bit of passion. There is nothing overtly sexual but their relationship is strong and I thought that was something refreshing to see on TV. For my money, there is too much sex and violence and not enough old-fashioned family entertainment.'

The role certainly called for versatility. David had to milk a cow, handle a horse, drive a lorry, row a boat and for one scene he had to eat no fewer than seven cooked breakfasts before the director was satisfied. Fortunately, he has always loved his food, although he felt that seven breakfasts at a single sitting was rather pushing it.

'When they brought in the cow, the director said to me breezily, "Do you know how to milk a cow, David?" When I simply answered, "Yes, I can do that for you," he was stunned. But at one time or another in my life I have been called upon to turn my hand to most things. With cows you have to be a bit careful, though. If you get in their way, it's tough luck.'

When the cow arrived she was quite happy to be milked by David but less enthusiastic about the television crew's lights. 'She kept turning away from them and pinning me against the wall,' he said. 'And when a cow wants to move around she is a big heavy animal and you can't do a lot to stop her. In the end, I just had to get out of there. She was a nice cow but I didn't want to get hurt.

'The truck was a bit of a poser, too. Apart from anything else, it was left-hand drive, 50 years old and had a crash gearbox, which means you have to double de-clutch. They introduced me to it about three minutes before I had to drive it. But I managed to get it going without any fuss — just like Pop Larkin!'

As work on the series went on, the cast began to realise that they were working on something special. Pam Ferris said, 'People mistake David for Del-Boy but that means they don't realise Del-Boy is a brilliant artistic creation of his. In *Darling Buds* people believe Pop Larkin is him. He is a very talented actor and great fun to work with. The first time I met him I gave him a peck on the cheek and said, "That's the first of many." '

Pam and David both found that they piled on the pounds as life with the Larkins revolved very much round eating. David packed on an extra one-and-a-half stones and went on a diet while Pam expanded up to 16 stone. She said, 'The Larkins are such powerful characters. They're so pro-life. They're into giving, loving, making love, eating and being generous — with themselves. And they spend so much time eating. They start the day with a huge breakfast, then there's a mid-morning sandwich snack, a proper cooked lunch, high tea of ham off the bone or kippers, followed by a full hot supper, finished off with cocktails.

'We both ate so much while filming. We couldn't cheat with just a tiny scrap of food on the end of a fork, we had to shovel it in just like the Larkins. Once we did a scene where David and I were eating chocolate and pickled onions in bed.

'Then, on another day, we re-shot the same scene eating kippers. I never want to see another kipper in my life. And that scene was eventually cut.'

Pop and Ma Larkin certainly captured the affection of the nation. When the video version of the series was rushed into the shops it sold £1 millon worth of copies in the first four days and HE Bates' classic novels staged a sudden revival in sales. The truth of their relationship, of course, was that although they lived so happily together with their huge family they were never actually married. Although he was blissfully content with his Ma, Pop somehow never quite managed to make it official.

This cheerfully unmarried condition mirrored David's happy and long established real-life relationship with Myfanwy Talog, the attractive Welsh actress who shared his life until her sad death from cancer at the age of 49 in March 1995, made all the more tragic because twice Myfanwy thought she had beaten the disease.

Born in Caerwys, Clwyd, daughter of a school attendance officer and a bus conductor, Myfanwy's career began in the late 1960s and was really launched with the huge success of *Ryan and Ronnie*, a comedy double act on Welsh and English television in the early 1970s.

After that, Myfanwy appeared in many of the long-running Welsh television series of the 1970s and 1980s and in the latter half of the '80s she became a national institution in S4C's soap opera *Dinas* in which she played Cynthia Doyle, a characteristically salt-of-the earth Welsh woman.

Myfanwy was well established in the BBC Wales studios when she and David first met when David was on tour in a play in South

Wales in the mid-1970s. He was immediately smitten by Myfanwy's striking blue eyes, natural red hair, handsome appearance and sense of fun and thereafter she and David remained very close.

Myfanwy was credited by David's friends for the tasteful decoration which transformed the stylish country home set in an acre of land which the couple shared in Wendover, near Aylesbury. Friends felt she could have had a second career as an interior decorator and at home with David she was always a vivacious hostess. Although Myfanwy worked a lot in her native Wales and David's work commitments meant he was frequently away from home, they were as close to being married as it is possible to be without the certificate.

Certainly Myfanwy was a great favourite with David's mother, Olwen, who often referred to her as the 'daughter-in-law'. Olwen was especially pleased her youngest son had fallen for a Welsh girl and Olwen made it clear she would have been very happy if Myfanwy had become David's wife.

Olwen fretted about her younger son. 'He has everything in his career,' she said as *Darling Buds* took David to a new pinnacle of popularity. 'But I'm worried that will be all he has. He might end up missing out on the honey in life. He's always worked terribly hard, even now he doesn't need to. When he was younger he told me he wanted to concentrate on his career and didn't have time to settle down. Now he's gone to the top of his career, he still won't marry and have children. I'd be very happy if he'd settle down with Myfanwy but I've given up expecting him to do that. He won't hear about marrying.'

David and Myfanwy frequently visited his mother who, until her death, still lived in a humble council flat not far from the Lodge Lane home which was demolished to make room for a car park some 25 years ago.

David had suggested a home in the country for his mother in her twilight years but she was fiercely independent and preferred to stay near her old friends. As she got older, David said, 'I would like to help her more, but what can you do?'

Although Olwen could not understand why David did not marry, David was reluctant to change the status quo. He said, 'If you have been living with somebody and you suddenly get married, then statistically quite often that ends in disaster. Maybe the reason is that you are near to breaking up and you feel insecure and decide to get married and that brings it to a head.' David did not want to risk it.

David has been irritated by suggestions his unmarried status could indicate he is gay. 'Just because I'm not married doesn't mean I'm a woofter,' he said. 'Not that it has got anything to do with anyone else what I am in that department. I happen to prefer women but there are lots of people of all persuasions. I just don't think it's important, or anyone's else's business.

'There are so many showbiz people who are bent or lesbian or whatever, but what the hell does it matter? How does that affect anybody's ability to be a good actor?'

As a young actor, David once said in an interview that marriage was like, 'throwing yourself in the river when you only want a drink'.

But as his relationship with Myfanwy continued to blossom he said, 'That was a flip remark that has come back to haunt me. I really am not against marriage but I'm fine as I am. Call us constant companions. We are very happy with the way things are. We are both busy so we do not see that much of each other, but that suits us fine. This arrangement works for us. It's nice, it's refreshing. It means that when we get together we have got things to talk about. It is something to look forward to.'

As David was happy to declare publicly that Myfanwy was 'the great love of my life', there were certainly times when Myfanwy wished she was Mrs Jason. More than once she was heard to chide David over the breakfast table as she read descriptions of herself in the morning newspapers as 'David Jason's constant companion'. That press tag did no justice to the love, devotion and stability Myfanwy provided for David in his acting career.

David, for his part, gave Myfanwy unstinting support in 'the great fight' as Myfanwy called her battle against cancer which began when she discovered a lump in her breast while on holiday abroad in 1990. 'My initial thought was, This is the end,' she said.

Myfanwy was warned that a malignant growth, which she and David nicknamed 'the Alien', could mean her losing her breast. David insisted on being with her when she went into hospital for exploratory surgery. Myfanwy recalled, 'We told the surgeon, "We trust you utterly. Just do what you have to do."' The tumour was removed and her breast saved and three years later Myfanwy was back on stage and, she said, 'feeling fantastic'. But the disease was to take a fatal hold.

Throughout her brave five-year battle, Myfanwy worked alongside charities, talking about her illness and trying to remove some of the stigma surrounding it.

After undergoing surgery and radiotherapy, Myfanwy later spoke of her ordeal and how it had brought her even closer to David. 'We faced everything together right from when I first found out,' she said. 'It improved our relationship and it strengthened what we had between us.'

David frequently broke away from filming commitments to be with Myfanwy and hold her hand as she was wheeled in for treatment. 'David has been a tower of strength,' she said at a time when she thought her cancer was in remission. 'I cannot stress enough how important it is to have the support of loved ones. David made all the difference.'

On the occasions when she was not with David, Myfanwy had lived in a small cottage in the village of Taff Wells six miles north of Cardiff. But not long before Myfanwy became seriously ill for the last time, David bought the lovely old house near Chequers with its lake and its swimming pool not far from the house that had been his home for so long. A friend said, 'That house was bought for Myfanwy. David was devoted to her. I think in his way he felt guilty they never married. But nobody gets that close to David. They never have and as he gets older he becomes even more reluctant to open up to anyone. He loved Myfanwy as much as he's able to love anyone. But while some people were convinced he'd wed her when it became obvious how ill she was I knew he wouldn't. David is very, very single-minded. He is kind and considerate and funny and all the rest but nothing deflects him from where he wants to go. He and Myfanwy lived apart for much of their 18-year relationship. She had her life and career in Wales and he liked his own space to himself from time to time.'

Myfanwy adored their new home and, ill and weak as she was, gained much pleasure from watching David roll up his sleeves to tackle some of the renovations or busy himself in the garden.

The £500,000 house was set in several acres of land which, as David was soon to discover, backed on to the Prime Minister's official country residence. At the time, it was John Major. Tory-voting David was delighted.

When David first moved in he received the most unlikely of visits — the Special Branch came knocking on his door. It's difficult to say who was the more astonished — the Special Branch officers when the man they immediately recognised as Del-Boy opened the door, or David when he found top security men on his doorstep checking him out. They asked David to be vigilant and told him that, now that they knew of David's existence, they might be able to look after him, too!

The thought of Del-Boy being asked to keep an eye out for the Prime Minister was comical enough. But it was a supreme irony that Special Branch had delivered their request to a man who had once made millions of TV viewers laugh playing a hapless espionage agent in *The Top-Secret Life of Edgar Briggs*.

It was early in 1995 when David was filming new episodes of the detective series *A Touch of Frost* when Myfanwy's condition seriously deteriorated. Frequently, he drove the 200 miles from Yorkshire to be with her as the end drew near and he was at her bedside at the Florence Nightingale Hospice, Stoke Mandeville, when she died.

'It is with great sadness and with a heavy heart that I have to announce that after a five-year courageous, noble fight of so many battles against the dreadful disease of cancer, Myfanwy has finally lost the war,' David announced in a statement.

'I would like to thank everyone for all their kind concern and thoughts in this dreadfully sad moment in my life.'

David was devastated. He threw himself into his work and five weeks after Myfanwy's death he was back in front of the cameras filming new episodes of *A Touch of Frost*. 'Her death left a gap I had to fill,' he later explained. 'I did it by working. It was my salvation — but it was difficult. Some days I didn't want to go to work. But I had to. It helped concentrate the mind that I was really working 24 hours a day because when I wasn't filming I was learning lines.

'Those six months before Myfanwy's death and the three to four months afterwards were really painful.' Gradually, after Myfanwy's death the friendship between David and Myfanwy's aged father Glyn grew stronger as they reached out to each other and shared their grief. Myfanwy's father knew how happy David Jason had made his daughter and they spent the second anniversary of her death together. David and Myfanwy had tried to keep the seriousness of her condition from her family until towards the end.

That Christmas, David had to face up to the festivities without Myfanwy for the first time in 18 years and he turned to brother Arthur for comfort. Arthur and his family and sister June joined him at his home in Buckinghamshire.

Ten months on from the tragedy as a new series of *A Touch of Frost* hit the screen, David still could not bring himself to speak openly about Myfanwy's death and the disease that had struck her down. 'I find it hard to talk about it,' he confessed. 'Yet I know it would help if I was a bit more outgoing. It would help me and help the campaign against this dreadful disease.'

Although David and Myfanwy would have made loving parents, David does not regret his lack of children. 'Sometimes when you see your friends' kids, you think they're lovely, those kids. But I've got to be honest; I've never been a person who has craved for the company of my own children.'

Not that he can't be paternal. David rescued a stray mongrel dog he found in his garden one night. He and Myfanwy were enjoying dinner at home with friends and family when David's cousin went outside to fetch something from her car. Suddenly David and Myfanwy heard her screaming and they rushed outside to find her shouting that something in the darkness had licked her hand.

David grabbed a torch and soon spotted a frightened and injured labrador-sheepdog-cross bitch furiously scavenging for food in the garden. It was too scared to approach them and David dashed into the house for some warm milk and something to eat. In the morning the food had gone but the dog was still there. David got in touch with the owners who said they didn't want the dog back and so he and Myfanwy decided to keep her.

One of its back legs was badly injured and one day while David was working on *Only Fools and Horses* he received a telephone call from Myfanwy to say that the vet had advised that the leg had to be amputated or the dog would have to be put down. The poor animal could not walk for weeks after the operation and David carried her with him everywhere, gently cradling her in his arms. David had already christened the dog Peg so that seemed highly suitable and she became an integral member of the household. Friends or David's mum babysat the dog when both David and Myfanwy were away together and Peg managed to get around just fine with a single back leg.

★   ★   ★

The business of acting does not come easily. David is a perfectionist and if he can't quite capture a role it worries him enormously. He still remembers his only panto appearance, in Newcastle towards the end of the 1980s, when he felt he had not quite got his character right. He suffered terrible stomach cramps and the doctor told him it was colon trouble. But once the panto opened and the audience started laughing the pain went away. 'I felt I was not good enough for the audience,' said David.

He no longer stays in hotels when working away on location because he is such a light sleeper he found himself staying awake making sure everyone had come back in. 'Even if I went to bed at 10 o'clock at night I could not sleep because I was counting all the people. Knowing that 502 was not back. I could not get to sleep until he came in.

'Then someone would put the telly on or have a shower,' he said. 'Now I try to rent a house if I'm away from home.'

Many times David tried to persuade his mother to move into a luxury home near him but she preferred to stay near her friends and lived in Finchley until she died. David said, 'We are a very independent family, like a lot of families that lived through the war. My mother was defiant, a very proud lady, so it was difficult to do anything for her. She was wonderful, bless her cotton socks. She had a tremendous spirit. What can you do with someone who is independent and wants to be on their own? I could suggest whatever I like and she'd go, "No, I'm all right."'

David fiercely protects his private life. And he loves his exotic holidays where he can remain happily anonymous. Well, for most of the time that is true but when he and Myfanwy were thousands of miles from home on the Cayman Islands he thought he had completely escaped because the mainly American tourists had never clapped eyes on Del-Boy. 'But the fellow who ran the diving school was a Welshman. He recognised me right away. I told him, "Don't say anything," but he let it out to this American woman who I was. She was amazed I did the voice for Dangermouse.'

That was just enough to accord him the instant celebrity status he was struggling so desperately to avoid. 'They all went potty,' he recalls.

'I'd just been diving and they rushed up demanding my autograph. I could have throttled the woman. There I was, thousands of miles from home, thinking I was totally incognito and I suddenly become famous for being a cartoon!'

It's a long way from Lodge Lane, Finchley, to the Cayman Islands and it's a journey that David Jason's single-minded determination to make it as an actor has helped him to make.

But he never forgets his humble origins. He recalls once seeing a pineapple in a greengrocer's priced at a time when pineapples were a real luxury at thirteen shillings and six pence. 'I wondered who could possibly spend that amount of money on a single fruit. It was more than my mother paid in rent on our little terraced house.'

Now he could afford to fill his conservatory with pineapples. David, in fact, lives sensibly and simply and never flaunts his hard-earned wealth. 'I am not an extravagant man,' he said. 'I'm not for the boat in the marina and the helicopter in the Home Counties.'

He is well aware that an actor with his popular appeal in America would be a multi-millionaire and he is also a victim of his own remarkable ability to make the difficult business of acting look desperately easy.

David said, 'People say to me, "Woor, it must be wonderful, I wouldn't mind your job. It must be great to be famous."

'You would be surprised at the number of people who sit around watching a piece of filming, watching me do something, and when we go for another take they say, "You're not going to do it again, are you?"

'Then after they have been there for two or three hours they will say, "Isn't this boring? It would drive me up the wall." And they have only been there for three hours. Then you realise they are the sort of people who couldn't handle it anyway. They want what they think they want, which is the "fame" if you like. And that is supposed to be pleasant but, in fact, is very hard to handle.

'They want a lot of money, and to swan around in swimming pools like Larry Hagman and have 10,000 acres in Beverly Hills and a Rolls-Royce and all that. I'm sorry, but that happens in America. It does not happen here.

'They also have the idea that once you have that "fame" that it is a panacea, a sort of magic fairy that has come and all your troubles will be solved. They think being famous must be like being in heaven, that you are like a god walking on clouds with nobody touching you because you have money and you have fame and everybody bows and it is wonderful. But it ain't like that.

'It is very difficult to say to people that what you put in right at the very beginning — in anything, not just in acting — affects your reward at the end. Reap as ye shall sow, I suppose.

'I did not go into the theatre thinking one day I want to be rich and famous. I knew 99.9 per cent of the people who want to be actors never even make a decent living at it. The people who go in really believing in themselves, and really wanting to do it, perhaps a small percentage of them make it and turn that corner into being successful.

'I became an actor, because I wanted my work to be recognised, not because I wanted to be famous. I know I have a high profile and I am delighted to do good work that is popular but I don't enjoy the endless recognition.'

David believes that the best comedy actors do not get the recognition and the critical acclaim that their dramatic counterparts inspire. He said, 'Nicholas Lyndhurst once showed me something written in a newspaper. Some Page Three girl had said, "I want to get into acting. I want to start off in comedy and then get into real acting." That's the sort of attitude that gets quite a long way up my nose.'

David worries about his business more than most actors. He is frustrated that his awards and his colossal comedy success have not brought film offers. 'If I were in America, in my situation I think I would have had real film chances, like Danny de Vito from *Taxi* or Alan Alda from *M*A*S*H*. If you're a success in TV over there, they make movies with you and finally you become an international movie star. Who have we got? Bob Hoskins had to fight his bollocks off to get a film that he really believed in, *The Long Good Friday*, and that gave him status but why do we have to go to America to become international stars? We should be able to do it ourselves.' But the fame side of the success he could cheerfully live without.

'People say to me, "Go on, you love it, really." Well, no, I don't. When I was struggling, it was a different ball game, because it was all part of the aggression of wanting to succeed. I couldn't get my face in the paper if I killed someone in those days. Now I still find it hard to come to terms with the people who find my life interesting.

'Ronnie Barker is the man in my business who has inspired most of my respect. I understood and agreed with the way he got out of the business. He did not want to dribble on for ever and neither do I. I haven't reached it yet but I will know when the time to go has come.'

There are moments, David concedes, when he really does seriously wonder what his life has come to. These questioning moments usually occur when he is filming at night, usually in some deep discomfort due to the elements.

One such moment occurred during the making of *The Bullion Boys*, a one-off film David made when he returned briefly to the BBC after his *Darling Buds of May* triumph.

'There I was making *The Bullion Boys*,' he recalled, 'standing in the rain, drenched to the skin, freezing cold, at four in the morning on a January night in Liverpool. That's when I questioned what I was doing with my life. I bet they don't do this to Tom Cruise, I told myself. All he seems to do is put his tongue down Nicole Kidman's throat or fly around in an aeroplane.'

The Bullion Boys was a film based on a true story about a bunch of Liverpool dockers who seize a golden chance to get rich. The film was set in 1940 at a time when the German armies are on the march and England is under threat of invasion. To safeguard the country's gold reserves, a top-secret plan is drawn up to move the priceless cargo from the Bank of England to a bank in Liverpool. Only a handful of policemen, a group of senior bank officials and a gang of dockers have been told about the bullion transfer. But it gives dockers leader Billy Mac, played by David Jason, a chance to hatch an ingenious plan to 'sample' the cargo.

His scheme involves a clever 'interruption' to the conveyor belt rolling the bars of gold to the Liverpool vaults which allows the dockers to replace the genuine gold bars with fake replicas.

The role was picked out by David's agent from the dozens of scripts which regularly arrive on her desk for him. She insisted that he read it and David was instantly hooked by the story. 'It was such a good yarn,' he said. 'That's what attracted me to it. It was a good once-upon-a-time *Boy's Own* adventure story. What also attracted me to *The Bullion Boys* was the brains of Billy Mac in working out an ingenious way to get the gold right from under the noses of the guards. It was nothing short of sheer genius.

'I also felt that this kind of film had been missing for a while. When I was a lad I'd spent so much time in the cinema I'd seen all those old British "B" movies that this country used to do so very well and I felt *The Bullion Boys* had all the values to be an entertaining film in the old-fashioned sense.'

Much as he loved the script and the whole tone and ingenuity of the story, David could see no way he could take the role of Billy Mac. He was simply too busy with the final episodes of *Darling Buds of May*, a first series of *A Touch of Frost* and an *Only Fools and Horses* Christmas Special.

'I reluctantly told the BBC it was impossible,' he said. 'I said I'd love to do it but I just couldn't fit it in. But I also told them I knew how annoyed I'd be when I eventually saw *The Bullion Boys* with someone else starring in it knowing it could have been me. That's when they came back and said that if I was that interested in playing Billy Mac, would I be prepared to film it the following year? When I said "Yes" they said they would be prepared to wait for me — which was wonderful.' *The Bullion Boys* was duly postponed for a year to accommodate him.

David had plenty of time to think about the role and one challenge he was patently going to have to face was producing a convincing Liverpool accent. He had never played a Liverpudlian before and he went so far as to ask the director whether it was essential for Billy Mac to be a Liverpudlian hoping the answer would not be in the affirmative.

'I asked if it was necessary for Billy to be a Scouser and he replied it was,' said David. 'So I asked once again if he'd really prefer him to be Scouse and he said "Yes". He wasn't getting my signals at all and so I knew that it was going to be a toughie to get the accent right. I knew I simply had to learn to speak Scouse.

'It's a very difficult accent to do and I didn't suppose for a minute that I was going to be able to fool real Scousers but I wanted to get my accent near enough. It was important to me that Billy should sound from that area.'

To that end, David sought out London voice coach Jo Washington who besides giving him a few lessons also furnished him with audio tapes, pages of notes, and instructions on sounds for him to reproduce to help him towards a Liverpool accent. With typical dedication, David took them all with him when he managed to snatch some precious time away with Myfanwy in Miami before filming of *The Bullion Boys* began.

He spent much of the Florida holiday uttering Scouse encouraged by Myfanwy. Coming from north Wales, Myfanwy was familiar with the Liverpool accent. She had encountered it many times while living on the north coast of Wales where it's possible to look across to Liverpool.

It was while he was in Miami with Myfanwy that the news became official that David had been awarded the OBE.

He had, of course, been notified of the honour long before but he had obeyed to the letter the instruction to keep it a secret. He had not told a soul, not even his mother or Myfanwy.

On the day he knew the announcement would be made to the media back in England, David had arranged for himself and Myfanwy to have a convivial lunch with friends. Naturally, he was itching to share his joy with Myfanwy and he devised a neat way of finally letting her in on his secret. Excusing himself from the lunch table, he put in a telephone call to his secretary back in London who excitedly offered her congratulations and confirmed that his OBE was now headline news.

'I came back to the table,' he recalled, 'and I decided that what I would do was write down my address to give to Myfanwy to pass on to our friends at the table. I duly wrote it down on a piece of paper, gave it to Myfanwy and, as she glanced at it, I took it back from her and said, "Hang on, there's something missing." She looked at what I'd written and asked what. That's when I wrote the initials "OBE" after my name and handed it back to her. She did a double-take. She was absolutely stunned.'

When the penny dropped, Myfanwy flung her arms round a beaming David and she whooped for joy. Their lunch guests sprang to their feet and joined in with back-slaps and handshakes. The waiter was quickly summoned to bring champagne.

'After all the euphoria and the champagne had been consumed, I got up from the table to phone my mum,' said David. 'I was very excited when I called her up and asked her if she'd heard the news.

And can you believe what she said? She said, "Yes I have. I suppose it'll cost money now for me to speak to you. What I want to know is when are you coming round to mend my cooker?" I was phoning her from the other side of the world about my OBE and all mum wanted to know was when I was going to fix her cooker! Actually, it was wonderful because it brought me straight back down to earth.'

Miami had become something of a favourite resort for David and Myfanwy after he had flown there to film a feature-length Christmas Special for *Only Fools and Horses* called *Miami Twice* in which he played two roles — Del and a Mafia boss.

In Florida for *Miami Twice*, David had been given the star treatment and had been chauffeured around in a huge limousine. With press photographers desperate for pictures of Peckham's favourite son filming abroad, Myfanwy, who had accompanied him, travelled some distance behind in an Espace so she and David were not photographed together.

If David had been brought down to earth by his mum asking for her cooker to be mended, back in England filming *The Bullion Boys* brought David down to earth with even more of a bump.

Rarely offscreen, David was sometimes working 16 hours a day. It was a gruelling schedule. 'The glamour of films doesn't really exist any more,' said David after completing the scene in which he found himself soaked and cold at 4.00am. 'They're trying to make films in a shorter time and extend the working day.'

As Billy Mac, the moustache he had grown for *A Touch of Frost* was shaved off and his hair dyed black under the cap he wore for much of the film. 'I had to keep on colouring it,' said David, 'and, of course, there were times when it was neither fish nor fowl and I'd go into a restaurant and hear people saying, "Look! Doesn't he dye his hair badly." I felt like putting a notice round my neck saying, "I'm sorry my hair's like this. I'm growing it out for my next character. It's part of my job."'

At least he had the satisfaction of ultimately knowing it was all worthwhile. *The Bullion Boys* attracted an audience of 14 million and a good reaction from the critics.

The closing scenes of *The Bullion Boys* called for David to play Billy as an 85-year-old grandfather. The make-up department transformed him into a frail figure with wisps of white hair. He was just as convincing an octogenarian as the old men Dithers and Blanco he had played on TV years before. 'But this time it was murder sitting in a make-up chair at five in the morning for four hours and being able to drink just through a straw,' said David. 'I didn't like seeing myself in the mirror aged 85. It made me think I'd not long to go now ...'

David Jason has always enjoyed a good working relationship with Yorkshire Television. He got on well straight away with David Reynolds who directed him in *A Bit of a Do*. When they met for the very first time for lunch at Reynolds' home, the two men hit it off instantly. Reynolds had an old mongrel which David took an immediate liking to during a pre-lunch stroll in the garden.

On their walk, David noticed that an area of the garden was sopping wet and Reynolds was embarrassed to explain a drain was blocked and he was getting someone round to fix it. 'Don't worry about that,' said David and promptly took off his jacket, rolled up his sleeves, got down on his hands and knees and quickly cleared it. Reynolds was extremely grateful though somewhat taken aback. He and Yorkshire Television were hoping to conclude a multi-million-pound deal to create a brand-new series and here was his potential star on his hands and knees with his arm up a drainpipe. But, in the end, he signed the deal for hundreds of thousands of pounds and fixed the drains for free.

Reynolds and, indeed, the crews David worked with at Yorkshire TV found him to be wonderfully professional in his work, an actor who talked not just to the bosses but everyone on the team to make sure everybody was happy.

They discovered that he made no ridiculous demands and for their part Yorkshire TV paid him handsomely, provided him with a cottage and a car and generally looked after him very well.

It was during his run of successes with Yorkshire TV that the ITV company offered David an exclusive deal to leave the BBC to come and work solely for Yorkshire. The offer would have made David an instant millionaire but Yorkshire felt they could justify such a fortune because of the output they were getting from him.

David turned it down, largely because he did not want to be tied down and also because of loyalty to John Sullivan who still had more episodes of *Only Fools and Horses* up his sleeve. As it transpired, he chose to stay with Yorkshire because of the quality of scripts and directors for his next project *A Touch of Frost*. Even so, David was unprepared for events which led to his taking on the role of detective Jack Frost based on the best-selling novels by RD Wingfield.

'Basically, it was a touch of me being head-hunted,' David later recalled with undisguised satisfaction. 'Yorkshire TV took me out to lunch while I was working on *Darling Buds* and said, "What would you like to do? How do you see your future progressing?" I was amazed. My knife and fork dropped on to the plate and I nearly choked on the decent wine they had bought.

'It took me completely by surprise. It was the first time

anything like that had ever happened to me. Although it's probably quite normal in America, it's not normal in this country to ask an actor what he wants to do. Usually the project comes first and then the actor is offered it. But here *they* were asking *me* what I wanted to do.

'Throughout the lunch, we talked about various ideas and I explained I'd always liked detective series. I watch the *Starsky and Hutch* and *Cagney and Lacey*-type of series but for me they have never been as interesting as *Inspector Morse*, the *Wexford* series, and *Taggart* and *Columbo*. I like the sort of detective who unravels the mystery, not the ones who go around blowing people away.

'During the lunch I said I felt there was an area which British TV had been missing out on — a copper who was a bit off-the-wall, a bit odd, a down-to-earth detective who had more than one job to do, perhaps three or four like most coppers do. I felt there was room for a detective who has to deal with the cut-and-thrust of life and the dross and the terrible things that happen, a man who is overworked but has a sense of humour, a man who has a sense of sympathy for the victims for a change and isn't just out to beat up the crook. So Yorkshire TV said, "Right, leave it to us."

'*Frost* was just one of three books Yorkshire came up with and as soon as I'd read it I said, "That's the one. Get me *Frost!*" I knew it would be a tremendous challenge but one of the reasons I wanted the challenge of taking on a major dramatic role like Frost was that it had never been offered to me before. *Porterhouse Blue* had done a great deal for me but after that I was never offered those parts again. Basically I went back into the comedy box and once you are in the comedy box it's very difficult to be taken seriously. When I read the first *Frost* script I thought, Bloody hell, this is good.'

Only a handful of top British actors are considered certainties when it comes to delivering big ITV audiences consistently. Most drama chiefs would place John Thaw, Dennis Waterman, George Cole, James Bolam and Sean Bean in this category. Given a script of quality, sound production values and an able and accomplished director, these stars are reckoned to be bankers that guarantee solid audiences.

Now, due to the remarkable ratings success of *A Touch of Frost*, David Jason is the most bankable of them all. He tops the lot. Since *Open All Hours*, Jason's name has only ever been associated with success, while even the much-acclaimed John Thaw has the blot of *A Year in Provence* on his CV.

But when David signed to play Detective Inspector Jack Frost in a brand-new police drama series for Yorkshire TV, it still represented something of a risk. His acting credentials were deeply rooted in comedy but, ironically, it was a scene from an episode of *Only Fools and Horses* which convinced everyone at Yorkshire TV of David's capabilities as a serious actor.

It was the scene at the hospital when Raquel is giving birth to Del's baby. One moment he prompts a big laugh by grabbing Raquel's oxygen mask to gulp in a huge lungful of air for himself before rushing out of the delivery room to tell Rodney and Uncle Albert, 'It's a baby!' — having completely forgotten to discover whether it is a boy or a girl.

Next, he stands by a window cradling his son in his arms and movingly talks to the sleeping infant and promises him a secure future. 'It was exciting to see such a great comedy actor as David become a great tragedian,' Vernon Lawrence observed. 'When you look at him in something like that birth scene in *Only Fools and Horses*, he makes you cry. Such talent is amazing.'

A Touch of Frost producer Don Leaver was of the same opinion. 'When we first started, we knew David as a serious actor from *Porterhouse Blue*,' he said. 'And although it was comedy, the sequences where Raquel was having her baby in *Only Fools and Horses* really showed his range. We knew he had a lot to bring to the role of Frost.'

As Yorkshire TV supremo, Vernon's instinct was that David would comfortably manage the sharp change in direction which the role of Frost clearly required.

In the first episodes, Frost would be a detective investigating such crimes as multiple murders, violent armed robbery and the poisoning of a football star — a stark contrast with Del-Boy's petty schemes and scams and Pop Larkin's golden-hearted, what's-mine-is-yours way of life.

Vernon felt sure Jason's huge following would warm to him. The dark nature of the crimes Frost was set to investigate would be offset by viewers seeing David playing Frost as an unperturbable cop who was still a caring, compassionate man who retained his humour and his humility after years of seeing the worst of human nature. Vernon's gut reaction and intuition told him David's fans would empathise with him as Frost and the show would be a success.

'I knew how good David was,' he explained. 'I was confident of David, I knew the story was good but what I wasn't confident of was whether we would take David's entire audience with us. That's what concerned me.'

To banish those doubts, Yorkshire TV decided to commission a survey to discover the public's likely reaction. The survey quizzed 3,000 people after the following introduction, '*A Touch of Frost* is a new thriller series featuring David Jason as never seen before, starring as a hard-nosed detective faced with the roughest backstreet crimes. Jack Frost is an intuitive Detective Inspector yet he is by no means a model policeman. Rash, sloppy and disorganised, he has a healthy disregard for the rules but always cracks the case despite unorthodox methods.'

The survey posed a number of questions about the popularity of detective series in general, the *Frost* books in particular, and the public's perception and appreciation of Jason as an actor. Happily for Yorkshire, the results proved to be highly encouraging.

Only 2 per cent polled said they would not watch *A Touch of Frost*. Of those who said they would watch, 58 per cent said their main reason for tuning in would be David Jason and 38 per cent said it would be because they enjoyed whodunnits. Even Yorkshire TV's proposed Sunday night slot for *A Touch of Frost* met with firm approval.

The fact that Frost would not have a regular woman in his life — Frost's wife was to die of cancer in the opening episode — also won plenty of backing. Asked if it was important that David Jason's character had a girlfriend or a wife, a total of 84 per cent said no.

The survey held only one cautionary note for Yorkshire TV. A total of 78 per cent stated they most associated David with comedy roles and only three per cent with serious roles.

Intensive research and analysis before the launch of a major TV series is common practice in American television. But it was only the second time Yorkshire TV had ever used such a survey to back up its programme plans.

'It's something that all self-opinionated TV producers and directors naturally go against,' said Vernon. 'In our arrogant way — and you have to be to do the job in the first place — we all think our gut reaction and intuition tells us what the public wants. But because of the incredible costs of programme-making, we are forced into making sure we are going along the right lines.

'By and large, an awful lot of what we had felt all along about the project was vindicated by the research. The only thing we did from the findings was to shorten part one of the first episode by five minutes and put it into part two. Some felt it was a bit long and concentration started to flag.'

As the opening two-hour film was to cost £3 million with a further three shows costing another £3 million, the £10,000 spent on the research seemed a trifling sum to pay.

Fortified by such favourable statistics, Yorkshire TV felt more confident than ever that they were on to a winner with Jason and *A Touch of Frost*. But as the launch date approached, Yorkshire mounted an expensive, carefully targeted advertising campaign in the press.

Vernon explained, 'We had two sets of people we thought would watch the show — the Jason addicts and the people who love programmes like *Inspector Morse* and *Taggart*. We were therefore trying to attract people who weren't Jason addicts and others who might not watch the show because it's not a genre they love.

'Our biggest problem was to convert the audience into accepting David in something they had never seen him in before, playing a detective in an opening episode in which his wife dies of cancer, where there are murders, and a prostitute's daughter is abducted.'

Naturally, David himself was as anxious as anybody to find out whether the public would warm to him as a detective. 'Taking on *Frost* in the first place was quite frightening for me,' he confided. 'The challenge was to convince people of my worth as a serious actor. It would have been very easy to do just comedy and avoid the risk of projects like *Frost*. But then what would have happened if I'd stayed where I was and the audience had tired of comedy from me?'

He was genuinely and openly relieved when early previews of *Frost* indicated he had little to fear. After the first two-hour film had been shown to a private audience he was jubilant. 'Some people said they thought I could never do this sort of thing,' he said. 'But those who have seen *Frost* confessed that they forgot about me after the first few minutes and they got drawn into the story.'

That two-hour opening film of *A Touch of Frost* was screened on 6 December 1992 and pulled in the incredible audience of nearly 18 million, an audience share of 73 per cent of people watching TV at the time. It was way beyond Yorkshire TV's expectations and the first series reached an average audience of 16 million.

David was overjoyed and had only one tiny quibble. 'We haven't been quite as faithful to the book as I would have liked,' he said. 'Frost is painted a bit darker in the books. He's much more anti-Establishment. But what works in literary terms does not necessarily work on TV, unfortunately.

'I've had one or two criticisms but then life wouldn't be any fun if we were all the same, would it? What's nice is that a lot of people have appreciated the efforts that went into the change of image.

'Sometimes the police are painted badly on television and I hope *Frost* redresses the balance the other way to a degree. He's a rather old-fashioned policeman, a policeman like we want them all to be. He's honest, he cares, he has no time for the criminal but believes the victim should be cared for. I enjoy playing Frost, not least because he's got a lovely sense of humour and that's fun to get across. You'd imagine with his lonely personal life he'd be a bit depressing. But not a bit. There are lots of facets to him. I admire him because he's opinionated and because he's totally dedicated which is one of the reasons he's lonely at times.'

The role of Frost proved a physical challenge for David quite apart from asking him to achieve a major change of direction. While filming the final episodes of *The Darling Buds of May*, he had piled on the pounds. For a small man, he was now considerably bulky and he knew it.

'I realised that wouldn't look right for Frost,' he said. 'Frost would look lean and hungry. On my TV set at home I had a picture of myself in my dinner jacket at an awards ceremony and I remember putting on the same dinner jacket after not wearing it for a year and thinking I'd better have a button moved. When I later saw photos of myself, I realised it wasn't the button's fault. I was like the Michelin man. I was huge.

'During the filming of *The Darling Buds of May* I was eating 24 hours a day. The problem was that the food on the set was real and one morning we were filming two different episodes. Spread over the two shows were five scenes which all took place at breakfast which I had to eat with great gusto. So that morning I had no less than five breakfasts.

'It finally got to the point where I felt I couldn't take bacon and eggs any more and I asked for fish instead. I had to tuck into a huge cod and for different camera angles I had to eat it several times. In the afternoon, for tea we had huge slices of bread, ham and cheese even though we weren't hungry. I just went up like a balloon.

'For *Frost*, I knew I had to put myself on a strict, mainly fish diet. I cut out biscuits and toast and anything in between meals and when I was hungry I'd just eat a couple of apples or an orange instead of tucking into a sandwich. Because I'm naturally a slim and not overweight man, it fell away quite quickly. I lost a stone-and-a-quarter on this strict diet and although it was hard I'm glad I did it.'

David also chose to set a personal example about cigarette smoking in *A Touch of Frost*. 'Frost is a chain-smoker in the books and that was very much part of his character,' he says. 'But I felt we should be socially aware and mindful that a lot of people were trying to give it up. So I told Yorkshire TV I wasn't going to chain-smoke on screen. For a start, I'd fall over dead — although I do smoke a bit, maybe a few cigarettes in the evening but none during the day. What I asked was: do we need this socially? It's not a good idea any more to smoke. So we hit on the idea of making Frost a smoker who is giving up the habit. That way, the idea was there all the time but I didn't actually chain-smoke.

'I had to smoke a couple of cigarettes but mainly I was lighting up and being told to stub it out. I feel I must set an example. It's the same with swearing on TV. I always ask: do we need it? I want more people to watch me. Not less. That means families watching and I believe you can be real on TV without resorting to language of the gutter. I don't like going past a bus stop and hearing loads of kids aged seven or eight effing and blinding.

'When I was a kid, I used to get a whack if I said the word "bloody". And if we were standing at a bus stop being a bit rowdy we'd get a clip round the ear from a man who'd say, "Cut that out, there's ladies present." We might have pulled a face behind the man's back but we certainly shut up.

'So if I don't like swearing, why should I encourage people to do it? I feel the question as far as TV goes should be: "Can we avoid it? Do we need it?" People may say, "Ah yes, but people swear in real life." Yes they do. But do you like it?'

Eschewing the sex and violence which has often been so

fashionable in TV cop shows, *A Touch of Frost* captured that crucial audience of both men and women and prospered beyond everyone's hopes at Yorkshire TV.

But after the remarkable ratings for the three 1996 Christmas episodes of *Only Fools and Horses* when Del and Rodney did finally become millionaires, Yorkshire Television executives could be forgiven for some anxiety as they prepared to launch their final series of *A Touch of Frost* just six weeks later. Would David's triumphant return as Del-Boy over Christmas have harmed the public's perception of him as Jack Frost, they wondered. After all, a staggering 23.4 million viewers had watched the final episode with the first two of the three pulling in over 22 million each. These were the sort of figures that had not been seen since the early 1970s in the days when there were only three television channels. Once again the image of David Jason as Del-Boy had been stamped firmly in the nation's mind.

But if producer Martyn Auty had any real fears for his new batch of four two-hour dramas, they were quickly dispelled when the first episode *Penny for the Guy* was screened on ITV on 9 February 1997. It was a strong storyline centred on a major case of kidnapping following the discovery of the body of a young boy dumped in a shop doorway. Frost knows he is dealing with a cool customer capable of amputating a child's little finger. But he comes close to losing his own cool when he realises he's got his man but doesn't have a scrap of evidence.

Once again, David and *Frost* delivered. An audience of 16 million viewers tuned in, a staggeringly high rating considering the alternative BBC attraction ranged against *Frost* was the popular drama *Ballykissangel*. David's return to the *Frost* beat thus decimated the BBC's traditional dominance of the Sunday night ratings and that set the tone for another compelling series in which Frost investigated child abuse, juvenile murder and kidnapping, armed robbery and an apparent suicide.

The new series featured two adaptations from the original *Frost* book. Both were written by Malcolm Bradbury whose writing connections with David dated back to *Porterhouse Blue*. 'Although Malcolm hadn't done much detective drama, he took to the genre like a duck to water,' said Auty. 'And his name helped us attract top directors.'

For his part, Malcom Bradbury appreciated the challenge. 'I enjoyed adapting the two episodes because Frost is a very strong character,' he said. 'I have favourites like Agatha Christie, Edgar Wallace and Reginald Hill who created *Dalziel and Pascoe*. The best always have that well-defined central character, so you are writing about an individual who is also a policeman. So for that reason you can put Frost in the same league as Inspector Morse.'

For devotees of *A Touch of Frost*, there were several changes to savour. A little more was revealed of Frost the man as he became involved with three women, although not at the same time.

Previously, viewers had witnessed Frost living over an Indian restaurant after his house had burned down. Now viewers saw him staying with — indeed, in bed with — ex-good-time girl Kitty (Gwyneth Powell) before moving on to another woman.

The four episodes also saw Frost working out of a new police station. Yorkshire TV already had the building but designed a new set from scratch to reflect the modern look. Despite a new canteen, however, Frost was still seen munching on his fast food snacks, especially his old favourites, bacon sandwiches. Frost was also given a computer — but mistook it for a microwave and left a pork pie on top of it.

As in previous series, Frost also found himself working with new colleagues and had to deal with his prickly relationship with DS Liz Maud, played by Susannah Doyle. Two faces new to *Frost* — but not to David — included Gwyneth Strong and Arthur White, David's brother. Gwyneth had, of course, played Rodney's wife Cassandra in *Only Fools and Horses* and now she was cast as a high-flying plain clothes officer DS Bailey who gave Frost an uncomfortable interrogation. 'I enjoyed that scene immensely,' Gwyneth enthused. 'After so many years as Cassandra, it felt like I had the power on my side for a change.'

David was pleased to say that he felt the new series achieved the high quality viewers had come to expect. 'It's difficult to be inventive and meet those standards we have set ourselves,' he said. 'We avoid being predictable by being a little more off-the-wall in the cases Frost has to investigate.'

In one important scene, David had to be filmed wading into a river in the middle of winter. 'It's one of the perks of the job,' he joked. But there were other moments to treasure. 'We had a massive demolition "caterpillar" truck on location to film a house being knocked down and I got to drive it between shooting. It was really fantastic but knocking down a brick wall is not as easy as you might think.

'Then I went up in a helicopter when we were filming at the end of the pier at Blackpool. Some guys running joyrides offered to take me up for a spin. I told the director and producer and they went white.

'Earlier in the year, I'd managed to fly a Harrier jump-jet. They reach speeds of 500 knots and it was a totally exhilarating experience. It was the ultimate ride.'

David and his brother Arthur shared some excellent comic scenes in the last series of *A Touch of Frost*. Arthur played quirky collator Ernie Trigg, the copper in charge of the station files and the source of endless meticulously ordered information who became one of Jack Frost's closer confidants. The brothers worked wonderfully well together and it gave Arthur the chance to move, for a moment, out of the shadow of his more famous younger brother.

Arthur said, 'In the early days people would say to Dave, "Aren't you Arthur White's brother?" Now it's the other way round, of course."

Although the brothers shared a bedroom as youngsters they were not close as teenagers. Arthur is very cautious about talking publicly about his relationship with his brother but he did try to describe his feelings. 'Being an elder brother by seven years makes one hell of a difference. For example, when David was still at

school I was preparing to go in the Army to do my National
Service. By the time I came back, he had changed and so had I. So
our early beginnings of getting to know each other as brothers
were interrupted and never quite matured until later. I remember
the days of the Blitz and parts of people's bodies landing on our
roof. David and I used to share a crystal set.

'I remember when I had become an actor, my wife Joy and I
had a party and David, still an electrician, was invited and said to
Joy, "They are bloody theatricals, no one wants to talk to me."
And apart from us, no one did, except my old friend Edna Dore
who spoke at great length to him. She was a great help in
changing his mind about "bloody theatricals". Gawd bless her, we
still say.

'We share a mutual respect of each other's work, and a
brotherly bond of love. I introduced him into the theatre, getting
him his first job. And my first advice as he finished work was —
"No, I'm not introducing you into the world of TV," as at the time
I was co-starring in *Crane, Orlando, A Place to Hide*, and so on. I
said to him, "Go out into Rep and learn like I had to." He did!
And the rest, as they say ...

'We have worked a lot together in the early days of his TV
work. In fact, we did a commercial together where I played a
ventriloquist and David played my dummy. It came from larking
about down the Green Room Actor's Club I had introduced him
into. I shoved my hand up his jacket after someone had said,
"Who's working him?" Our natural inborn sense of comedy and
timing and David's ability to become a vent doll had them in
stitches. We even went around some clubs hoping we would make
a good sideline living with act.

'I have very fond memories of our days when we were out of
work, spent taking my wife's Mini to bits and putting it back
together, jugs of cheap wine afterwards with Joy's superb dinners.
We'd have theatre chat around the table, and play games of
Monopoly. We watched the first moonwalk with my son Russell.
David got him up to see history even though he was only one year

old. I am vastly proud of his achievements.'

On 2 March 1997, ITV screened the emotional finale to *A Touch of Frost*. David had millions of viewers dewy-eyed as he shed genuine tears on screen as Frost grieved over the death of a woman friend. The scene was all the more moving because the nation knew he was drawing on the harrowing personal experience of watching his beloved Myfanwy Talog's own decline towards death. 'It was an incredibly difficult scene to do,' said David, 'the hardest I've ever done.'

7

The Dynamic Duo

No one could ever accuse TV's dream team pairing of David Jason and Nicholas Lyndhurst of being out of their depth or having their heads in the clouds. But that's precisely where the two stars often longed to be after a gruelling day's filming.

Away from the screen, both David and Nicholas are action men who share a passion for flying and for the sea.

Nicholas grew up on the coast in Sussex and was always in the water. He could swim by the time he was three and he remembers quite clearly that as a little lad his idol was always a character called Fishboy, a brilliant underwater hero who featured in a comic called *Buster*. Nicholas wanted to be Fishboy and every day he'd be on the beach either swimming, scuba diving, fishing or just messing about in boats. As he grew up, he also learned to surf, riding the waves on an old piece of plywood until he was able to afford the proper equipment.

'I'm a complete water nut and surf all the year round,' he says.

'There's nothing better than a couple of hours surfing, being carried along on waves that are 3ft, 4ft, 6ft high.'

Nicholas is also a sailing enthusiast and when he escapes the television cameras he's been known to head straight off for deep waters in a friend's catamaran. 'When the sun's shining and the water's lapping all around you, there's no better place on earth,' he says.

But all the sailing, surfing and swimming caused problems for Nicholas on *Only Fools and Horses* because Rodney wasn't supposed to have a tan. 'Rodney was supposed to be pale, puny and pasty-faced,' he says, 'and if I did catch the sun I had to tone down my tan with whitener.'

For someone so comfortable in and around water, it was inevitable that Nicholas would also, like David Jason, eventually want to venture deep under the waves. So deep-sea diving was added to Nicholas's list of water sports. 'We actually worked together for about five years before David and I realised we both dived,' he says. 'We were hoping to dive together when we were filming *Only Fools and Horses* in Miami but we ran out of time.'

Like David, Nicholas has had the odd anxious moment while diving, notably the day he found himself caught up in a fishing net. 'As I struggled, my tank got caught and I was trussed,' he recalls. 'But before I got too panicky my mate Brian cut me free. It could have been fatal had he not been there.'

Apart from his passion for the sea when he was a little boy, Nicholas also adored model aircraft and was totally fascinated by anything that flew. Some of the happiest hours of his early life were spent throwing Frisbees or flying model gliders in the field behind his home in Sussex.

He says, 'As a young boy, I was always dreaming about flying, about anything that flew — I wanted anything that defied gravity and carried that through to adulthood.'

His passion for flying became irresistible once his mother Liz had paid for a trial flying lesson as a surprise present for his 16th birthday. He found it so exhilarating that he knew at once that he just had to qualify as a pilot one day. In his last year at drama school, Nicholas took a part-time job working in a chemist's at the weekend for £4.80 and his thoughts seriously turned towards making a career for himself in the RAF.

All the while he was a drama student, he simply could not scrape together the money for regular flying lessons. But by 1986, the success of *Only Fools and Horses* meant he could afford to take flying lessons at Goodwood not far from his home in Sussex.

Nicholas's first solo flight was on 16 October 1986 in a PA38 Tomahawk and it came at the end of 12 hours of dual instruction and after he had spent the morning practising what are termed 'touch and goes' — circling the airfield, coming down to land then opening the throttle and going round again. After two hours of this he had taxied back when his instructor got out of the plane telling him with a grin, 'You'll probably find it lighter without my weight.' Nicholas was on his own.

'There wasn't time to get nervous,' he remembers, 'but I was so timid that when I asked air-traffic control for permission to taxi I must have sounded like an eight-year-old girl!' Happily, Nicholas soon took a grip of his nerves, moved into position, accelerated up to 55 knots and took off on what for him was an unforgettable flight.

Equally memorable was the first time he landed a plane by himself. 'It was terrifying!' he said. 'We were about 3,000ft up and the instructor said, "I want you to pick out a field and pretend you are going to land." I started to descend and went through the pre-landing check. We did this several times then headed for base.

'When we were near the aerodrome, the instructor said, "Go through the pre-landing drill again." I did and then waited for him to take control but he didn't and we were getting lower and lower. The ground was zooming nearer and nearer. I kept looking across at him but he just sat there with his arms folded grinning at me. Then he said, "You've come this far, you might as well take her in." As soon as we were down my arm turned to jelly. But it was a wonderful moment.'

Since his first flight, Nicholas has flown solo hundreds of times over the south of England and achieved his long-held ambition of qualifying as a pilot in 1989. That was a sweet moment for him because there was a time when he wondered whether he really had what it takes to qualify, having to pass seven exams and read volumes of material. But his dedication paid off.

Through the years, flying has been an endless source of pleasure for Nicholas. 'It's an indescribable feeling to be up in the air surrounded by clouds and to look down and see the miniature towns and countryside below,' Nicholas explains. 'I love the feeling of power, of being in control of an aircraft. It's a little like surfing and trying to master the waves; a sort of battle — man against Nature's forces.'

One of Nicholas's most enjoyable roles was playing an aircraft mechanic called Chalky in the First World War film *Gunbus*. 'There were a lot of old aircraft,' he recalls, 'all my favourites, and I spent most of my time talking to the pilots and drooling over the instrument panels and controls.'

Nicholas believes the adage which says that if you want to learn about yourself, then learn to fly. 'So true,' he says. 'My favourite poem is one written by a Spitfire pilot who died on his first patrol in the Second World War. The poem refers to his feelings for flying and how a pilot can "reach out and touch the face of God".'

★   ★   ★

David Jason will similarly go to any lengths to get away from it all. When the pressures of fame and constant recognition build up too much he loves to escape high into the clouds or deep into the ocean. Autograph hunters and nosy journalists are left very far behind because action man David's idea of relaxation is following one of his two favourite dangerous sports, flying a glider hundreds of feet above his fans or scuba diving in the depths off the remote Cayman Islands.

He is honest enough to accept that the perilous nature of both pastimes is part of the appeal. 'I suppose the edge of danger is quite attractive,' he says frankly.

'But that is part of the challenge. I am a very physical person and I get an indescribably warm feeling doing things that are a real physical challenge. I am not a big one for just lying on a beach sizzling in the sun for hours on end. I think I would get pretty bored with that pretty soon. I can't play ball games very well, I can't hit a tennis, golf or snooker ball. But I do love to get involved with something physically demanding.'

That enthusiasm for a challenge has brought David into real life-threatening danger in both air and sea.

He learned to fly a glider at the London Gliding Club in Dunstable, Bedfordshire, where he shared the hire purchase payments on a glider with a few close friends. It took him six months' practice and training before he made his first solo flight. David always found it very exhilarating until the day he took off in completely the wrong mood.

'I was flying with not the right attitude of mind. I went up when I had had a row with somebody and I took this aircraft up and, because the row was more on my mind than flying the aircraft, when I came into land my mind was not really on the job. And I really messed it up, messed it up badly. I did a ground loop and ripped the bottom out of the aeroplane. It was a very hairy moment. I thought, this is it, I've had it. What a bloody stupid way to go.

'I was coming in far too fast, and there was a cross wind and I was just coming in too quickly and got it all wrong. If a wing touches the ground — which you must never do — it's all right if you are travelling really slowly, but if you are moving at quite a high speed then you can go into a ground loop. The whole plane spins and does a somersault. My wing tip hit the ground and the plane went right over and I thought I was a goner. I was terrified. It was not a very pleasant experience.

'Amazingly, I was not injured. I couldn't believe I had got out of it without a scratch. I was all right but I ripped the bottom out of this aeroplane, and I was very shocked. It put me off flying for a bit. It made me wonder what I was doing up there for a while. Why do I do this? I thought. But it is all part of the challenge.'

He is also a qualified and experienced diver after becoming interested in the sport when he saw an underwater film on television at the age of 18. During his several spells of summer seasons at Bournemouth, he startled the rest of the cast by arriving on the packed beach complete with aqualung equipment. 'They fell about in hysterics when I began getting into my rubber wet-suit, pulling on the flippers and mask,' recalls David. But when he returned from the sea with a dozen tasty mullet 'their expressions changed to hunger'.

But there was no mullet on the menu much more recently when David took a week's holiday in the Cayman Islands and encountered a crisis 100ft down. 'Two years ago I went to the Caymans and completed a dive master course. It was a full, concentrated week and I dived every day and when I had finished diving at four o'clock I went back to study the diving manuals and took all the tests. I spent seven solid days diving and studying. It was really a way of switching off and I wanted to be better at diving than I was, that's why I enrolled for the course.

'The problem happened on my first dive. Would you believe it? It would have to happen on the very first one. One of the things you have to do to qualify as a dive master is to conduct a dive, supervise other divers. You start by briefing them on board the ship, take them through the dive and then bring them all safely to the surface. Instructors watch you at every stage.

'I gave the initial briefing and provided the dive plan which was to do a 20-minute dive to 100ft below the surface and then carefully come up. You always ensure that you have more than enough air to get through the exercise safely. You make sure you are never on what they call the "high profile" for decompression. You need a safety margin.

'And to make sure you don't come up too fast, you always get all the people on the dive into a decompression spot. You make a three-minute safety stop at 15ft for total insurance. And one of the things you insist on, if you are in charge of the dive, is that the others do not go below you.

'Anyway, it was my responsibility to control everything. And I was watching one of the guys on the dive — half your experience is that you are taught to observe people carefully, and try to make nervous people feel calm — and he is putting weights into his life jacket. So I went up to this guy and said, "Do you really need all those weights?" He said he had about 12 pounds.

'That's heavy, and he had not got a wet suit on. He was putting all these weights in his life jacket. I felt I might have trouble with this guy unless I was careful.

'So, we all got in the water and swam down to 100ft and I am in charge of five people on my first dive. Suddenly, I see this guy below me and he is down to 110ft and sinking. I went down and motioned to him to go up and he went up. Then when I turned round again, he started to go down again. I motioned to the others to stay where they were. And this guy is going down to 120ft. I kept waving at him to get up but he kept constantly sinking down again.

'Soon, we need to go back up and all this messing about meant I was beginning to run short of air. I was very unhappy with him because all the time I spent chasing after him meant I was pushing the limit to my decompression time. I was really not very happy because every time I went down for him meant that my profile was getting higher which might mean another decompression stop which I wanted to avoid.

'Eventually, we are just about to return to the surface and this bloody guy signals that he is running low on air. I went over to him again and saw his dial was right on the red for danger. He was supposed to have told me, the man in charge, long before, so I could have aborted the dive safely. He had exhausted a lot of his air inflating the device to keep bringing himself up.

'So I signal to everyone to go up and we all get to the decompression stop. And there is a hang bar at 6ft which is another slight safety measure. This guy should still have been all right. But he goes to the hang bar and he signals he is completely out of air. I am starting to worry a bit now, and I looked at these two instructors just floating there watching me with their arms crossed. And they didn't do anything. They turned their backs. I was really panicking then because I had to share the last of my air from my mask with this guy. I had to calm him down and put my mask on his face. Somehow, I got him up to the steps and on board. But it was all I needed on my very first test.

'I was quite polite to this guy afterwards when he said he was all right. I told him he must remember the rules. But when we got back to the shore the two instructors came up to me and said, "Well, you have learned something today. But you were far too easy on that guy who ran out of air. You should have given him a really big bollocking. That guy endangered his own life but he also endangered yours. If anyone ever does that again you must give them a real dressing down."

'But that is what you take on when you start diving. If you want the responsibility of being a dive master, that is what it is all about.'

It can take David Jason anything up to 20 minutes to do the

simplest of shopping. He can spend five minutes choosing a shirt, perhaps, and another 15 politely having to put up with other shoppers slapping him on the back, asking for autographs, enquiring after Rodney, or pleading with him to just come over and say a quick hello to the wife.

The extraordinary mateyness with which the general public regards David, plus the genuine affection they have for such characters as Del-Boy, Granville and Pop Larkin, means that the actor's life is all too often not his own.

Once, at a party, a fellow guest was asking David to do something for a charity and when David said he was sorry but he simply could not fit it in, the man's wife grabbed David in a headlock and would not let go.

There was even an occasion when David was followed into a gentleman's lavatory by a fan who attempted to shake his hand while it was otherwise engaged.

If you spot David at a restaurant it's more than likely his back will be to the entrance. If he faces the majority of diners there is every chance his meal will be constantly interrupted by strangers just wanting to say hello.

Top showbusiness writer and author Gareth Pearce was astonished at the reaction of fellow diners while lunching with David at L'Etoile restaurant in Charlotte Street in 1988 when he was enjoying unparalleled success in *Only Fools and Horses*. This was a smart restaurant where the lunch bill came to £68 a head.

'Two men separately came over with their table napkins and asked David to autograph them,' Pearce recalls.

'They had actually taken the trouble to buy the napkins from the manager of the restaurant just so they could get David's autograph. Also, while we were there a bubbly woman from Inverness staying at the Meridian Hotel in Piccadilly for a couple of days, rushed up and greeted David like a long-lost friend. She was a complete stranger to him. Then, when we left the restaurant, a pretty girl raced up to David in the street and planted a kiss on his cheek. The popularity of the man was, and is, astonishing.'

Pearce's lunch with David took place just 17 days before Christmas and, looking ahead to the festivities, David commented, 'I want to go home, lock the door, sit in front of the TV and relax. I can understand people who want to have drinks and parties. For me, that can happen any time during the year. I want to be able to turn off at Christmas.

'I shall be going to see my brother and sister at Brighton. They might have a few people around, which is great if I know them. But if I don't, I have to start talking again about all the things I do.'

Fame does not rest easily on David's shoulders. 'I'd love to do the work I do and have the benefit of being able to go to a restaurant or pub or anywhere and be totally anonymous like everyone else,' he says. 'The fame, the intrusion, the lack of privacy is very odd. It's just something I don't enjoy.

'People think they'd enjoy it. They think it would be wonderful to be recognised. But it's not.'

The days when David felt able to use public transport have long gone. 'If you get trapped on a train you're public property,' he points out. 'I had a nasty experience when I was working in Hammersmith and travelled by underground from my flat. I met a wally who attacked me for nothing. He was quite smart, but he had a big chip on his shoulder.

'He saw me at 9.30am and started to have a go and push me about. I had a big bag with me containing my cheque book, wallet and lots of personal stuff and I thought that if I put it down he'd have a partner somewhere who was going to whip it away. But if I was to whack him one, there was no way I could hit him with a bag around my shoulder. So I had to take this rather humiliating experience.

'He didn't hit me. He just knocked my hat off. There were all these people looking. It can happen to anybody but I thought,

Oh, do I need this in my life? Do I need to go to rehearsals like this? No, dammit, I'll either go by taxi or by car.'

David was not so lucky the night he went to the aid of a girl he saw being attacked in London's Soho. He had been dining with a friend and while his friend went ahead to find a taxi, David saw a woman being punched by a man across the street. There was another man egging the thug on, but bravely David decided to intervene.

'I went over and said, "Can I mediate?" which was a really stupid thing to do but I was afraid and I thought that by trying to be reasonably nice they'd be reasonably nice back.

'Unfortunately, the two guys, who had their backs to me, took offence and I got really badly beaten up. I said, "Excuse me, is there some problem?" and I don't remember much after that except my head ringing and in total shock I realised I was being hit. I got seven shades beaten out of me.'

One of the thugs punched David so hard in the face that he fell backwards into a wall some yards away. Then they put the boot in.

'I remember falling on the floor and thinking that I was really going to sort the problem out,' he says. 'And then I passed out.'

The thugs continued to beat David senseless until his friend reappeared with a taxi and dragged David away by his jacket collar and into the cab.

'He bundled me into a taxi and the last thing I remember before passing out was seeing one of the blokes hitting the woman again as we drove past. We went back to my friend's flat and each time I had a bath I discovered more bruises. I was a real mess. I should probably have gone to hospital.

'Strange as it sounds,' he reflects, 'I thought I could make people stop hitting each other and talk. It was very naïve and it's made me think about going to the rescue of damsels ever since. I'm not one of the world's natural fighters — I'm just too busy trying to survive.'

Just before *The Darling Buds of May* brought David a whole new wave of affection from the general public, he admitted, 'I hardly go out at all. It's not bad where I live because they've got used to me. But I still don't go out very much socially to pubs only because it does create an interest.

'People do want to come and talk to you and buy you a drink and I can't blame them for that. They want to know what's going on with Rodney and when we are coming back on TV. You can never really relax wherever you sit. People come up and are usually very nice but you can never get away from yourself.

'So what I tend to do is to go and see friends and go round to dinner with them or stay in. I watch an awful lot of television. I mess about with my motorbikes. I only do it because I know what's going to happen if I go anywhere.'

The constant attention of the fans has become a particular burden for David to bear when he goes shopping.

'I have to steel myself,' he admitted. 'If I want to go and buy a pair of shoes, I think, Do I really need these shoes or this tie? I tend not to buy clothes.

'I don't want to go and buy anything so I save it all up until I think I have to go. I know what's going to happen. It's not much fun when people shout at you in the street. Again, you can't blame them.

'I find it a bit of a strain to keep having to explain to people what I'm doing and what Ronnie Barker or Nick Lyndhurst is like. It makes you very tired. So I found that I was staying in more and more. But in order to stay in, I needed something to do.'

To this end, David has developed a hobby he can enjoy at home — restoring motorbikes and old fairground machines. The outbuildings at his Wendover home are a treasure trove of old machines of all descriptions and his frequent partner in grime is Brian Cosgrove. Whenever David Jason is in the north of England, he stays at Brian Cosgrove's home near Manchester. Brian says,

'My wife always laughingly refers to herself as his northern landlady. I think he first stayed when he was in a play in Wilmslow and he would come back late at night and Angela would cook him meat and two veg and we would sit and talk until one or two in the morning as he eased down after his performance.

'We do share an interest in old machines, but we also have an understanding not to talk about it too much. We do both enjoy that sort of do-it-yourself small engineering, but once a thing like that gets talked about too much and written about too much in magazines and people ask you about it then it somehow takes the edge off it.

'But it is one of those things where you get your old clothes on and get covered in oil and have a darn good time "being normal". You get back to the time when you were a young fellow before you had done anything and there is something very nice about that, something very relaxing, and something very private that I am reluctant to spoil. We just want to enjoy it.'

The two men have worked together on a variety of old machines, from aged fairground sideshows to vintage motorcycles. 'It is nice facing little challenges of whatever we are working on rather than the big challenges of everyday life. We work well together because David is very good mechanically and I bring the artistic side to it. And in our own ways we each have ways of solving problems in whatever we are working on. I do it in an artistic way but David has a great engineering talent.

'He is particularly good with old motorbikes. He can take them to bits and put them together again with great ease. But if you put together two chaps with those different approaches it works well. And we just love to work together, we each enjoy what the other guy does. It gives us both a feedback. We are forever saying, "It's great what you've done there, terrific." It happens in such a little way but it is important. It's like telling a keen gardener what a smashing garden he has produced. The lift we both get from it is important. It is one of life's little pleasures and we both prize and protect it.'

Brian's love for machines encompasses everything from pinball to penny slot. But there was one fairground machine in particular which fascinated David called Marvo the Mystic which featured a doll with a cone in his hand. When a penny was inserted in the slot, the eyes went up and down, the wand was waved and, with the help of a cone, he could make things disappear.

David was so enthralled by this machine that he went on and on at Brian asking him how much he wanted for it. Finally Cosgrove said, 'If you really want it so much, why don't we make one? We'll take it to bits and build it again.'

Next time David was in Manchester, he and Cosgrove went down into Cosgrove's cellar and took the Marvo machine apart.

'For the next two years, we rebuilt it,' David says proudly.' Twice I was on tour and I used to stay with Brian working on Marvo the Mystic. Brian is a great artist whereas, as he says, I tend to concentrate on the mechanical side. I'm a great one for mechanical things. I suppose it's because I was an electrician and I was taught engineering.'

If fame has made David somewhat reclusive, those who work with him say they have never seen him get angry with fans however rudely they might have been interrupting his life.

Writer David Nobbs travelled on a train with David from London to Leeds and witnessed a stream of wellwishers and fans who all wanted to ask about Rodney or to call him a plonker or a dipstick for the 400th time that morning. The breakfast that David was trying to eat was cold by the time they arrived. As they got off the train, Nobbs remarked that such attention must be difficult to deal with. Nobbs said, 'David just looked at me and said, "Well, those people are the reason why I am not still an electrician."'

His fan mail appears to cover all ages and two fan letters in particular stick in David's mind. The first followed the episode in which Rodney got married and Del-Boy was left all on his own at the reception. It was a wonderful, bitter-sweet moment and soon afterwards David received a letter from a woman who said that after seeing this scene her three-year-old daughter had not been able to get to sleep and had ended up crying all night and that the only thing she wanted in the world was for Del to go and live with her. It was not the first time David had been aware that *Only Fools and Horses* is watched by people of all ages.

The second letter that David has never forgotten came from a woman who wrote to him to say that every appearance he made on TV had a strange effect on her cat. 'The cat loves you,' ran the letter. What tickled David pink was that to prove it the woman had enclosed a photograph of her puss gazing adoringly at the TV with David on the screen!

8

Private Lives

In the very first series of *A Touch of Frost*, Frost's screen wife had died of cancer and subsequent series revealed that, after years of loneliness, Frost had enjoyed a love life brightened by occasional passionate flings.

The parallels in David's own life were apparent for all to see when, by October 1996, 18 months after Myfanwy had died, there was a new woman in his life. She was beautiful former Yorkshire TV assistant Gill Hinchcliffe who first emerged at David's side, happily basking in his reflected glory, at London's Royal Albert Hall where David received a standing ovation as he accepted a Special Recognition award at the National Television Awards presentation.

Gill, who had joined Yorkshire TV as a secretary and had steadily worked her way up, had first met David when he was making *A Bit of a Do* and they had subsequently worked together on *A Touch of Frost*. Gradually they became close although David bristled at suggestions that the romance might have begun before

Myfanwy's death. He was adamant it had blossomed long afterwards but a long-serving Yorkshire TV employee noted, 'Gill often used to be in the bar with her boyfriend who was much older than she was. We thought he was her father but he was pretty unhappy at the suggestion and was always very protective. Gill always liked older men. She said she felt more comfortable with them than "boys" as she called them of her own age. Gill is a very striking lady and if David hadn't noticed her he must have been the only guy in the bar who didn't. But, of course, he is absolutely right to resent suggestions their relationship began when Myfanwy was still alive. It was a good story but it just was not true. Nothing really sparked between them until long afterwards, we could all see it happening on the production. It wasn't at all sudden, they just gradually seemed to be spending a lot of time with each other.

'Gill was totally smitten. David can be quite charismatic and very, very funny. At first she was quite in awe of him. Anyone who has seen him act knows what an incredible talent he has and wherever he goes, even though he's a little guy, he just has this amazing presence. When he comes into a room, if he's in the mood, he can completely dominate any occasion.

'Gill told a pal they were really good friends for quite a long time before they became lovers. He was very respectful and old-fashioned even. There were lots of bouquets of flowers and candle-lit dinners for two. I guess Gill's warmth and David's loneliness was the start of it. Everyone in the crew was delighted when they got together, they make a lovely couple.'

Gill, an attractive 37-year-old blonde, and David looked radiantly happy arm-in-arm at the star-studded party after the awards. Even the Spice Girls were momentarily ignored by photographers as they jostled each other for pictures of David Jason with the new woman in his life who, it was noted, bore some resemblance to Myfanwy with her sparkling eyes, ready smile and cropped hair.

Taking Gill to the awards was a very public statement by David that he had found love again and that he now did not care who knew it. Nor, it seemed, did Gill's mother. 'They are meant for each other. They make a wonderful pair and they are very much in love,' said Mrs Hinchcliffe at her home at Mirfield, near Dewsbury, West Yorkshire.

Gill's mother had been impressed with David when Gill brought him home to tea one day. 'He's a wonderful man, very considerate and charming,' she said. 'And she's a wonderful girl who deserves happiness. She's not extrovert or bubbly — just very nice. Gillian is very grown up and knows what she is doing. Her romance with David was certainly no surprise to us.'

Unlike Myfanwy, Gill had observed David's work at close quarters during her time at Yorkshire TV and she was very aware of the effort he always put in and the strain he had been under to continue with *A Touch of Frost* while trying to come to terms with his grief over Myfanwy. Gill saw the way he worried away at his lines to get them absolutely perfect and how he found it difficult to wind down after a performance.

Gill was understanding and she was also a soft shoulder for him to rely on. But it was not until David and Gill flew out to the Montreux TV festival as guests of the BBC in the spring of 1997 that he was able to reveal the extent of Gill's influence in his life. 'She's great,' he said. 'People are always asking me to do things all the time and I find it hard to relax. But she shields me from all of that pressure. She takes all my phone calls and keeps me relaxed so that I have to do the minimum of work. It's so nice to have someone as lovely as her who is so caring and loving, especially after what I've been through.'

Gill has been a calming influence and when she and David flew off for a romantic holiday on the Caribbean island of Providenciales, David was able to see 1997 stretching ahead of him with no TV projects firmed up. He was physically and mentally exhausted and it was his first real carefree holiday for many years. During their sun-filled fortnight at a luxurious £2,000-a-night villa overlooking the sea, David did nothing more strenuous than swim, snorkel and hire a four-wheel-drive Suzuki to see the local sites on the island which covers only 28 square miles. On secluded beaches they lovingly held hands as they strode into the sea. But even behind dark glasses and by now sporting a small grey beard, he still found his fame had followed him to such a remote setting. As David was emerging one day from the sea with Gill, a young British holidaymaker looked up and exclaimed to his parents, 'Look, it's Del-Boy! What are you doing here, you dipstick?'

As Christmas approached, David made plans to spend the festivities with Gill at his eighteenth-century farmhouse. It was a joyous occasion, so different from the year before when he was still mourning Myfanwy's loss.

Together, they both sat down to watch the last episodes of *Only Fools and Horses*. Just a few months before, David's loyal fans had voted him Favourite Situation Comedy Performer at the BBC's Auntie's All-Time Greats awards ceremony celebrating the Corporation's 60th birthday.

That award was another treasured moment in a remarkable year for David. It was a year in which he had found new love and rounded off *Only Fools and Horses*, the TV series which had enthralled, entertained, and endeared him to the nation.

Four months later Gill was with him glowing with pride again as her famous lover received yet another standing ovation when David scored a double triumph at the BAFTA Awards. He won the Best TV Comedy Performance award for the *Only Fools and Horses* Christmas Special and the show itself was named Best TV Comedy. 'Lovely jubbly,' said David as he collected his award. Gill helped to persuade David to take time off for himself for the first time in a long time, so at the start of 1977 he announced he was to have a year off.

The real David Jason is a complex mixture. The towering talent that has transformed his life comes with a large slice of insecurity and a strange reluctance to open up even to his closest friends. Richard Harris, the acclaimed playwright who penned *Stepping Out* and *Outside Edge*, was a very good friend to David when they were young men.

The couple were introduced by David's friend and business partner Malcolm Taylor and met in Edinburgh when David starred, with Virginia Stride, in Richard's farce *Albert and Virginia* that was on at the Arts Theatre. Richard recalls, 'David was very energetic and very good in the play. When we met we were both totally unknown and both beginners. He had just finished working as an electrician and was just starting out as an actor. He was a very funny guy and a great mimic but never in my wildest dreams did I imagine he would go on to such fame and fortune.

'For a time we were pretty close, going on holiday several times to Corfu, me and my wife, Malcolm and his wife and David. We always had an enormous laugh. David always seemed very easy-going. Gradually we drifted apart over the years but I always watched his rise and rise with interest. Then he got *No Sex Please — We're British* and I could see him building a nice career.

'Then, years later, I saw David again when I was asked to write the television adaptation of first *Darling Buds of May* and *A Touch of Frost*. It was interesting work and I was delighted to do it, thinking that it would be nice to renew my old friendship. But when we met again it was almost as if he didn't know me. During all the time we were working on the same projects, I don't think David and I exchanged more than ten words. He had changed. There was no reaching out. We never had a drink together and we never had a meal together. I thought it was strange. I think he has become very, very private. I thought we were friends from way back and while I did not particularly want to wallow in nostalgia I did have lots of happy recollections of laughs we had enjoyed together. But he did not seem to want to take a single step down memory lane.

'Malcolm Taylor arranged for us all to get together and have dinner one night but it turned out to be a rather dismal evening. David was very unforthcoming. I think perhaps he has got to the position in life where he thinks everyone is after something from him. David just did not want to know. He certainly did not want to have any of those "Do you remember the time we all did so and so?" conversations. It was very strange because we had lots of laughs when we were younger. Good God, many a time he slept on my floor when he didn't have tuppence, but he didn't seem to want to open up on that at all.

'I loved adapting *A Touch of Frost* for television and David seemed to enjoying playing the role. I did the first ten hours of *Frost* but he never once said to me that he thought the scripts were any good. People might think he landed me the work but that's not the way it was. I was surprised he wanted to forget the old days. He obviously liked working on my writing because he told other people so, but he certainly never found time to tell me, which would have been nice, but there we are.

'When David won his awards, I dropped him a note saying "Well done", but I never got anything in return. Make of that what you will ... I hadn't spoken to him for about 20 years in between. I was very disappointed to renew an acquaintance with someone with whom I was fairly close and find there was no desire from him to remember those days.

'He has always kept himself very much to himself and he does so even more now. I don't think he is very comfortable with being a star. It must be terribly difficult. I think he is haunted with anxiety about when he is going to make the wrong move. Let's face it, these days you've only got to say the name David Jason and you've got a successful television series. He has not had a flop recently. He had all his flops when he was young. He had lots of chances. *Only Fools and Horses* is a marvellous creation and his other work is tremendous. *Porterhouse Blue* was terrific.

'As a young man, he was very determined to do well. We had a lot of laughs and a lot of fun but there was also a very dark side to him. He used to get incredibly frustrated when he didn't get the breaks. He had a lot of insecurity inside him, as much as any creative person I've known. Now he is very protective of his privacy. I was just disappointed he was protective with me, an old mate. Fame is a funny thing. It must be very, very hard being that famous.

'There was one particular scene in *A Touch of Frost* that took my breath away. I wrote the scene and the director directed it but there was just something about the way that David played it that surprised us both. He was brilliant. He just had this look that told you everything that only a great actor can convey. The face tells you everything. He is a very human actor, that humanity is very evident. It's in his face. Both the comic and the sad side are so very real and he shares that with the audience. And he burns with this incredible energy. It's almost impossible not to watch him. He has come an awful long way from being a Finchley electrician. But he always was a solitary sort of chap. Now he's even more so.'

Virginia Stride, the actress who starred with David in *Albert and Virginia* now lives only a few miles from David's mansion. She'd like to renew their old friendship, too. 'David was so alive, he was great to work with,' said Virginia. 'When I realised we lived so close I thought it would be nice to get in touch for old times' sake and I wondered if he might open our village garden fête but his brother Arthur warned me off. He said David was a recluse these days so I didn't bother any more.'

The story of the relentless rise and rise of David Jason does have its sad side. As a boy and a young man there is no doubt that David was the life and soul of any occasion. His clowning and mimicry and love of life shone through his early years but it also obscured the steely determination underneath.

A friend who was close to David as a young man said, 'Once, we had had too much to drink and he suddenly opened up and said how much it meant to him getting on in life and making a name for himself as an actor. I had my ambitions, too, and agreed. But he gripped my arm and his eyes burned into me as he said, "You don't understand. My brother didn't make it. My twin, I mean. So it's all down to me. I must make it. I just have to."

'I didn't think anything of it. I didn't even know that David's twin brother had died. Then another pal warned me not to mention it. He said, "It's the one thing that really gets to him. He feels it's like part of him died so he has to try that much harder at everything."'

The sociable fun of David's early years are in stark contrast to his life now. He lives in splendid isolation in his mansion, with Tony Blair as his new neighbour and Special Branch as his local neighbourhood watch. And it's only at home that he feels really happy. He is very, very careful about who he lets into his domain. Ronnie Barker, John Sullivan, Nicholas Lyndhurst and other trusted friends from the business come to dinner. But the house was bought really for Myfanwy. She loved the space and the scope it provided for her flair for decoration. But after she died, David found it very difficult to be there on his own. Memories of Myfanwy were in every room and David threw himself into work to try to buy some time and space between him and his tragedy. Now his relationship with caring Gill has blossomed, friends say somehow the great house feels happy again.

But David's favourite times are not spent hosting glittering dinner parties. Instead he much prefers the moments spent tinkering in his garage with something mechanical, such as one of his beloved motorbikes. One of the keys to the success of his love for Gill is that she loves to see him absorbed in his work. And she can sit for hours watching him with spanner or screwdriver dismantling some old engine, his mind relaxed and blissfully happy to be in a world where there are no autograph hunters yelling, 'Oi you plonker!'

They also love gardening together and doing anything practical. At the end of the day, David is a jobbing artisan, it's just that instead of making a few quid a day as an electrician he makes a few thousand as an actor. But he is haunted by the fear that it might all dry up.

Much of his insecurity is rooted in the knowledge that he is not really quite sure why he is so immensely popular and successful. He knows he can act most thespians off the screen, but there is also an undefinable 'X' factor which makes the public switch on to whatever he does on television.

Certainly, it is not money that drives Jason. Several times in his career he has turned his back on the most lucrative options. And a senior TV executive who has negotiated with David on a string of projects insists he is a joy to deal with. 'He is probably only about number five in the league of top British actor earners behind Thaw and Cole and Waterman and Bolam. But he is number one in terms of audience attraction. If I had a script that I wanted to turn into a successful drama or comedy then I'd go for David first, second and third.' And the people in charge of British television rate David as a second Chaplin, a comic genius who delivers fabulous performances and enormous audiences every time.

And the rewards can be enormous. The son of the fish porter who still grumbles about being ripped off when he bought a bicycle from a neighbour as a teenager is now a millionaire many times over. But there is a 47-year-old former leading man who will always be grateful to Jason's unselfishness. The actor, who agreed to talk to the authors on condition his identity was not revealed, said, 'I'd just done a 13-part series for the BBC and we had all been approached about a second run. I'd taken out a huge mortgage on a house on the strength of it and then suddenly I was hit by a wave of really bad asthma attacks. I'd had asthma as a child but this was much worse. It was a nightmare. One minute I was on top of the world, and the next I was out of work and unemployable in the job I loved.

'I've not worked as an actor since. But just when I was really on my beam ends, I was helped out by a large cheque from David Jason. I was absolutely stunned. I didn't know him that well. We'd only worked together once. But someone told him about my problems and without saying a word he had this cheque hand-delivered to my house. It meant I could keep the bank at bay while I sold the house again and it made all the difference in the world to me and my family. And I know other people he's helped as well, but he always does it quietly. The last thing he'd want to get is a reputation as a soft touch. But when people say he's tight, it makes me very angry. David Jason is a gent in my book, always will be.'

David certainly makes regular large contributions to a string of more conventional charities, but always insists so far as possible on anonymity. But then he can afford it. For the last series of *A Touch of Frost* he was paid £106,000 a film. The accountants at Yorkshire TV considered it money well spent when the show swept towards the top of the TV ratings. And that £106,000 will quickly be doubled by the 100 per cent repeat fee for the second screening. After that, repeats are paid on a slowly declining scale.

Even the penny-pinching BBC were made to pay handsomely for the sensationally successful three-part swan-song for *Only Fools and Horses*. David's ability to earn the Corporation a runaway win in the 1996 Christmas ratings battle earned him £69,000 for each of the three hilarious films.

With lucrative video sales, occasional voice-overs, and the re-runs of *The Darling Buds of May* on UK Gold, David Jason is by anybody's standards a very rich man. But apart from his home and his beloved Jaguar XJS he is always careful with his money. 'I was brought up to respect money and I'm not going to change,' he says. 'I drive a Jaguar because it is comfortable and I do a lot of miles. It's not a status symbol. And I live in the country because I like it. I love holidays so I spend a bit on them but I never spend just for spending's sake.'

In fact, David is very generous professionally. He always sets out to try to inspire a team atmosphere on all of his shows and he is much more likely to spend his off-duty moments laughing with the crew or his fellow actors than closeted away in his caravan.

But David is incredibly shy of commitment. He never married Myfanwy even though he knew it would more than anything have made her and his mother very happy. When ITV offered him a fantastic million-pound deal to sign up to work for them exclusively, he refused. He definitely did not want to shut the door on Del, but he is also very wary of anyone taking control of his life. A friend said, 'His insecurity is frightening. I tried to get him to relax once. I said, "David, you're a millionaire. You're the most popular actor in the country. You've got a lovely lady in your life. Why on earth can't you just lie back and enjoy life from time to time?" He looked at me as if I was talking Russian. He is a driven man and there's no changing him now.'

David agonises that his colossal comedy success has masked his dramatic achievement. Although he loves playing Del Trotter he is always incensed if people or newspapers confuse him with the character. 'Why do they call me David "Del-Boy" Jason?' he raves. 'You never hear anyone talking about Alec "*Bridge over the River Kwai*" Guinness.'

When the authors of this book met David we went once to one of his favourite restaurants, The Wife of Bath at Wye, and it proved one of the most revealing evenings. David was polite and forthright. He answered every question with considerable candour, but you couldn't begin to call him a happy man. He was certainly down to earth, passing the budget-busting wine list back to the waiter and asking if he wouldn't mind popping across the road to the pub for a couple of pints of beer.

9

Wedded Bliss

D uring the 20 years they worked together making *Only Fools and Horses*, David Jason and Nicholas Lyndhurst developed a bond both on screen and off that even the very closest of friends rarely establish.

As actors they were unselfishly loyal and supportive of each other throughout, both of them working hard to create and then maintain and improve their remarkable on-screen rapport as the Trotter brothers.

Together they shared the good times on set, the laughter and the acclaim. Together they put in the long hours of filming and endured the disappointment of the initial lukewarm response to *Only Fools and Horses* from both the BBC and the general public.

As actors, they grew in stature together, thanks to the phenomenal popularity of the series. And, naturally, they grew, too, as individuals.

Nicholas was only 20 years old when he first took on the role of Rodney. Tall, pencil slim and gangling, he looked young and he was young. David, at 40, was exactly twice his age and, as the years rolled by, David was able to watch from close proximity his co-star maturing from a boy into a man — both as Rodney and as Nicholas.

As Rodney's elder brother, Del always lent him a protective hand. Del had taken Rodney under his wing when their mum had died and had helped to raise him. And so it was no surprise to find that David Jason had a few tears in his eyes when they came to film the episode in which Rodney finally stretched his wings and flew the nest by marrying his sweetheart Cassandra, played by Gwyneth Strong.

It was inevitable, too, that David would be similarly moved when he witnessed Nicholas becoming a married man in real life. The shy, self-conscious boy he had first met when barely out of his teens, was by now a confident 38-year-old man with a beautiful young bride at his side.

As weddings go, the joining together of Rodney Charlton Trotter and Cassandra Louise Parry in matrimony in 1989 could hardly have been more different from the real-life marriage of Nicholas Lyndhurst to gorgeous ballet dancer Lucy Smith in 1999.

And as for wedding receptions, it's hard to imagine a wider contrast between the basic celebrations of the Trotter nuptials in the Nag's Head and the sumptuous wedding reception for Nicholas and Lucy held at one of Britain's grandest historic country estates.

But, fittingly, looking on proudly but misty-eyed on both occasions was David Jason. David, as Del-Boy, was Best Man at Rodney's wedding, and he was a distinguished guest at Nicholas Lyndhurst's own marriage ten years later.

David has confessed he was genuinely moved to tears when the regular cast got together to film Rodney's wedding to Cassandra and, similarly, David had a lump in his throat as Nicholas wed his beautiful bride Lucy.

It was a brilliant, memorable, landmark episode of *Only Fools and Horses* when Del's 'little bruv' Rodney married his long-time love Cass. That episode, called *Little Problems* and originally transmitted on 12 February 1989, two days before St Valentine's Day, certainly remains one of David's favourites and would be very high on the list of most *Only Fools and Horses* fans.

'It was a sad moment for Del and for me,' David recalled. 'We cried real tears together. It was emotional because Nick and I have worked so closely together and I knew that Del realises for the first time that Rodders has grown up. It was a nostalgic moment, probably the most emotional in my life.'

Rodney finally wed Cassandra two days after his drunken stag night during which he slurred to pal Denzil that Del was 'the bestest bloke in the world'. With one arm draped around his elder brother's shoulders, Rodney told him, 'You've done everything for me in my life.' Generously, Del had promised to give Rodney £2,000 for a deposit on a flat and managed to come up with the money, even though it ultimately cost him a beating from the feared Driscoll Brothers to get it.

As *Only Fools and Horses* fans remember with relish, Rodney's stag night ended hilariously when he arrived home minus his trousers and with a learner driver's red L-plate pinned to the front of his boxer shorts.

Every TV wedding holds a fascination for viewers and Rodney's and Cassandra's was no exception. The vast army of faithful fans of *Only Fools and Horses* were captivated by the prospect of watching Rodney and Cassandra officially become man and wife. They duly did so at the local Peckham Register Office amid sniggers of incredulity among the assembled guests when the registrar read out Rodney's middle name during the exchange of vows.

Much to the merriment of his chortling friends, it was revealed that Rodney had been given the second name of Charlton.

Rodney, to his excruciating embarrassment, had been named Charlton after the local South London football team, Charlton Athletic, and not, as Boycie's wife Marlene had supposed, after the Hollywood screen idol Charlton Heston.

It was a wedding to remember. But, after the exchanging of the marriage vows, the similarity to Nicholas Lyndhurst's own wedding ended there.

While Rodney got married in a register office in Peckham, Nicholas Lyndhurst took his vows with Lucy at the picturesque thirteenth-century church of St Mary in East Lavant, West Sussex, two miles north of his home town of Chichester. Nicholas was born and raised in the nearby towns of Emsworth and Selsey.

For her nuptials, Cassandra wore a simple, cream dress with a hemline cut just above the knee. Cassandra's only bridal extravagance on her big day was a large bow tied at the back of her wedding dress.

Nicholas's bride Lucy, on the other hand, arrived for her wedding ceremony in style in a vintage 1930s white Bentley and stepped out to gasps from onlookers in a beautiful ivory crêpe silk wedding gown with a stunning, hand-beaded, ivory silk veil held in place by a silver diamante tiara.

As perhaps befits the most famous residents of Peckham's Nelson Mandela House tower block, the Peckham-style post-wedding celebrations to mark the splicing of Rodney and Cassandra were held at their local, the Nag's Head, in the unromantic setting of a drab, dingy, dimly lit room with a dartboard, cheap faded wallpaper, clashing red and orange peeling paintwork and a threadbare carpet. Jellied eels were the highpoint of the wedding menu. The lowpoint was Boycie's Great Dane called Duke planting his front paws firmly on the food table to snaffle up the crumbs.

The most poignant moment was when Del was left alone after the newly-weds and the guests had departed, a scene played out with the voice of Mick Hucknall in the background singing Simply Red's big hit 'Holding Back the Years', which, as we've discovered, was a moment carefully constructed to create maximum poignancy, after John Sullivan suggested the track to David.

Certainly, there was nothing that in any way could be described as cheap when Nicholas and Lucy received their guests after their church wedding. Their reception was held in the glorious splendour of Goodwood House which has been home to successive Dukes of Richmond. Built in the 17th-century and nestling in 12,000 acres of rolling West Sussex countryside, the grand estate is famous for its horse and car racing events.

Earlier in the day, Nicholas's marriage to Lucy had been the perfect fairytale conclusion to a seven-year romance which had been conducted in great secrecy. Only close family and friends of the couple had known about the romance and among those privileged few was David Jason. Just as Del had watched Rodney's and Cassandra's relationship develop, so, too, David had witnessed Nicholas and Lucy's romance blossom while respectfully heeding their wish for privacy by keeping his knowledge of their love for each other to himself.

Like others among the trusted ring of family and friends, David dutifully kept quiet about his co-star's burgeoning love for Lucy to allow it to grow and flourish out of the spotlight. The couple had been afraid that if their love affair had become public knowledge, they would have been besieged by the press wherever they went.

Right from the very start, theirs had been a courtship so laced with romance that it might have been orchestrated by Cupid himself. Nicholas, frequently so gauche, clumsy and dull as Rodney when courting girls in *Only Fools and Horses*, proved himself to be brimful of romance, charm and chivalry when it came to the wooing of Lucy.

Ironically, Lucy first set eyes on Nicholas one summer's evening when he was exuding anything but masculine appeal. Nicholas was playing a gay kitchen fitter in the stage show *Straight and Narrow* at the Wyndhams Theatre in the West End and Lucy was a member of the audience.

Lucy, just 19 at the time, was a dancer with the English National Ballet company who were presenting *Cinderella* at the Coliseum Theatre close by and it was perhaps only natural that she should check out the production being staged down the road.

Lucy was thrilled when she discovered that an actor of the calibre of Nicholas Lyndhurst was playing the leading role and, with the help of her Equity actors' union card, she secured a price reduction for a seat in the front row and took along one of her best friends, another dancer called Alice Crawford, for company.

The two girls found they enjoyed the show so much that they booked seats to go back and see the play again the very next night. Once again they managed to acquire seats in the front row. There are many who will testify that Nicholas is professional to the core as an actor but it was so unusual to find the same two pretty girls in front row seats on successive nights that even Nicholas could not fail to notice them.

After the show, Lucy and her friend showed how much they had enjoyed the play by going round to the stage door and leaving a bottle of champagne for the cast. They also left a note inviting the cast to come and see *Cinderella* at the Coliseum. Then they headed for the Tube station and home, but on the way they passed the pub where the cast of *Straight and Narrow* were enjoying a post-performance drink.

On that balmy summer evening, Nicholas was sitting outside the pub sipping his drink unnoticed by passers-by. The cap which he regularly wears to hide his familiar features was pulled down but not so as to obscure his sight. And when Lucy and her friend entered his field of vision, he recognised them as the two girls in the front row and quickly figured from the graceful way they were walking that they must be ballerinas. He felt sure they must be the girls who had left the champagne and the note. Fellow *Straight and Narrow* actor Pete Jonfield agreed with this assessment and, at Nicholas' urging, went up to the girls and invited them over to join him and Nicholas for a drink.

Nicholas clicked with Lucy straight away. He had been struck by Lucy's beautiful, large, blue eyes when she was sitting in the front row at the theatre. Now he was looking straight into them and they were just as bewitchingly beautiful.

Not long afterwards, it was Nicholas's turn to see Lucy performing on stage and leave a note for her backstage. He eagerly accepted her invitation to see *Cinderella* and afterwards left a note which simply read, 'Teach me to dance.'

The mutual admiration for each other's work took Lucy back to see *Straight and Narrow* a further five times, prompting Nicholas to send her a jokey card declaring that, because she had seen the play so often, she had won herself a prize of two glasses of wine. For further details Lucy was asked to phone a certain number which, of course, turned out to be Nicholas'.

They arranged to meet up for their first date but it almost never happened. Lucy turned up at the appointed hour but there was no sign of Nicholas. When a full half-hour went by and still he had not turned up, Lucy feared she had been stood up. She was on the point of resignedly setting off for home again when a panting Nicholas came running up full of apologies. He had genuinely been delayed by the sudden unexpected arrival of a friend he hadn't see for some time and felt he couldn't just rush off without at least an exchange of a few pleasantries and a bit of a chat.

That first date lit the initial spark of love for Nicholas and Lucy who had never had a boyfriend before. But with Lucy travelling all over the world as a ballerina and Nicholas's TV and stage work often taking them in different directions, their romance was inevitably lit by a slow-burning fuse.

They kept in touch regularly by phone and by fax and gradually they became closer. But Nicholas was determined that their love should remain under wraps to protect Lucy from being pestered by the press on her travels as a ballerina. Lucy readily agreed. Whenever she was questioned about boyfriends she would admit to having a man in her life but to put people off the scent she said that he was a Swedish pilot! No one could call Lucy a liar, however, because there was more than a grain of truth in that. Nicholas was, after all, a qualified pilot and spoke some Swedish.

The couple managed to keep their relationship a secret for five years until they were pictured together for the first time in 1997 at the BAFTA awards in London. By then they were very much in love, although it's fair to say that Nicholas had had an inkling that Lucy was going to be Miss Right almost from the very start.

Nicholas's star dressing room at the Wyndham's Theatre had, as all theatres do, an intercom to the stage so he could hear what was going on. Before the curtain went up, the stage was, of course, empty, but the microphone was powerful enough to pick up the audience talking among themselves. On her frequent visits to see the show, Nicholas was able to tell that Lucy was in the front row again with Alice because he could hear them laughing and chatting away.

In preparation for each night's performance, it was Nicholas's habit to go up into the wings of the theatre and pause for a few moments in thought. That particular evening, he pulled back the curtain an inch or two to take a peep at the front row and there was Lucy looking relaxed and happy in the front row, and he admits, 'There was no voice in my head, there was no great surge of emotion, it was just a very quiet feeling of "that's her".'

It was in April 1998, on Lucy's 25th birthday, when Nicholas popped the question to Lucy in the most romantic style. Lucy had been hoping that Nicholas would buy her a bicycle as a gift and when she woke up on her birthday she was thrilled to find a bike waiting for her and jumped on it immediately.

But there were plenty of other presents waiting for Lucy to unwrap including a few little packages for her long-treasured doll's house. Nicholas had previously bought her several items for the doll's house and Lucy was delighted at the prospect of having a few more when Nick told her to delay opening the tiniest gift to the last.

The final small, carefully wrapped item took Lucy's breath away. It was the most beautiful diamond and platinum engagement ring. Nicholas had taken the ring out of its box and had wrapped it just as if it was another little doll's house treasure so it came as a complete surprise to Lucy when she opened it. As the reality sank in, Nicholas asked her to marry him and Lucy could not refrain from bursting into tears of joy as she said, "Yes, please." In another typically romantic gesture from Nicholas, the magic of this delightful moment for the couple was all being recorded for posterity on video.

Although there is a 12-year age gap between them, neither of them has ever found it a problem and Nicholas and Lucy were duly married on 1 September 1999. Among the 100 guests was David Jason, inwardly glowing with pride at his co-star's big day. Del had seen Rodney off on his new journey in life as a married man. Now David was doing much the same with Nicholas.

Only Fools and Horses has always been a team effort and as well as David, looking avuncular with a grey moustache, smart grey suit, blue shirt and yellow patterned tie, Nicholas had also invited Tony Dow, the director of *Only Fools and Horses*, Ken McDonald who played Mike, the barman of the Nag's Head, John Challis who played Boycie and John Sullivan, the writer of the show. Together they flanked Nicholas and Lucy to pose for photographs in the grand elegance of Goodwood's Yellow Drawing Room designed by Charles, Third Duke of Richmond to house a series of magnificent full-length royal portraits by such revered artists as Canaletto and Van Dyck.

This time, jellied eels were *not* on the wedding menu. Instead, the wedding feast included Thai lobster salad, breast of chicken in Madeira sauce, and caramelised lemon fudge tart with raspberry sauce. In his speech Nicholas brought a smile of approval to David's face when he recalled how he had been smitten the moment he had first set eyes on Lucy. 'Since that day, I have fallen in love with her every day,' he said.

The glorious Goodwood estate has an aerodrome which was used as a take-off and landing point for British fighter planes during the Second World War and it is still very much a functional aerodrome today. It's from here that Nicholas frequently indulges his passion for flying in a Piper Tomahawk and, very aptly, it was by air that Nicholas and his new bride left Goodwood.

On Goodwood's front lawn they clambered aboard a helicopter and were whisked into the sky before the pilot swooped low in front of Goodwood House to give the guests a farewell glimpse of the new Mr and Mrs Lyndhurst beaming and waving.

As one guest jokingly remarked, 'The Peckham posse would never have believed it!'